NEW SLAVERY

A Reference Handbook

Other Titles in ABC-CLIO's
CONTEMPORARY
WORLD ISSUES
Series

Affirmative Action, Lynne Eisaguirre
AIDS Crisis in America, Second Edition, Eric K. Lerner and Mary Ellen Hombs
Censorship, Mary E. Hull
Children's Rights, Beverly C. Edmonds and William R. Fernekes
Feminism, Judith Harlan
Hate Crimes, Donald Altschiller
Human Rights, Second Edition, Nina Redman and Lucille Whalen
Pornography in America, Joseph W. Slade
Prisons in America, Debra L. Stanley and Nicole Hahn Rafter
Privacy Rights in America, Leigh Glenn
Sexual Harassment, Second Edition, Lynne Eisaguirre
Women in the Third World, Karen L. Kinnear

Books in the Contemporary World Issues series address vital issues in today's society such as terrorism, sexual harassment, homelessness, AIDS, gambling, animal rights, and air pollution. Written by professional writers, scholars, and nonacademic experts, these books are authoritative, clearly written, up-to-date, and objective. They provide a good starting point for research by high school and college students, scholars, and general readers, as well as by legislators, businesspeople, activists, and others.

Each book, carefully organized and easy to use, contains an overview of the subject; a detailed chronology; biographical sketches; facts and data and/or documents and other primary-source material; a directory of organizations and agencies; annotated lists of print and nonprint resources; a glossary; and an index.

Readers of books in the Contemporary World Issues series will find the information they need in order to better understand the social, political, environmental, and economic issues facing the world today.

NEW SLAVERY
A Reference Handbook

Kevin Bales

**CONTEMPORARY
WORLD ISSUES**

ABC-CLIO

Santa Barbara, California
Denver, Colorado
Oxford, England

Library of Congress Cataloging-in-Publication Data

Bales, Kevin.
    New slavery : a reference handbook / Kevin Bales.
        p.   cm. — (Contemporary world issues)
    Includes bibliographical references and index.
        ISBN 1-57607-239-8
    1. Slavery—History—20th century.   I. Title.   II. Series.
    HT867.B37 2000
    306.3'62'0904—dc21

                                                    00-010873

06 05 04 03 02 01 00   10 9 8 7 6 5 4 3 2 1

ABC-CLIO, Inc.
130 Cremona Drive, P.O. Box 1911
Santa Barbara, California 93116-1911

To
Ernst Borinski

Contents

Preface, xiii
Acknowledgments, xvii

1 Introduction, 1
　　Slavery Defined, 2
　　How Many Slaves? 3
　　The Nature of Contemporary Slavery, 4
　　How Slavery Changed into Its Modern Form, 5
　　Old and New Slavery Compared, 7
　　The Question of Race, 10
　　The Forms of Contemporary Slavery, 12
　　Examples of Contemporary Slavery, 15
　　　　Lives up in Smoke, 15
　　　　Slavery in the City of Lights, 16
　　Slavery and Globalization, 18
　　Who Is Responsible for Global Slavery? 20
　　The Role of the State and the United Nations: International
　　　　Law and Slavery, 21
　　Trafficking in People, 23
　　Groups and Strategies Working against Slavery, 25
　　　　Examples at the International Level, 25
　　　　Examples at the National and Regional Level, 26
　　　　Examples at the Local Level, 28
　　Liberation and Rehabilitation, 31
　　What Can We Do? 32
　　References, 33
　　Notes, 33

2 Chronology, 35

3 Biographical Sketches, 49

4 Facts and Documents, 73
    Facts and Figures, 74
        The Slavery Index, 74
        The Spread of Slavery, 75
    Key International Laws and Conventions on Slavery, 77
        Slavery Convention of the League of Nations (1926), 78
        The Universal Declaration of Human Rights (1948), 79
        Supplementary Convention on the Abolition of Slavery,
            the Slave Trade, and Institutions and Practices
            Similar to Slavery (1956), 79
        Convention on the Rights of the Child (1989) (Excerpts),
            82
        ILO Convention Concerning the Prohibition and
            Immediate Action for the Elimination of the Worst
            Forms of Child Labour (1999) (Excerpts), 83
    Reports, Evidence, and Testimony about the Different
            Types of Slavery, 83
        Bonded Labor, 83
        Contract Slavery, 90
        Chattel Slavery, 92
        War Slavery, 97
        Slavery Linked to Religious Practice, 103
        Forced Labor, 105
        Commercial Sexual Slavery and Trafficking
            of People, 111
        Domestic Slavery, 125
        Child Labor and Slavery, 128
        The Worst Forms of Child Labor, 130

5 Directory of Organizations, 135
    Africa, 137
    Asia, 138
    Europe, 139
    North America, 150
    South America, 162
    South and Southeast Asia, 163

6 Selected Print Resources, 169
    Books, 169
    Briefings and Reports, 181
    Newsletters and Periodicals, 184

7 Selected Nonprint Resources, 187
    Audiotapes, 187
    CD Roms, 188
    Exhibits, 190
    Pamphlets, Photographs and Digital Images, Posters, and
        Press Kits, 191
    Videotapes, 193

Glossary, 207
Index, 211
About the Author, 227

Preface

This book is about the newest forms of one of the oldest institutions on earth. Slavery has been part of human existence since the dawn of history. Slaves have tilled the soil, swept the floors, prepared the food, and worked and worked and worked in any number of ways from the very beginnings of civilization. In almost every culture and society there has been, at one time or another, slavery. In all of those societies slavery has reflected the ideas, the economy, and the power relationships of the moment. At times slavery has been about legal ownership of one person by another. At other times it has been about controlling people, but not about owning them as property. Though it has taken many forms through history, slavery has always been a kind of relationship between people. It is a personal as well as a social relationship, and it is almost always an economic relationship, for slavery is about making a profit from the work of others. Sometimes it is also a legal relationship. The important point is that slavery is dynamic, reflecting local customs and practices, but also changing over time.

When the world is changing rapidly, slavery changes rapidly as well. Slavery has always been part of war, for example. In the past, slaves might be taken on the battlefield or captured in raids. In the Crusades of the Middle Ages, enslaving the enemy was part of the strategy for victory, as well as a way to finance the war effort. In the twentieth century mass slavery became part of the mass warfare of 1939–1945. The German war effort relied on millions of enslaved men, women, and children. Many of these slaves worked to construct the very weapons that would be used to enslave others. Since World War II the pace of social and technological change has accelerated. As the twentieth century turned into the twenty-first, very rapid change was sweeping the world. The end of colonialism, the population explosion, and the end of the Cold War, followed quickly by the globalization of technology, culture, and the economy, have brought tremendous changes. Some of these changes have been in the way that slaves are taken, controlled, and used.

Today slaves are cheaper than they have ever been in human history. The population explosion has created a vast supply of potential workers, and the rapid economic changes of the past fifty years have ensured that many of these people are desperate and vulnerable and easily enslaved. Because they are so cheap, slaves today fulfill a new role in the economy. They are no longer valuable property; they are used and disposed of according to the whims of their slaveholders. But the profits they generate are remarkably high, even though they are normally used in only the most basic kinds of work. Today slavery is a very profitable business.

Slaves are found in almost every country. Altogether there are millions of slaves in the world—concentrated in the developing world, but exploited in the United States, Europe, and Japan as well. The rapid change in the way slavery operates means that governments and other organizations are still trying to come to understand today's slavery. Most people still think of slavery in terms of the slavery of the American South in the mid-nineteenth century. The reality is much more fluid and more difficult to see. As part of the criminal economy, slavery is hidden from view. But as part of the global traffic in human beings and their exploitation, we know that it is growing. This book aims to illuminate slavery as it exists today and to show how it is changing.

It has to be recognized that we do not know a great deal about slavery in the world today. Since most people believe that slavery was abolished long ago, few people are conducting research on it or campaigning against it. Governments and other organizations are just coming to grips with the volume and extent of slavery in the economy. So this book is just a beginning, a starting point for people who want to be part of the quest to understand slavery. Reading it, using it, should help to clarify what we now know (and what we still need to learn) about slavery. It points to the sources, organizations, and people that will carry the reader still further. The aim of this book is not to have all the answers but to be a tool that will help you find the answers to your own unique questions about slavery.

Chapter 1 defines slavery and gives examples of slavery today. It gives estimates of the number of slaves in the world and describes their conditions. The process of change that has created new forms of slavery is traced, and the key factors that make up slavery are discussed. In order to clarify the nature of slavery, the slavery of the American South in 1850 is compared and contrasted to the slavery of today. Since the notion of "race" or ethnicity is much less important to an understanding of contemporary slavery, this shift from slavery based in racism to slavery centered on vulnerability is explained.

Slavery takes several forms around the world, and these are also listed in the first chapter. Case studies provide examples of these forms. The process of globalization is linked to changes in the nature of slavery, and this process and those changes are examined. Once a picture of contemporary slavery has been drawn, this question is addressed: Who is responsible for global slavery? Many people look to the United Nations to lead on the issue of slavery, so the role of the UN and its work are examined. One of the areas that the UN is especially concerned with is the transport, and often enslavement, of illegal migrants. This is called human trafficking, and it is a growing problem.

Other groups and organizations are involved in the work against slavery. Examples of these organizations with descriptions of their work are given for the international, national, and local levels. Many of these groups are concerned with directly liberating slaves and then helping them through rehabilitation, and that process is considered. Chapter 1 concludes by considering the important question, What can we do?

Chapter 2 presents a chronology of slavery worldwide, with emphasis on key events in the past century; Chapter 3 contains a selection of biographical sketches of persons active in contemporary antislavery work and a few historical figures as well. Most of the individuals included in the biographical sketches will be unfamiliar to readers. Since slavery is barely recognized publicly, it has to be said that antislavery workers are even less well known. The ones listed here are just a sample, some suggested by antislavery activists and some from my own experience of researching slavery around the world. Younger people active in antislavery work have been singled out for inclusion. Of course, many people around the world work to combat slavery in near anonymity. In the developing world, as you will read in these sketches, working against slavery can be a dangerous business, and researchers and campaigners have been killed trying to free slaves. Those who work at the more dangerous grassroots level often prefer to keep their identities secret to protect their families.

For that reason the names of some real heroes in the struggle against slavery may never be known.

Chapter 4 presents facts, data, evidence, and firsthand testimony about modern slavery. After some basic statistics about slavery are identified, the key international laws and conventions on slavery are reviewed. Relevant excerpts from these laws and conventions are reproduced here with brief introductions. Most of Chapter 4 is given over to reports, evidence, and testimony about different forms of slavery. These may be press reports, radio transcripts, interviews, statements to the United Nations, or the personal accounts of being a slave. Evidence is given for each of the following types of contemporary slavery: bonded labor, contract slavery, chattel slavery, war slavery, slavery linked to religious practice, forced labor, commercial sex slavery and trafficking, domestic slavery, and slavery linked to child labor.

Organizations concerned with fighting slavery are listed and described in Chapter 5. These include international, national, local, and overseas groups. A special effort has been made to provide links, mostly through the Internet, with organizations in the developing world that are so often ignored in Western media. The information about all these organizations was up-to-date at the time of writing, but remember that these are fluid and dynamic collections of human beings, and so they will be changing, reorganizing, restructuring, and expanding or contracting like all human groups.

Chapter 6 lists print resources. Slavery receives relatively little attention, and the number of printed works is not great, so the resources given here range widely around the world and are, I think, the best and most useful. In an area concerned with a human rights violation like slavery, much of what is written is produced by campaigning groups rather than academics or professional writers, so many of the listed works are briefing papers or reports. A few periodicals are also listed. In many ways the nonprint resources, listed in Chapter 7, are more rich and varied than the print resources. Many filmmakers have worked to open up the subject of slavery and have produced investigative programs exploring the issue and the lives of slaves. These are listed along with other resources, such as exhibitions, posters, press kits, and digital images that can be down loaded from the Internet.

Kevin Bales
Oxford, Mississippi

Acknowledgments

This book benefited from the help, guidance, and hard work of a number of people. Foremost among these is Sally Ramsden, a London-based journalist well known for her work in development and human rights. She provided the research behind much of this book. Catherine Prior helped to construct the database used in Chapter 4. In the United States, Jenni Trovillion, Caroline Tendall, and Jacob Patton did a superlative job on Web-based searches and editing. The London-based organization Anti-Slavery International holds one of the best archives and information centers on contemporary slavery; without access to that resource this book could not have been written. Mary Matheson, Mike Dottridge, David Ould, Becky Smaga, Jen Escher, Jeff Howarth, and Beth Herzfeld, all Anti-Slavery International staff, guided me through their library and checked my work to make sure I and my associates had not missed anything. Much of the work on this book was done while I was on a sabbatical leave from my post at the School of Sociology and Social Policy at the University of Surrey Roehampton in England. The support of the University of Surrey Roehampton, and especially Professor Graham Fennell, was very important. The writing was made much easier by the hospitality, support, and stimulating company provided by the Croft Institute for International Studies at the University of Mississippi and its director, Professor Michael Metcalf. The errors and omissions in this book, of course, all belong to the author.

1

Introduction

Most of us think that slavery ended a long time ago—or that if it does exist, it only happens in poor countries far away. Maybe that is one reason why Hilda Dos Santos stayed in slavery for so long in the well-to-do suburbs outside Washington, D.C. Hilda had worked as a domestic servant in her native Brazil for many years, and when her employers, Rene and Margarida Bonnetti, asked her to move with them to the United States in 1979, she agreed. Once in the United States, the Bonnettis stopped paying Hilda and locked her into a life of slavery. She cleaned the house, did the yardwork, cooked the meals, cared for the pets, and even shoveled snow without gloves, boots, or a coat. Her bed was a mattress in the basement, and she was not allowed to use the showers or bathtubs in the house. Her food was scraps and leftovers, and when Hilda made mistakes in her work, she was beaten. Mrs. Bonnetti once poured hot soup over her face and chest when she didn't like the way it tasted. When a cut on Hilda's leg became infected the Bonnettis refused to provide medical care. A stomach tumor grew to the size of a soccer ball without any help from the Bonnettis; a neighbor finally took her to the hospital. It was there that social workers were alerted to her situation and the law stepped in. She had been in slavery for twenty years.

Hilda Dos Santos is typical of many slaves in the world today—poor, vulnerable people tricked into slavery. Her case demonstrates that slavery is alive and well. If her case was unique it would be shocking enough, but Hilda is one of hundreds, perhaps thousands, of slaves in the United Sates, and one of millions of slaves in the world. The slavery she suffered is much the same as the old kinds of slavery we learn about in history. It is still about one person controlling another, taking away an individual's free will and abusing and stealing his or her life and livelihood. But slavery today is also different, for slavery has evolved into new—and in some ways more destructive—forms that stretch through our global economy to touch us wherever we are.

This book will introduce you to modern slavery around the world, to slaves and slaveholders, and to the people that are working to stop slavery. It will explain how slavery has changed since the Atlantic slave trade of the nineteenth century and why racial differences are no longer very important in slavery. We'll look closely at some instances of real slavery and consider what these cases have in common. And we'll examine how slavery fits into our global economy and what international organizations are doing to fight it. But first we have to think about how we can understand and define this ancient yet dynamic and changing thing that we call slavery.

Slavery Defined

Since the abolition of legal slavery in the nineteenth century, the word "slavery" has been used to describe many different things: prostitution, prison labor, even the sale of human organs. More than 300 international slavery treaties have been signed since 1815, but none have defined slavery in exactly the same way. Many definitions of slavery focus on *the legal ownership of one person by another,* since most slavery in the nineteenth century took that form. But it is important to remember that slavery has been part of human history for thousands of years. Some of that time slavery was about legal ownership of people, but at other times it was not.

Before we can define "slavery," we need to recognize the characteristics and conditions that make it what it is. Slavery is a relationship between two people. It is both a social and economic relationship, and like all relationships it has certain characteristics and rules. The key characteristics of slavery are not about ownership but about how people are controlled. The core characteristic of slavery throughout history, whether it was legal or not, is *violence.* The slave master or slaveholder controls a slave by using or threatening violence. Slavery is about no choices at all, no control over your life, and a constant fear of violence. This is the key to slavery. Violence brings a person into slavery. Many people who become slaves are tricked into it. Many people, following a trail of lies, walk into enslavement, but what keeps them there is violence. Once enslaved, there are all sorts of ways that slaves are held in slavery—sometimes it is the way the slave gives up and gives into slavery, sometimes it is about the personal relationships that develop between slaves and slaveholders—but the essential ingredient is violence.

The second key characteristic of slavery is *loss of free will;* slaves are under the complete control of someone else. There is no other person, authority, or government the slave can turn to for protection. Slaves must do as they are told or they will suffer. The third characteristic is that slavery is normally used to *exploit* someone in some kind of economic activity. No one enslaves another person just to be mean; people are enslaved to make a profit. Most slaveholders see themselves as normal businesspeople. They have little interest in hurting anyone, in being cruel or torturing people; it is just part of the job. Slavery is about money. If we put these characteristics together we can define slavery in this way: *Slavery is a social and economic relationship in which a person is controlled through violence or its threat, paid nothing, and economically exploited.*

In some ways this is a narrow definition. It excludes many things that people have called "slavery" (like the selling of human organs), but it includes all those relationships that most people agree are slavery, and it is broad enough to include many kinds of slavery around the world.

A definition that works for many different types of slavery is important because slavery, like all human relationships, changes over time. The main characteristic of slavery is control through violence, but that can take many forms. The conditions in which slaves live around the world vary enormously. In those few places where old styles of slavery are still practiced, like Mauritania, there are long-term, often lifelong relationships between slave and master. In most countries slavery is more short-term and dangerous.

How Many Slaves?

No one knows how many slaves are in the world. Slavery is illegal in virtually every country, and that means it is usually hidden from view. But if we carefully review all the information available about slaves around the world, we can estimate that there are perhaps 27 million slaves alive today. Where are all these slaves? The biggest part of that 27 million, perhaps 15 to 20 million, is in India, Pakistan, and Nepal. Slavery also is concentrated in Southeast Asia, in Northern and Western Africa, and in parts of South America, but there are some slaves in almost every country in the world, including the United States, Japan, and many European countries. To put it in perspective, today's slave population is greater than the population of Canada and six times greater than the population of Israel.

Slaves tend to be used in simple, nontechnological, traditional work. The largest proportion works in agriculture. Other kinds of work include brick making, mining and quarrying, textiles, leather working, prostitution, gem working and jewelry making, cloth and carpet making, domestic servantry, forest clearing, charcoal making, and working in shops. Much of this work is aimed at local sale and consumption, but slave-made goods filter throughout the global economy. Carpets, fireworks, jewelry, metal goods, steel (made with slave-produced charcoal), and foods like grains, rice, and sugar are imported directly to North America and Europe after being produced using slave labor. In countries where slavery and industry coexist, cheap slave-made goods and food keep factory wages low and help make everything from toys to computers less expensive.

The Nature of Contemporary Slavery

As a human relationship, slavery has changed over time. Of course, slavery remains the same in that one person has complete control of another person, but exactly how that happens changes from time to time and place to place. Slavery today is different from slavery in the past in three important ways. First, slaves today are cheaper than they have ever been. The cost of slaves has fallen to a historical low, and they can be acquired in some parts of the world for as little as $10. Second, the length of time that slaves are held has also fallen. In the past, slavery was usually a lifelong condition; today it is often temporary, lasting just a few years or even months. Third, slavery is globalized. This means that the forms of slavery in different parts of the world are becoming more alike. The way slaves are used and the part they play in the world economy is increasingly similar wherever they are. These changes have come about very quickly, occurring, for the most part, in the past fifty years. What has made these new forms of slavery possible?

How Slavery Changed into Its Modern Form

There are three key factors in the emergence of this new kind of slavery. The first is the *dramatic increase in world population* since World War II, which has increased the supply of potential slaves. In a classic example of "supply and demand," the increase in population has also driven down their price. Since 1945 the world population has tripled from about 2 billion people to over 6 billion. The greatest part of that increase has been in those countries where slavery is most prevalent today. Across Southeast Asia, the Indian subcontinent, Africa, and the Arab countries, the population boom has more than tripled populations and flooded countries with children. Over half the population in some countries is under the age of fifteen. In countries that were already poor, the sheer weight of numbers sometimes overwhelms resources. Especially in those parts of the world where slavery still existed or had been practiced in the past, the population explosion radically increased the number of people who could be enslaved and drove down their price.

The second key factor is *rapid social and economic change.* This has been caused in part by the population explosion, which created global conditions that make new forms of slavery possible. In many developing countries the postcolonial period brought immense wealth to the elite and continued or increased the poverty of the majority of the population. Throughout Africa and Asia, the past fifty years have been scarred by civil war and the wholesale looting of resources by dictators, who were often supported by the powerful nations of Europe and North America. Countries with little to sell on the world market have been put deeply into debt to pay for the weapons the dictators needed to hold on to power. Meanwhile, traditional ways of agricultural life and farming were sacrificed to concentrate on cash crops needed to pay off those foreign debts. As the world economy grew and became more global, it had a profound impact on people in the Third World and the small-scale farming that supported them. The shift from small-scale farming to cash-crop agriculture, the loss of common land shared by all the people in a village, and government policies that pushed down farm income in favor of cheap food for city workers have all helped to bankrupt millions of peasants and drive them from their land. All across the Third World the slums and shantytowns that surround big cities hold millions of these displaced people. They come to the cities in search of jobs but find they are competing for jobs with thousands of other people. With little income and no job security, they are powerless and very vulnerable.

Some national and global policies and trends also threaten these vulnerable displaced people. Although economic modernization may have good effects as well, particularly in improvements to health care and education, the political focus in many developing countries concentrates on economic growth rather than on sustainable livelihoods for the majority of people. So while the rich of the developing world grow richer, the poor have fewer and fewer options, and in the disruption that comes with rapid social change, slavery can become one of those options.

The end of the Cold War and the ending of state control of the economy in the former Soviet Union also served to widen the opportunities for slavery. William Greider explained it well:

> One of the striking qualities of the post–Cold War globalisation is how easily business and government in the capitalist democracies have abandoned the values they putatively espoused for forty years during the struggle against communism—individual liberties and political legitimacy based on free elections. Concern for human rights, including freedom of assembly for workers wishing to speak for themselves, has been pushed aside by commercial opportunity. Multinationals plunge confidently into new markets, from Vietnam to China, where governments routinely control and abuse their own citizens. (Greider 1997, 37)

Government corruption is the third key factor that supports this new form of slavery. Just having large numbers of vulnerable people doesn't automatically make them slaves. In order to turn vulnerable people into slaves on any scale, violence must be used. One of the basic ideas about democratic government is that it should have a monopoly on the means of violence. The military and the police are generally the only ones who can use weapons and commit violence legally. Normally they do so to protect citizens from crime, including criminal or illegal violence. But if anyone in a society can use violence freely for their own ends, without fear of being arrested and locked up, then they can force others into slavery. To do that on any scale requires government corruption, especially police corruption. In some countries the police act as slave catchers, pursuing and punishing escaped slaves. Often police require that people holding slaves pay them weekly for police "protection." For the slave-using businessperson, payments to the police are just a normal part of business. When laws against kidnapping are not enforced, those who have the means of violence (often the police themselves) can harvest slaves.

Old and New Slavery Compared

The population boom, the vulnerability of poor people in the Third World, and government corruption have led to new forms of slavery. For the first time in human history there is an absolute glut of potential slaves. It is a dramatic example of supply and demand. There are so many possible slaves that their value has fallen and fallen. Slaves are now so cheap that they have become cost-effective in many new kinds of work. Their value is so low that it has completely changed the way they are seen and used. Slaves are no longer major investments. This fact has changed the nature of the relationship between slaves and slaveholders. It has also dramatically changed the amount of profit to be made from a slave as well as the length of time a person might be enslaved. And it has made the question of legal ownership less important. When slaves were expensive, it was important to safeguard that investment by having clear and legally documented ownership. Slaves of the past were worth stealing and worth chasing down if they escaped. Today slaves are so cheap that they are not worth securing permanent ownership. The fact that ownership of slaves is now illegal is not really a problem for slaveholders; slaves are disposable.

Disposability means that the new forms of slavery are less permanent. Across the world the length of time a slave spends in bondage varies enormously. It is simply not profitable to keep slaves when they are not immediately useful. Although most are enslaved for years, some are held for only a few months. In countries where sugarcane is grown, for example, people are often enslaved for a single harvest. Since they are used only for a short time, there is no reason to invest heavily in their upkeep. There is also little reason to insure that they survive their enslavement. Although slaves in the American South in the nineteenth century were often horribly treated, there was still a strong incentive to keep them alive as long as possible. Slaves were like valuable livestock; the owner needed to make back his investment. There was also pressure to breed them and produce more slaves, since it was usually cheaper to raise new slaves than to buy adults. Today no slaveholder wants to spend money supporting useless infants.

The key differences between old and new forms of slavery are these:

Old Forms of Slavery	New Forms of Slavery
Legal ownership asserted	Legal ownership avoided
High purchase cost	Very low purchase cost
Low profits	Very high profits
Shortage of potential slaves	Surplus of potential slaves
Long-term relationship	Short-term relationship
Slaves maintained	Slaves disposable
Ethnic differences important	Ethnic differences less important

This is clarified when we look at a specific example. Perhaps the best-studied and best-understood form of old slavery was the system of slavery in the American South before 1860, particularly the use of slaves in cotton cultivation (see, for example, Ransom 1989). Slaves were at a premium. The demand for slaves was reflected in their price. By 1850 an average field laborer was selling for $1,000 to $1,800. This was three to six times the average yearly wage of an American worker at the time; in today's money it would equal around $50,000 to $100,000. Despite their high cost, slaves generated, on average, profits of only about 5 percent each year. If the cotton market went up, a plantation owner could make a very good profit on his slaves, but if the price of cotton fell, he might be forced to sell slaves to stay in business. Ownership was clearly demonstrated by bills of sale and titles of ownership, and slaves could be used as collateral for loans or to pay off debts. Slaves were often brutalized to keep them under control, but they were also maintained as befitted their sizable investment. And there was, of course, extreme racial differentiation between slaveholder and slave. The racist element was so strong that a very small genetic difference—being one-eighth black and seven-eighths white—could still mean lifelong enslavement (Genovese 1976, 416, 420).

A point of comparison to the old slavery of the American South is the agricultural slave in debt bondage in modern India. In India today land rather than labor is at a premium. India's population has grown enormously; the country currently has three times the population of the United States in one-third the space. The glut of potential workers means that free labor must regularly compete with slave labor, and the resulting pressure on agricultural wages pushes free laborers toward bondage. When free farmers run out of money, when a crop fails or a member of the family becomes ill and needs medicine, they have few choices. Faced with a crisis, they borrow from a local landowner enough money to meet the crisis, but having no other possessions they have to use their own lives as collateral. The debt against which a person is bonded, that is, the price of a laborer, might be 500 to 1,000 rupees (about $30 to $60). The bond is completely open-ended; the slave must work for the slaveholder until the slaveholder decides the debt is repaid. The debt might be carried into a second and third generation, growing under fraudulent accounting by the slaveholder, who may also seize and sell the children of the bonded laborer against the debt. The functional reality is one of slavery, but five key differences exist between this and old slavery.

The first difference is that no one tries to assert legal ownership of the bonded laborer. He or she is held under threat of violence, often physically locked up, but no one asserts that he or she is in fact "property." The second difference is that the bonded laborer is made partially or wholly responsible for his or her own upkeep, which results in cost savings for the slaveholder. A third difference is that if a bonded laborer is not able to work, perhaps due to illness or injury, or is not needed for work, he or she can be abandoned or disposed of by the slaveholder, who takes no responsibility for maintenance. The fourth difference has to do with race; the ethnic differentiation is not nearly so rigid as that of old slavery. Bonded laborers may well belong to a different caste than the slaveholder, but this is not always the case. The key distinction is about wealth and power, not caste.

Finally, a major difference between old and new slavery is in the profit to be made on an enslaved laborer. Agricultural bonded laborers in India generate one of the lowest profits found across all contemporary slavery, but they can still produce over 50-percent profit per year for the slaveholder. This high profit is due, in part, to the low cost of the slave in terms of the loan advanced, but the profit is still smaller than most other forms of modern slavery since it reflects the low returns on old-fashioned, small-scale agriculture.

Agricultural debt bondage in India still has some characteristics of older forms of slavery, such as the fact that the slaves will be held for long periods. A better example of new forms of slavery is the young women put to work in prostitution in Thailand. A population explosion in Thailand has resulted in a surplus of potential slaves. Rapid economic change has led to new poverty and desperation. Young Thai women and girls are often initially lured from rural areas with the promise of work in restaurants or factories. There is no ethnic difference; if anything, the difference is rural (slaves) versus urban (slaveholders). The girls might be sold by their parents to a broker or be tricked by an agent. Away from their homes they are brutalized and enslaved and sold to a brothel owner. The brothel owners place the girls in debt bondage and tell them they must pay back their purchase price plus interest through prostitution. The calculation of the debt and the interest is, of course, completely in the hands of the brothel owners. Manipulating the figures to their advantage, they can keep the girls as long as they want, and they don't need to show any legal ownership. The brothels do have to feed the girls and keep them presentable, but if they become ill or injured or too old, they are disposed of. In Thailand today this often happens when a girl tests positive for HIV. This form of "contract" debt bondage is extremely profitable. A girl aged twelve to fifteen can be purchased for $800 to $2,000, and the costs of running a brothel and feeding the girls are relatively low. The profit is often as high as 800 percent a year. This kind of return can be made on a girl for five to ten years. After that, especially if she becomes ill or HIV positive, the girl will be dumped.

The Question of Race

In the new forms of slavery, race means little. Ethnic and racial differences were used in the past to explain and excuse slavery. These differences allowed slaveholders to make up reasons why slavery was acceptable and even benefited the slaves. The *otherness* of the slaves made it easier to use the violence and the cruelty necessary for total control. This otherness could be defined in almost any way—a different religion, or tribe, or skin color, or language, or customs, or economic class. Any of these could be used to separate the slaves from the slaveholders. Maintaining these differences required tremendous investment in some very irrational ideas, and the crazier the justifying idea, the more strongly it was insisted upon. The "Founding Fathers" of the United States of America had to go through moral, linguistic, and political contortions to explain why the "land of the free" only applied to white people.[1] Many of them knew they were lying, that they were betraying their most cherished ideals. They were driven to it because slavery was worth a lot of money to a lot of people in Colonial America. They still went to the trouble of legal and political justification because back then they felt they had to make moral excuses for their economic decisions.

Today the morality of money overrides most others. Most slaveholders feel no need to explain or defend their choice to use slavery. Slavery is a very profitable business, and a good profit is reason enough. Freed of ideas that restrict the status of slave to "other" and of ideas that say you can't enslave your own people, modern slaveholders use other criteria to choose slaves. When you can enslave people from your own country, your costs are low. Slaves in the American South were very expensive, in part due to the fact that the first generation of them had to be shipped thousands of miles from Africa. When you can go to the next town or region for slaves, transport costs fall to a minimum. The question isn't "Are they the right color to be slaves?" but "Are they vulnerable enough to be enslaved?" The criteria of enslavement is not about color, tribe, or religion; it is about weakness, gullibility, and vulnerability.

It is true that in some countries there are ethnic or religious differences between slaves and slaveholders. In Pakistan, for example, many enslaved brick makers are Christians, and the slaveholders are Muslim. In India slave and slaveholder may be of different castes. In Thailand they might come from different regions of the country. But in Pakistan there are Christians who are not slaves, and in India some members of a caste are free while others are enslaved. Their caste or religion simply reflects their vulnerability to enslavement; it doesn't cause it. Only in one country, Mauritania, does the racism of old slavery persist. In Mauritania, black slaves are held by Arab slaveholders and race is a key division, but this is the last and fading survival of old slavery. Of course, some cultures are more divisive than others. Cultural ideas in Japan very strongly separate Japanese people from everyone else, and so enslaved prostitutes in Japan are more likely to be Thai or Philippine women, though they may also be Japanese. The key difference is that Japanese women are not nearly so vulnerable and desperate as Thais or Filipinas. And the Thai women are available for shipment to Japan because Thais are enslaving Thais. The same pattern occurs in the oil-rich states of Saudi Arabia and Kuwait, where Muslim Arabs might enslave Sri Lankan Hindus, Filipino Christians, or Nigerian Muslims. The common denominator is poverty, not color. Behind every assertion of ethnic difference is the reality of economic disparity. If every left-handed person in the world were made destitute tomorrow, there would soon be slaveholders arguing that slavery was perhaps the best thing for them. Modern slaveholders are color blind, but they are predators acutely perceptive to weakness. Although slavery has been around for thousands of years, these predators are rapidly adapting it to the new global economy.

The Forms of Contemporary Slavery

Slavery has never existed in a single form. In some ways every relationship of slavery that links two people might be unique, but there are patterns in these relationships. There are several forms of slavery common enough to have their own names. The three main types given here are not an exhaustive list, but they do represent the prevalent forms of slavery today, under which most modern slaves are held:

Chattel slavery is the form closest to old slavery. A person is captured, born, or sold into permanent servitude, and ownership is often asserted. The slave's children are normally treated as property as well and can be sold by the slaveholder. Occasionally, these slaves are kept as items of conspicuous consumption. This form is most often found in Northern and Western Africa and in some Arab countries, but it represents a small proportion of slaves in the modern world.

Debt bondage is the most common form of slavery in the world. A person pledges him/herself against a loan of money, but the length and nature of the service is not defined, nor does his or her labor diminish the original debt. The debt can be passed down to subsequent generations, thus enslaving offspring, or "defaulting" can be punished by seizing or selling children into further debt bonds. Ownership is not normally asserted, but there is complete physical control of the bonded laborer. Debt bondage is most common in South Asia.

There are in fact two distinct forms of debt bondage. In many cases of debt bondage, the slaves' work (and indeed their very lives) become *collateral* for the debt. This means that all of their work belongs to the moneylender until the debt is repaid. This establishes the trap of bondage—since all their work is the property of the lender until the debt is repaid, debtors are unable to ever earn enough to repay the debt by their own labor. This arrangement is a common form of the debt bondage in India. In other places the work of the debtor may, supposedly, be used to pay off the debt, but through false accounting or charging very high interest, repayment remains forever out of reach. In the first form the agreement that changes the debtor and all his or her work into collateral pretty well means the debtor will never be able to repay his or her debt. In the second form it is a violation of the loan agreement, when the value of the work is not really used to pay off the loan, that traps the debtor.

Contract slavery shows how modern labor relations are used to hide new forms of slavery. Contracts are offered that guarantee employment, perhaps in a workshop or factory, but when workers are taken to their place of work, they find they are enslaved. The contract is used as an enticement to trick persons into slavery; it is also a way to make the slavery look legitimate if necessary. Ownership is not asserted, and if legal questions are raised the contract is produced, but the slave is under threat of violence, has no freedom of movement, and is paid nothing. This is the most rapidly growing form of slavery, and it is probably the second largest form today. Contract slavery is most often found in Southeast Asia, Brazil, some Arab states, and some parts of the Indian subcontinent.

These types are not mutually exclusive. Contracts may be issued to chattel slaves in order to conceal their enslavement. Girls trapped into prostitution by debt bondage will sometimes have contracts that specify their obligations, but not always. The important thing to remember is that *people are enslaved by violence and held against their wills for exploitation.* The labels we apply to the types of slavery are useful to help us keep track of the patterns of enslavement and for what they might suggest about how slavery might be attacked. The labels reflect the nature of the relationship between the slave and the slaveholder, but these relationships are fluid and changeable.

In addition to these three main types of slavery, several other kinds account for a small part of the total number of slaves. Most of these tend to be restricted to specific geographical regions or political situations. A good example of slavery linked to politics is what is often called *war slavery* and includes government-sponsored slavery. In Burma (Myanmar) today there is widespread capture and enslavement of civilians by the government and the army. Tens of thousands of men, women, and children are used as laborers or bearers in military campaigns against indigenous peoples or on government construction projects. The Burmese military dictatorship doesn't suggest that they own the people they have enslaved—in fact, they deny that they enslave anyone—but the International Labor Organization (ILO), U.S. State

Department, and human rights organizations confirm that violence is used to hold a large number of Burmese people in bondage. War slavery is also a feature of the ongoing civil war in Sudan.

In some parts of the Caribbean and in Western Africa, children are given or sold into domestic service. They are sometimes called *restavecs*. Ownership is not asserted, but strict control, enforced by violence, is maintained over the child. The return on the enslaved child is not in terms of profits generated but in the domestic services provided. It is a culturally approved way of dealing with "extra" children, and some are treated well, but for most it is a kind of slavery that lasts until adulthood.

Slavery can also be linked to religion, as with the *devadasi* women in India, or the children who are ritual slaves in Ghana.[2] Each year, several thousand girls and young women are given by their families as slaves to local fetish priests in southeastern Ghana, Togo, Benin, and southwestern Nigeria. The girls are given to the priests in order to atone for sins committed by members of their families, often rape. The girls may, in fact, be the products of rape, and their slavery is seen as a way of appeasing the gods for the crimes committed by their male relatives. The girls are given to a local priest as a slave when they are about ten years old, and it is required that they must be virgins. The girl then stays with the priest, cooking and cleaning, farming, and serving the priest sexually until the priest frees her, usually after she has borne several children. At that point the slave's family must provide another young girl to replace her. Ghana's Constitution forbids slavery, but the practice is justified by villagers and priests as a religious requirement.

As can be seen by the preceding cases, slavery comes in many forms and can be found in virtually all countries. A recent investigation in Britain found young girls held in slavery and forced to be prostitutes in Birmingham and Manchester.[3] Enslaved domestic workers have been found and freed in London and Paris. In the United States textile workers have been found locked inside a factory and working under armed guards. Enslaved Thai and Philippine women have been freed from brothels in New York, Seattle, and Los Angeles.[4] This list could go on and on. Almost all of the countries where slavery "cannot" exist have slaves inside their borders, but, it must be said, in very small numbers compared to the Indian subcontinent and the Far East. Altogether slaves constitute a vast workforce that supports the world economy we all share.

Examples of Contemporary Slavery

Lives up in Smoke

In a recent survey over a third of all American high school students said that they used tobacco at least once in the last month. That students should be doing something so stupid is alarming, but what is even worse is that many of them were supporting slavery as they smoked. Almost 300,000 students said that they had been smoking *beedis,* small flavored cigarettes from India. Would they have done so if they knew that most beedis are made by slave children?

In the southern Indian state of Tamil Nadu, outside the big city of Madras, are small towns where millions of beedis are made. On the outskirts of one of these towns lives an eleven-year-old boy named Vikram. He and many of the other children in his town are slaves. When Vikram was nine his younger brother became very ill. His family is very poor, and the only way his parents could buy medicine was to borrow money from a local man. This man controls the production of beedis in their village. This moneylender used the loan as a way to take Vikram into debt bondage. Since Vikram's parents had nothing else to give as collateral, the moneylender said they must pledge Vikram against the debt. His parents' choice was a terrible one: to save the life of their youngest son, they must put their oldest son into bondage. For the moneylender it was business as usual, and he had obtained another slave for just a few dollars. Today none of the work that Vikram does pays off the debt. He is basically the property of the moneylender until his parents can find the money for repayment. Two years after it was first made, the debt has grown with extra charges to about $65.

Vikram works from six in the morning until nine at night, with breaks for breakfast and lunch. Each day he rolls about 1,500 beedi cigarettes by hand. Each beedi is smaller than a normal cigarette, and instead of paper the tobacco is wrapped in a leaf from the kendu tree. Since no glue is used, each beedi must be tied shut with a thread and a tiny knot. Sitting cross-legged on the floor with a tray of tobacco and kendu leaves on his lap, Vikram's hands fly through the motions of wrapping, rolling, and tying the beedis. He has to work very quickly, like a machine, if he is to make the number required of him everyday. If he is sick, he still has to work, and if he fails to deliver the full number, his debt will be increased. He can watch the world, or a very small piece of it, from the porch where he sits rolling the beedis, but he cannot be part of it. Some of the local children go off to school in the mornings; he sees them go as he rolls beedi. In the afternoon other children play around the village, and Vikram watches but cannot join in. His childhood has been taken by the moneylender to provide virtually free labor and high profits.

In some ways Vikram's slavery could be worse. At night he is allowed to go home for supper and to sleep with his family. Of course, this is very clever of the moneylender, since it means that he doesn't have to provide food or lodging for his slave. Vikram, like so many modern slaves, was very cheap to buy and is also very cheap to maintain. Until recently a boy in Vikram's position would have little to look forward to except years spent rolling beedis. Many children have had their whole childhood taken by beedi rolling. When they become young adults the moneylender will often turn them to other kinds of work, since their larger hands are not as nimble for rolling beedis. When they finally stop rolling beedis, they are young men with no education and little experience of the world. Their job prospects, if they can get away from the moneylender, are dismal.

Slavery in the City of Lights

In France I interviewed an animated twenty-two-year-old woman, who told me of her life as a slave in Paris:

> I was raised by my grandmother in Mali, and when I was still a little girl a woman my family knew came and asked her if she could take me to Paris to care for her children. She told my grandmother that she would put me in school and that I would learn French. But when I came to Paris I was not sent to school, I had to work every day. In their house I did all the work, I cleaned the house, cooked the meals, cared for the children, and washed and fed the baby. Every day I started work before 7 a.m. and finished about 11 p.m.; I never had a day off. My mistress did nothing— she slept late and then watched television or went out.
>
> One day I told her that I wanted to go to school. She replied that she had not brought me to France to go to school but to take care of her children. I was so tired and run down. I had problems with my teeth; sometimes my cheek would swell and the pain would be

terrible. Sometimes I had stomachaches, but when I was ill I still had to work. Sometimes when I was in pain I would cry, but my mistress would shout at me.

I slept on the floor in one of the children's bedrooms; my food was their leftovers. I was not allowed to take food from the refrigerator like the children. If I took food she would beat me. She often beat me. She would slap me all the time. She beat me with the broom, with kitchen tools, or whipped me with an electric cable. Sometimes I would bleed. I still have marks on my body.

Once in 1992 I was late going to get the children from school. My mistress and her husband were furious with me and beat and then threw me out on the street. I had nowhere to go, I didn't understand anything, and I wandered on the streets. After some time her husband found me and took me back to their house. Then they beat me again with a wire attached to a broomstick until I lost consciousness.

Sometime later one of the children came and untied me. I lay on the floor where they had left me for several days. The pain was terrible but no one treated my wounds. When I was able to stand I had to start work again, but after this I was always locked in the apartment. They continued to beat me.

Seba was finally freed when a neighbor, after hearing the sounds of abuse and beating, managed to talk to her. Seeing her scars and wounds, the neighbor called the police and the French Committee Against Modern Slavery (CCEM), which brought a case against Seba's abusers and took Seba into care. Medical examinations confirmed that she had been tortured. Today Seba is well cared for, living with a volunteer family. She is receiving counseling and learning to read and write. Recovery will take years, but she is a remarkably strong young woman. What amazed me was how far Seba still needs to go. As we talked I realized that though she was twenty-two and intelligent, her understanding of the world was less developed than the average five-year-old's. For example, until she was freed she had little understanding of time—no knowledge of weeks, months, or years. For Seba there was only the endless round of work and sleep. She knew that there were hot days and cold days, but she never learned that the seasons follow a pattern. If she had once known her birthday she had since forgotten it, and she did not know her age. She is baffled by the idea of "choice." Her volunteer family tries to help her make choices, but she still can't grasp the concept. I asked Seba to draw the best picture of a person she could. She told me it was the first time she had ever tried to draw a person, this is the result:

If Seba's case were unique it would be shocking enough, but Seba is one of perhaps three thousand household slaves in Paris. Nor is this slavery unique to Paris. In London, New York, Zurich, Los Angeles, and across the world children are brutalized as household slaves. And they are just one small group of the world's slaves.

Slavery and Globalization

Globalization is hard to define because it is still occurring and changing. But most people agree that globalization is the dramatic worldwide shift responsible for three key changes: (1) It is reducing the amount of time required to communicate with anyone, as well as making physical distance between people much less important; (2) it is leading to the emergence of global tastes and global ideas, from what is stylish in shoes and food to ideas about human rights and culture; and (3) it is reducing the importance of nations and increasing the importance of businesses or groups that are transnational.

These changes apply to slavery as well. In the nineteenth century slavery was, by definition, a social and economic relationship controlled by national governments. Slavery was given precise legal status within the boundaries of a country (or sometimes a state within a country), and removing a slave from that country meant automatic freedom. Unfortunately for contemporary slaves, defining slavery as legal ownership in a certain country or state means that many people think that slavery was abolished when countries stopped allowing legal slavery. Of course, slavery did not end when slavery laws were changed, and more important, the globalization of transnational organizations applies to criminal groups as well.

Globalization is seen in the ongoing loss of government control over international trade. When young people mounted big protests at the World Trade Organization meetings in Seattle in 1999, they were drawing attention to the fact that no one seems to be in control on international trade, which means that no one is protecting people from the worst outcomes of trade. The trade in human beings is also difficult for governments to control. The trade in people is sometimes called "trafficking" or "human trafficking." The United Nations estimates that $7 billion is made each year by trafficking in people. These profits flow across national borders, enriching criminal networks. Governments are used to enforcing law within their borders, but when people and profits are moved rapidly from country to country it is difficult for law enforcement to keep up.

The spread of production and products around the world is another mark of globalization. Today we are not surprised to see that our shoes are made in Italy, our shirts in India, our cars in Mexico, or that our fruit comes from Africa and our fish from Norway. Global businesses can pull together all of these products from around the world. Global slavery does the same. Slaves are recruited in one country to be sent to another, or they are shipped thousands of miles within the same country. It is true that in the nineteenth century slaves were moved long distances in a one-way traffic from Africa to the Americas, but the trade today sees slaves moved in many directions all around the world.

Before globalization, people were concerned with "fixed" capital investments, like factories or lifelong slaves, and with long-term planning. The globalized world is more concerned with flexibility than fixed capital, and with processes of production rather than permanence. The same is true of slavery. Slaves are so cheap now that they are not seen as long-term investments, just flexible resources to be used or thrown away as needed. And this more temporary, low-cost slavery is also becoming more common around the globe. Whether slaves are cutting sugarcane in the Caribbean, making bricks in Pakistan, or mining in Brazil, the nature of slavery is merging into a more global form. And because transnational companies now tie together the world's economy, we may be using or profiting from the work of these slaves.

Who Is Responsible for Global Slavery?

If responsibility for slaveholding is extended to those who profit from it, we have to confront a shocking ethical problem. Those who profit from slavery might include you or me or anyone. Pension funds or mutual funds may be buying stock (which is, after all, part-ownership) in companies that own companies that subcontract slave labor. Some key questions are, How many links have to stand between a slave and an "owner" for them to be held responsible? Is ignorance an excuse? If your job were to depend on the availability of slave-produced raw materials, where would you stand? There are, in fact, several layers of responsibility. But how much responsibility does the average person carry for the eradication of slavery? William Greider points out that

> The deepest meaning of the global industrial revolution is that people no longer have free choice in the matter of identity. Ready or not, they are already of the world. As producers or consumers, as workers or merchants or investors, they are now bound to distant others through the complex strands of commerce and finance reorganising the globe as a unified marketplace. The prosperity of South Carolina or Scotland is deeply linked to Stuttgart's or Kuala Lumpur's. The true social values of Californians or Swedes will be determined by what is tolerated in the factories of Thailand or Bangladesh. (Greider 1997, 333)

If people do not participate in slavery through investment, they almost certainly have through consumption. Slave-produced goods and services flow into the global market, making up a tiny but significant part of what we buy. But the sheer volume of our consumption overwhelms our ability to make responsible choices. We don't have time to research the living conditions of the people who produced everything we buy. And if we *could* ask these questions, how would we go about it? Is it the responsibility of the local supermarket to investigate labor relations around the world, or to get you the best food at the lowest price? We also have to think about what happens when we get answers we don't like. For example, Haitian men, women, and children have been enslaved to harvest sugarcane in the Dominican Republic—sugar exported to the United States and other countries. Is the average consumer ready to pay $5 for a candy bar if that is what it takes to ensure that the producers are not enslaved and that they receive a decent wage? When enough research reveals where and how slave-made goods enter our lives, there will be an even bigger question to face: How much is the average person willing to pay to end slavery? Meanwhile, most people assume that the problem should be dealt with by governments and the United Nations, yet the power of the UN turns out to be less than that of consumers.

The Role of the State and the United Nations: International Law and Slavery

When the now-defunct League of Nations was set up after World War I, one of its first major statements was a convention against slavery (a convention is an agreement made between countries that is less formal than a treaty). Commonly known as the 1926 Slavery Convention, it called on every country that signed it (and most countries have done so) to "prevent and suppress the slave trade; and to bring about . . . the complete abolition of slavery in all its forms." When the Universal Declaration of Human Rights was published by the newly formed United Nations in 1948, freedom from slavery was seen as one of the most fundamental of human rights. Article 4 reads, "No one shall be held in slavery or servitude; slavery and the slave trade shall be prohibited in all their forms." In 1956 a Supplementary Convention was added that included debt bondage, serfdom, and unfree forms of marriage in the UN's definition of slavery.

It is important to remember that only one arm of the United

Nations, the Security Council, has the power to punish countries or mobilize armed forces. It is the Security Council that decided, for example, to intervene in Kuwait, East Timor, and Kosovo. And even the Security Council has to rely on voluntary support from member countries. Most of the other UN organizations are primarily "talking shops." They investigate, review, discuss, put forward resolutions and conventions, but cannot require any country to act in a certain way. Slavery is an important concern within the United Nations, but it must compete with many other concerns. The United Nations is a large bureaucracy; slavery comes under the Economic and Social Council that was set up when the United Nations was formed. Within the Economic and Social Council is the Commission on Human Rights, and within that commission is the Subcommission on Prevention of Discrimination and Protection of Minorities. The commission and subcommission meet every year to consider human rights issues. Prior to these meetings a number of working groups get together to focus on particular issues; one of these is the Working Group on Contemporary Forms of Slavery. It calls for reports from groups like Anti-Slavery International on slavery around the world, and it passes resolutions calling on countries to enforce their own laws and the treaties they have signed. But like other parts of the United Nations, the working group cannot require or force countries to take action against slavery. Sometimes the Commission on Human Rights also appoints people to be special reporters or investigators on particular issues, like torture or the rights of women. So far, there has never been a special reporter on slavery, but many people believe that this would be an important step to highlight the extent of slavery today.

Other parts of the United Nations are also very concerned with slavery, especially the International Labor Organization. The ILO, for example, runs the International Program on the Elimination of Child Labor (IPEC), which is responsible for raising awareness and combating child labor. IPEC focuses on preventing child labor and the systematic search for alternative solutions in the form of decent employment for parents of child workers, and rehabilitation, education, or vocational training offers for children.

Child labor has emerged as one of the most important global issues of our time, and international cooperation on the issue has been strengthened over the past few years. Children who are enslaved, perhaps through debt bondage, are a special concern in the fight against child labor. One nongovernmental organization, the Global March Against Child Labor, with key support from IPEC, has developed a worldwide network of political leaders and activists in many countries, raising awareness and understanding of the issue. When child laborers from around the world marched on the United Nations in Geneva in 1998, their voices and example pushed politicians to enact much stronger rules in the new Convention on the Worst Forms of Child Labor, which includes child slavery. Around the world IPEC also sets up projects to get children out of the workplace and back into schools. In 1998–1999 an estimated 130,000 children benefited directly from "child labor–related services" provided by IPEC and its partners. The ILO also does in-depth investigations of slavery. In Chapter 4 you will find part of a report on the way the government of Burma has been enslaving its own citizens. By calling in independent experts and maintaining a staff of highly trained specialists, it brings together some of the most reliable information available on slavery today.

Another UN body that confronts slavery is the International Organization for Migration (IOM). For years, trafficking rings have thrived on the exploitation of women from developing countries. Recently countries of the former Soviet Union have become their latest targets. In Ukraine, women have become more economically vulnerable, and trafficking in women has become a dangerously booming "business." Lured by false promises and misled by false information on migration regulations, many women fall prey to unscrupulous traffickers, allowing their dream for a better life to be exploited. Helping stem the rising tide of trafficking in women, the IOM set up an information campaign that educated and warned women about the truth of trafficking. The result was a significant reduction in the number of women tricked in this way.

Trafficking in People

The size of the modern slave trade is very hard to measure. Its numbers are mixed with the smuggling of illegal immigrants, with forced migration, and with criminal networks. The United Nations estimates that around the world, four million people a year are traded against their will into some form of slavery or servitude. Most of these people come from Southeast Asia, Eastern Europe, and Latin America. In these parts of the world people and families that are poor and desperate will do almost anything to improve their lot. "Recruiters" take advantage of them, promising transportation and jobs in a new country. Once the recruiters have people away from their homes, they use violence to take control of their lives. The U.S. State Department estimates that as many as 50,000 women and children are smuggled into the United States each year to be forced into prostitution, domestic service, or as bonded labor in factories and sweatshops. Men are also brought into the country, but in smaller numbers.

Recent cases show the nature of the trade:

- In 1995, seventy-six immigrants from Thailand were liberated from a cockroach-infested garment factory in El Monte, California. Razor-wire fences surrounded the factory where they were forced to sleep and work up to sixteen-hour days. They were being held against debts supposedly amassed for their passage to the United States.
- In 1997, three men were convicted of kidnapping a twenty-two-year-old woman in China. They had brought her to the United States, raped her, and forced her to work as a prostitute. She was beaten, burned with cigarettes, and tattooed with a gang symbol before she escaped.
- In 1999, police in Atlanta, Georgia, broke up a smuggling ring that brought up to one thousand Asian women to the United States and forced them to work as prostitutes. The smugglers would fly the women to different cities in the United States to ensure variety in the brothels. Whereas the women were given just enough money to cover basic necessities, one brothel grossed $1.5 million over a two-year period.

Most slavery in the United States begins as a case of illegally smuggling people into the country. Federal prosecutors have made 150 cases of slavery or debt bondage in the past five years, but this amount is just the tip of the iceberg. Most of the victims are not able to communicate with officials if they escape, and most are also afraid to come forward. Told by the "recruiters" that they will be tortured or killed by the police if they are caught as illegal aliens, they keep quiet even in slavery.

For the traffickers the crime is very attractive. Crime networks from Asia and Eastern Europe have found that dealing in people makes as much money as dealing in drugs and with much lower risk. Immigrants from Asia pay as much as $50,000 to smugglers to get them into the United States; once in the country they can be locked up and forced to work twelve- to sixteen-hour days. Between the threat of violence and the psychological coercion based on fear of the police, the victims can be held and controlled for years. If traffickers are caught, the penalties are much lower than for smuggling drugs. If apprehended, the smuggler often pretends to be an illegal immigrant as well, and he or she will be deported but not punished.

Trafficking in people has boomed since the end of the Cold War as borders have become more open and more people have become economically vulnerable. The increase has governments scrambling to catch up. In early 2000 the U.S. Congress began consideration of a law that would increase punishments for people who smuggle or keep bonded workers. The United Nations has drafted a new convention on trafficking in persons, but it is still in the discussion stage. The European Union has also started work on new laws, but all of these governments are waiting for more research to be carried out to provide a picture of the extent and flow of this trade in human beings.

Groups and Strategies Working against Slavery

Examples at the International Level

Working to stop this traffic in people and to bring slaves to freedom are a number of organizations around the world. One of the most important of these is Anti-Slavery International. Founded in 1839, it is the oldest human rights organization in the world. It grew from an organization led by Thomas Clarkson that mounted the public campaign that brought about the abolition of the slave trade in the British Empire in 1807. From that time to the present the organization has been campaigning, researching, working with governments, raising awareness, and working with people in countries around the world to end slavery. Remarkably, it is much smaller today than it was in the 1800s, but from its base in London, England, its influence is felt in many countries.

Currently Anti-Slavery's work concentrates on these issues, which also shows the different types of slavery spread around the world:

- The exploitation of child labor; campaigning for the right of children to be protected from exploitative work.
- The commercial sexual exploitation of children, particularly when connected to the growth in travel and tourism.
- Abused migrant workers who are trapped and exploited by their employers.
- Bonded labor; landowners and businesspeople force whole families to work by keeping them in a never-ending cycle of debt.
- Early and forced marriage of women and children.
- Trafficking of women for sexual exploitation and all forms of forced prostitution.
- Forced labor; the illegal recruitment of workers by governments, political parties, or private individuals under threat of violence or other penalty.

In the past few years Anti-Slavery International has investigated the sale of children as domestic servants in West Africa and the plight of young boys enslaved on unstable wooden fishing platforms in the ocean around Indonesia. As one of the key organizations in the Global March, it lobbied the United Nations and ILO and then led the working group that helped the ILO pass the new Convention on the Worst Forms of Child Labor. Each year the organization gives the Anti-Slavery Award to someone who has worked to end slavery (you can read about some of the award winners in Chapter 3). Anti-Slavery International is especially active in the United Nations, where it is recognized as a regular participant; in 2000 it sent a delegation to the government of Nepal to urge its leaders to enact a law against debt bondage. Research and awareness-raising are key to its strategy to battle slavery. For many years the organization has been almost a lone voice keeping the issue alive with the press and governments. Today it makes films, produces reports, and provides teaching materials for schools.

Examples at the National and Regional Level

Rugmark

One of the worst industries in India for the abuse of child slaves has been rug and carpet making. If you have an oriental rug on your floor right now, there is a good chance it was woven by slave children. For many years campaigners in India tried to free and rehabilitate these bonded laborers, with only partial success. But a few years ago the Rugmark campaign set out to put the pressure not on the makers but on the buyers of carpets. Working from a tiny office with little funds, Rugmark organizers proposed that people should look for a special tag on handmade rugs that guaranteed that they were not made by slaves. To earn this "Rugmark," producers had to agree to only three things: not to exploit children, to cooperate with independent monitoring, and to turn over 1 percent of the carpet price to a welfare fund for child workers. Special effort was put into building up a sophisticated monitoring team that can detect fake labels, knows carpet making inside and out, and can't be corrupted. Today the German, United States, and Canadian governments recognize the Rugmark. The biggest mail-order company in the world plus major retailers in the United States, Germany, and the Netherlands now import only Rugmark carpets. In the United States you can find the stores selling Rugmark rugs on the organization's website, www.rugmark.org.

The most important aspect of the Rugmark campaign is its impact on the lives of bonded child laborers. The 1-percent contribution from producers has now made possible the building and staffing of two Rugmark-sponsored schools in India that serve a total of 250 students. The campaign itself has drawn the attention of other organizations; the German government and UNICEF now fund other schools in the areas that were once the recruiting grounds for child slaves. Helped to stay in school, the children aren't lured away to bondage. Confronted with buyers from the retail chains who insist on "slave-free" goods, the worst of the slaveholders have left the business, and other producers now do what is necessary to earn the Rugmark. It is a tremendous example of positive consumer power.

The American Anti-Slavery Group

Whereas Rugmark began with campaigners in India and worked toward Europe and the United States, the American Anti-Slavery Group (AASG) began in Boston, Massachusetts, and carries U.S. concerns and efforts to other parts of the world. The AASG was established in 1993 by Charles Jacobs, Mohamed Athie, and David Chand, who together broke the story of widespread slavery in the African countries of Mauritania and Sudan in the U.S. press. After representatives from the AASG testified before Congress in 1996, U.S. foreign aid to Mauritania was cut. In 1998 the organization launched an emancipation fund that helped secure the freedom of slaves captured in the civil war in Sudan. By 2000 they had helped emancipate nearly four thousand people, assisting families to redeem their relatives.

An important offshoot of AASG has been STOP—Stop Slavery that Oppresses People. STOP was founded in 1998 by a fifth-grade class in Denver, Colorado, that wanted to take action on behalf of children now held as chattel slaves in the Sudan. The students were in the middle of a history unit on American slavery when they learned that black people were still slaves in the Sudan—especially boys and girls their own age. That brutal fact was shocking, but the students refused to sit idly by. They began saving their lunch money toward purchasing the freedom of slaves. Some students even contributed cash given to them as birthday presents. In the end, they raised enough money to free two Sudanese slaves. At the same time, the children attracted both local and national media for what soon became a nationwide campaign toward redeeming slaves. Today the STOP campaign has helped raise over $70,000 and freed more than two thousand slaves. The original students' teacher, Barbara Vogel, has spoken before hundreds of teachers and educators about what students can do in the fight against modern-day slavery. Classes and schools across the country have now launched abolitionist campaigns of their own.

Examples at the Local Level

The Campaign for Migrant Domestic Workers Rights—Washington, DC

This chapter began with the story of Hilda Dos Santos, a woman held against her will and forced to work as a servant for a family near Washington, D.C. Unfortunately, her story is not unique. Other women, from Cameroon, from Ghana, and other parts of the developing world are being brought into the U.S. capital on permits (called A-3 or G-5 visas) that allow foreigners to bring their servants with them to the United States. Some of these workers are then enslaved, and several legal cases have been brought by the government against the employers. Few of these cases would have ever come about, however, except for the work of the staff and volunteers of Campaign for Migrant Domestic Workers Rights. The Campaign is a coalition of legal and social service agencies, ethnically based organizations, social action groups, and individuals devoted to protecting the rights of migrant domestic workers. Specifically, they focus on those domestic workers carrying A-3 or G-5 visas.

The A-3 visa was established for the personal employees and attendants of foreign diplomats stationed in the United States. The G-5 visa was established for the personal employees and attendants of employees of international organizations such as the World Bank, International Monetary Fund, Inter-American Development Bank, or Organization of American States. A-3 and G-5 visa holders come from all over the world. The most common countries of origin currently include the Philippines, Indonesia, Peru, India, Brazil, Sri Lanka, Mexico, Morocco, Chile, and Colombia.

Social service professionals and religious leaders have encountered numerous cases of abuse and exploitation of these domestic workers within the Washington, D.C., area and estimate that the problem is widespread. Abuse and exploitation range from wage abuse and contract violation to physical and even sexual abuse. Incredibly, though it is an organization fighting slavery in the nation's capital, the campaign has to run on a shoestring. Joy Zarempka, the young woman who coordinates the campaign, explained:

> Most Americans want to believe that slavery no longer exists, that it is just a racist vestige of the past. But, slavery is both colorblind and current. Americans need to be more vigilant and that is especially easier for young people who, by and large, are more observant and have better access to information. Before I began working on this issue, my own younger brother discovered a situation of domestic worker abuse right down the street from us and I didn't even know it was occurring. We need to learn to question situations that don't seem quite right—Is there someone in your neighborhood that you have seen go into a house and never come back out? Have you seen cleaning ladies and maids that don't seem to be allowed to go outside? Some people should even question themselves and ask if they treat their own housekeeper with dignity and respect.

The Committee Against Modern Slavery—France

In 1994 the French journalist Dominique Torres was investigating a story about the enslavement of domestic workers in Europe. She learned that such slavery had been found in London but felt sure that her own nation's capital, Paris, hosted no slavery. However, while visiting a small Paris church that was a center for escaped Filipina domestic slaves, she learned of more women who were still being held. Recruiting other journalists, Torres led the liberation of Mehret, a young woman from Eritrea held captive in the house of a diplomat in Paris. The media attention moved the French people to form the Committee Against Modern Slavery.

Today, operating from a small office, the committee has taken up more than 140 cases, liberating 142 domestic slaves, 27 of whom were children. Over one hundred slaveholders have been investigated, 31 of them international diplomats. The slaveholders come primarily from Arab and African countries, but three were from Israel and one from the United States. Their victims are mostly from Africa, the Philippines, Arab countries, and Poland. Committee investigators follow up all reports of possible slavery; the situation of Seba described earlier was a recent case. However, even if a slave is freed, a court case is difficult to win. The freed slave often has little understanding of what has happened and is unable to be a good witness, many times slaveholders flee the country before they can be arrested, and the other witnesses are rare. But whatever the outcome of the legal side of a liberation, the committee helps liberated slaves through medical treatment and counseling, training and education, and provides foster families where they can live in security.

The Informal Sector Service Center—Nepal

Organized in 1988, the Informal Sector Service Center (INSEC) was Nepal's first human rights organization. INSEC works in several areas, publishing, for example, the annual *Human Rights Yearbook for Nepal*. One of its key areas of work is with agricultural bonded laborers. Some forty thousand people are trapped in debt bondage in Nepal, yet by 1999 there was still no law forbidding it. INSEC has attacked this problem in several ways. By carrying out research around the country it has identified the main areas where debt bondage exists. In those areas INSEC has set up awareness and literacy programs. These programs help the agricultural workers understand their rights and teach them to read and write, skills that make it more difficult to enslave them in the future. The workers trained in the programs often organize themselves with the help of INSEC and then make a public stand against debt bondage. Meanwhile, INSEC is bringing legal cases to court to force the attention of government and press legislators for their help. By approaching the problem from many directions, INSEC, though relatively small and poor, is making dramatic progress. An especially innovative project recognizes the difficulty of traveling in a mountainous country like Nepal. INSEC workers provide radios to the poor around the country and broadcast a weekly program on human rights from the capital. "Listener Clubs" meet in rural villages to hear the program and then discuss it; the result is mass human-rights education at a low cost. All of these programs help liberate and rehabilitate bonded workers, but the two thousand trained to date are only a small part of the total in bondage, and even these are just beginning their process of attaining freedom.

Liberation and Rehabilitation

The human and economic relationships of modern slavery are complex. It would be so much easier to understand and combat slavery if there were very clear good guys and bad guys, if all slaveholders were cruel and all slaves yearned for freedom, if the solution to all slavery were simply to set slaves free. But being free means more than just walking away from bondage. Liberation is a bitter victory if it only leads to starvation or reenslavement. Freedom is both a mental realization and a physical condition. Ultimately, slaves have to find their own way into true freedom. The physical and psychological dependence they often felt toward their masters can make this a long process. If we expect an abused child to need years of therapy and guidance to overcome trauma, we can hardly expect equally abused slaves to enter society immediately as full citizens. It is true that many ex-slaves are phenomenally resilient, but the worst abused may need a lifetime of care. In the struggle to survive not just slavery but liberation, there is one striking parallel between the old slavery of the United States and the new slavery of today: When slavery came to an end in 1865 the slaves were just dumped; and so it is with slaves today. If slavery is to end, we must learn how ex-slaves can best secure their own freedom.

Liberation brings new problems. A lifetime of dependence cannot be swept away in an instant. A person denied autonomy, who has never had to make choices, can be paralyzed when confronting decisions. If we can learn anything from the lives of freed slaves, it is that liberation is a process, not an event. If we are serious about stopping slavery, we have to be committed to supporting freed slaves in a process that can take years. It means thinking very carefully about what slaves need in order to achieve true freedom. For example, we have to consider how to help slaves as people. What kind of care do slaves and ex-slaves need to attain a sense of freedom and personhood? Unfortunately, we know very little about the psychology of slavery or how to help its victims. To end slavery we will have to become experts in repairing the damage slavery brings to both mind and body.

We will also have to become experts in slaves as economic beings. Slaves have few skills. The jobs they do as slaves are not usually worth much on the free market. But if they are freed and can't support themselves, how will they avoid being enslaved again? Small children are dependent on their parents, who often expect them to do simple tasks around the house. Slaves are kept in a state of permanent dependence and are normally prevented from learning all but the most simple tasks. No one would dream of dropping an eight-year-old into the job market to compete for his or her livelihood, but this has happened to thousands of freed slaves. Around the world, only a tiny handful of people work to understand and build new economic routes from slavery to self-sufficiency. The economic process of becoming self-supporting parallels the growth to psychological independence.

From psychology to small-scale economics to large-scale law enforcement, much more research and development is needed. From the little work that has been done, it seems that there are several ways to help people to stay free: helping them to make the psychological adjustment to freedom; giving them access to credit; letting ex-slaves make their own decisions about what work they will do; overcoming corruption in the rehabilitation programs; the presence and oversight of powerful people on the side of ex-slaves; and that greatest of liberators, education.

What Can We Do?

Around the world people, especially young people, are fighting against slavery. Many of these people have to invent the strategies and actions that they will take because the modern abolitionist movement is just beginning. We have wonderful examples, such as Free the Children, where a group of twelve-year-olds has built up a powerful international organization. Even more inspiring are the lives of children liberated from slavery, children who have suffered terrible abuse and are not just rebuilding their lives but becoming leaders in the fight against slavery.

One of the things we know about slavery today is that it spans the globe and reaches into our lives. Whether we like it or not, we are now global people. We have to ask ourselves, Are we willing to live in a world with slaves? If not, we have to work to understand the links that tie us to slavery and then take action to break those links. If we don't do that, we are puppets, subject to forces we can't or won't control. If we don't take action we are just giving up and letting other people jerk the strings that tie us to slavery. Of course, there are many kinds of exploitation in the world, many kinds of injustice and violence to be concerned about. But slavery is important because it is exploitation, violence, and injustice all rolled together. There is no more potent combination of these three crimes. If there is one fundamental violation of our humanity we cannot allow, it is slavery. If there is one basic truth that virtually every human being can agree on, it is that slavery must end. What good is all our economic and political power if we can't use it to free slaves? If we can't stop slavery, how can we really say we are free?

One of the best ways to take action is to contact one or more of the organizations listed in this book to learn more about contemporary slavery and how you might contribute to eradicating it. Student groups and local organizations are popping up all over the United States that educate, lobby, raise funds, and campaign on slavery. All of them need volunteers.

References

Genovese, Eugene. *Roll, Jordan, Roll: The World the Slaves Made* (New York: Vintage, 1976).

Greider, William. *One World Ready or Not: The Manic Logic of Global Capitalism* (New York: Simon and Schuster, 1997).

Ransom, Roger L. *Conflict and Compromise: The Political Economy of Slavery, Emancipation, and the American Civil War* (Cambridge: Cambridge University Press, 1989).

Notes

Parts of this chapter have been adapted or excerpted from my book *Disposable People: New Slavery in the Global Economy* (Berkeley: University of California Press, 1999) by permission of the publisher.

1. See, for example, Benjamin Quarles, *The Negro in the American Revolution,* 1961; and David Brion Davis, *The Problem of Slavery in the Age of Revolution 1770–1823,* 1975.

2. Anti-Slavery Society of Australia, *The Forgotten Slaves: Report on a Mission to Investigate the Girl-Child Slaves of West Africa,* 1996. Also see Howard W. French, "The Ritual Slaves of Ghana: Young and Female," *New York Times,* January 20, 1997.

3. The Children's Society, *The Game's Up,* 1996; see also Maggie O'Kane, "Death of Innocence," *The Guardian,* February 12, 1996.

4. "Sex Slavery, Thailand to New York," *New York Times,* September 11, 1995.

2

Chronology

This chronology concentrates on the past century, but it starts with the ancient world just to illustrate the age-old nature of slavery.

c. 6800 B.C.   The world's first city grows in Mesopotamia. With the ownership of land and the beginnings of technology comes warfare in which enemies are captured and forced to work—slavery.

c. 2575 B.C.   Egyptians send expeditions down the Nile River to capture slaves. Temple art celebrates the capture of slaves in battle.

c. 550 B.C.   The mighty Greek city-state of Athens uses up to 30,000 slaves in the silver mines it controls.

c. 120   Slaves are taken by the thousands in Roman military campaigns; some estimates put the population of Rome at more than half slave.

c. 500   In England the native Britons are enslaved after invasion by Anglo-Saxons.

c. 1000   Slavery is normal practice in England's rural economy, as destitute agricultural workers place themselves and their families in a form of debt bondage to landowners.

c. 1250   The trans-Saharan slave trade carries between 5,000 and 25,000 slaves each year from West Africa to the

Mediterranean. From there they are sold into Europe and the Middle East.

c. 1380   In the aftermath of the Black Plague, Europe's slave trade revives to deal with the labor shortage. The slaves come from all over Europe, the Middle East, and North Africa.

c. 1444   Portuguese traders bring the first cargo of slaves from West Africa to Europe by sea, thus beginning the Atlantic slave trade. With the "discovery" of the Americas, it will greatly expand; by the time it ends around 1870, some 13,000,000 slaves will be taken from Africa.

c. 1550   Renaissance art is peopled with slaves displayed as objects of conspicuous consumption.

1619   A Dutch ship delivers twenty Africans to the English settlement at Jamestown, Virginia; they become the first African Americans and slavery begins in the American colonies.

1781   Holy Roman Emperor Joseph II abolishes serfdom, a form of slavery tied to land ownership, in the Austrian Habsburg dominions.

1789   On August 26, during the French Revolution, the French National Assembly adopts the Declaration of the Rights of Man, one of the fundamental charters of human liberties. The first of seventeen articles states, "Men are born and remain free and equal in rights."

1803   Denmark becomes the first country in Europe to ban the African slave trade. A law passed in 1792 takes effect in 1803 to forbid trading in slaves by Danish subjects and to end the importation of slaves into Danish dominions.

1804   After a slave revolt expels the French from the island of Saint Domingue, the island is declared independent under its original Arawak name, "Haiti."

1807   After prolonged lobbying by abolitionists in Britain, led by William Wilberforce and Thomas Clarkson, the British Parliament makes it illegal for British ships to transport slaves and for British colonies to import them.

1808   The United States bans further importation of Africans as slaves. At this point, there are about 1 million slaves in the United States.

1811–1867   Operating off the Atlantic coast of Africa, the British Navy's Anti-Slavery Squadron liberates 160,000 slaves. Freed from captured slave ships, they are returned to areas under British protection on the African coast, particularly Sierra Leone.

1813   Sweden, a nation that has never authorized slave traffic, consents to ban the African slave trade.

1814   The king of the Netherlands officially terminates Dutch participation in the African slave trade.

1814   During the Congress of Vienna, largely through the efforts of Britain, the assembled powers proclaim that the slave trade should be abolished as soon as possible. The congress leaves the actual effective date of abolition to negotiation among the various nations.

1820   The government of Spain, pursuant to a treaty with Britain, abolishes the slave trade south of the Equator. Slave trade in Cuba continues until 1888.

1825   Argentina, Peru, Chile, and Bolivia abolish legal slavery.

1833   The British Parliament's Factory Act of 1833 establishes a normal working day in textile manufacture. The act bans the employment of children under the age of nine and limits the workday of children between the ages of thirteen and eighteen to twelve hours. The law also provides for government inspection of working conditions.

1834   In Britain the Abolition Act of 1833 abolishes slavery throughout the British Empire, including its colonies in North America. The bill emancipates the slaves in all British colonies and appropriates a sum equivalent to nearly $100 million to compensate slave owners for their losses.

1837   In 1837, Thomas F. Buxton begins a campaign to abolish coolie labor in India. After the abolition of slavery, coolies (unskilled Far Eastern laborers) have become a preferred source of cheap labor. Buxton argues that coolie labor amounts to slavery, with workers often kidnapped, transported to the Caribbean, and forced to toil in appalling conditions.

1840   The new British and Foreign Anti-Slavery Society calls the first World Anti-Slavery Convention in London to mobilize reformers to monitor and assist abolition and postemancipation efforts throughout the world. A group of abolitionists from the United States travels to London to attend the convention, but Elizabeth Cady Stanton and Lucretia Mott, as well as several male supporters, leave the meeting in protest when women are excluded from seating on the convention floor.

1845   Thirty-six British Navy ships are assigned to the Anti-Slavery Squadron, making it one of the largest fleets in the world.

1848   After the revolution of 1848 in France, the new government abolishes slavery in all French colonies.

1850   The government of Brazil adopts the Queirós Law, which ends the country's participation in the slave trade. The law declares slave traffic to be a form of piracy, and it prohibits Brazilian citizens from taking part in the trade.

1861   By decree Alexander II, czar of Russia, emancipates all Russian serfs, who number around fifty million. The act begins the time of the Great Reform in Russia and earns Alexander II the title of "Czar Liberator."

1863   During the American Civil War, President Abraham Lincoln's Emancipation Proclamation takes effect, freeing all slaves in the United States. Lincoln also announces that blacks can be recruited into the military.

1863   The government of the Netherlands takes official action to abolish slavery in all Dutch colonies.

1888   Slavery ends in South America when the legislature of Brazil frees the country's 725,000 slaves by enacting the Lei Aurea (Golden Law).

1909   The campaign of the Congo Reform Association (CRA) to end forced labor in the Congo Free State succeeds. Set up in Great Britain in 1904 by E. D. Morel, the CRA has as its main objective the end of forced labor in the Congo Free State (later known as Zaire). King Leopold II of Belgium had undertaken personal administration of this huge territory and forced local people to produce rubber for sale in Europe, where an increasing number of cars and bicycles intensify demand for rubber tires. Workers who refused to labor for King Leopold's officials had their hands cut off and their houses burnt and pillaged. The "Red Rubber" campaign has sought to bring justice to the Congo.

1910   The International Convention for the Suppression of the White Slave Trade, signed in Paris on May 4, 1910, is the first of its kind. The convention obligates parties to punish anyone who recruits a woman below the age of majority into prostitution, even if she consents.

1913   Peoples' petition to the British Parliament shuts down the Peruvian Amazon Company. In 1909 W. E. Hardenburg, an American civil engineer, had arrived in London with accounts of the inhuman exploitation of indigenous Indians in Peru by the Peruvian Amazon Company, a British entity. In the ensuing four years the Indians have been trapped by debt and forced to work for the company, which

1913
(cont.)
has exploited the natives: "they flog them inhumanely until their bones are laid bare; . . . they torture them by means of fire, of water, and by tying them up, crucified head down" (*The Truth*, 1909). When journalists take up the story, there is a public outcry in Britain. The House of Commons mandates reports from both the company and the British Consul and establishes a Select Committee to investigate the allegations.

1915
The colonial government of Malaya officially abolishes slavery.

1918
The British governor of Hong Kong estimates that most households that can afford it keep a young child as a household slave.

1919
The League of Nations is founded. Its existence continues until the formation of the United Nations in 1946.

1919
The International Labor Organization (ILO) is founded to establish a code of international labor standards. Headquartered in Geneva, Switzerland, the ILO brings together government, labor, and management to solve problems and to make recommendations concerning pay, working conditions, trade union rights, safety, woman and child labor, and social security. The ILO will be brought into relationship with the United Nations in 1946.

1920
Buxton's campaign against coolie labor (see 1837) succeeds when the British colonial government bans the export of bonded Indian workers.

1923
The British colonial government in Hong Kong passes a law banning the selling of little girls as domestic slaves.

1926
The League of Nations approves the Slavery Convention, and more than thirty governments sign the document, which defines slavery as "status or condition of a person over whom any or all of the

powers attaching to the right of ownership are exercised." The convention charges member nations to work to suppress all forms of slavery.

1926   Burma (later known as Myanmar) abolishes legal slavery.

1927   Slavery is legally abolished in Sierra Leone, a country founded as a colony by the British in the eighteenth century to serve as a homeland for freed slaves.

1929   To achieve the abolition of slavery Burma begins to compensate slaveholders for their "losses."

1930   The Forced Labor Convention, a combined effort of the League of Nations and the International Labor Organization, meets to discuss how to protect the rights of colonial laborers.

1936   Pursuant to a treaty with Great Britain, Ibn Sa'ud, king of Saudi Arabia, issues a decree ending the importation of new slaves into his country, regulating the condition of existing slaves, and providing for manumission under some conditions.

1938   The Japanese military establishes "comfort stations" (brothels) for Japanese troops. Thousands of Korean and Chinese women are forced into sexual slavery during World War II as "military comfort women."

1939–1945   The German Nazi government uses slave labor throughout the war in farming and industry. Up to nine million people are forced to work until they are worn out, at which time they are sent to concentration camps.

1941   The campaign to protect children in Ceylon (Sri Lanka) from "adoption" succeeds with the passage of the Adoption of Children Ordinance Law, which ensures the registration of all children who are adopted and requires regular inspections to prevent adopted children from working as slaves.

1948   The United Nations produces the Universal Declaration of Human Rights. Article 4 provides, "No one shall be held in slavery or servitude; slavery and the slave trade shall be prohibited in all their forms."

1949   The Convention for the Suppression of the Traffic in Persons and Exploitation of the Prostitution of Others prohibits any person from procuring, enticing, or leading away another person, for the purposes of prostitution, even with the other person's consent. The convention consolidates earlier laws and will form the legal basis for the international protection against traffic in people until the present day.

1952   It is estimated that forty thousand Japanese children are sold into slavery for prostitution in this year alone. Brothel owners pay between $25 and $100 per child.

1954   China passes the State Regulation on Reform through Labor, allowing prisoners to be used as laborers in the *laogai* prison camps.

1956   The Supplementary Convention on the Abolition of Slavery, the Slave Trade and Institutions and Practices Similar to Slavery regulates practices involving the sale of wives, serfdom, debt bondage, and child servitude.

1957   The British and Foreign Anti-Slavery Society changes its name to the Anti-Slavery Society for the Protection of Human Rights. (In the 1990s the name will be changed to Anti-Slavery International.)

1960   Harry Wu is sentenced to serve nineteen years in the *laogai* slave labor camp system.

1962   Slavery is legally abolished in Saudi Arabia and Yemen.

1964   The sixth World Muslim Congress pledges global

support for all antislavery movements. Founded in 1926, the World Muslim Congress has consultative status with the United Nations and observer status with the Organization of Islamic Countries.

1973　　The UN General Assembly adopts the International Convention on the Suppression and Punishment of the Crime of Apartheid. The convention outlaws a number of inhuman acts committed for the purposes of establishing and maintaining domination by one racial group over another, including exploitation of the labor of members of a racial group or groups by submitting them to forced labor.

1974　　Mauritania's emancipated slaves form the El Hor (freedom) movement to oppose slavery. Leaders of El Hor insist that emancipation is impossible without realistic means of enforcing the antislavery laws and providing former slaves with the means of achieving economic independence. The movement demands land reform and encourages the formation of agricultural cooperatives. (The influence of El Hor was strongest between 1978–1982, though the organization still exists today.)

1975　　The UN Working Group on Contemporary Forms of Slavery is formed to collect information and make recommendations on slavery and slavery-like practices around the world.

1976　　India passes a law banning bonded labor.

1977　　The ILO adopts the Tripartite Declaration of Principles Concerning Multinational Enterprises and Social Policy, a set of recommended standards with no means of enforcement.

1980　　Slavery is abolished for the fourth time in the Islamic republic of Mauritania, but the situation is not fundamentally changed. Although the law decrees that "slavery" no longer exists, the ban does not address how masters are to be compensated or how slaves are to gain property.

1983   The civil war in Sudan breaks out again, pitting the Muslim north of the country against the Christian and Animist southern tribes.

1989   The National Islamic Front takes over the government of Sudan and begins to arm Baggara tribesmen to fight the Dinka and Nuer tribes in the south of the country. These new "militias" raid villages, capturing and enslaving the inhabitants.

          The UN Convention on the Rights of the Child seeks to promote the basic health care and education of the young, as well as their protection from abuse, exploitation, or neglect at home, at work, and in armed conflicts.

1992   The Pakistan National Assembly enacts the Bonded Labor Act, which abolishes indentured servitude and the *peshgi* (bonded money) system. However, the government fails to provide for the implementation and enforcement of the law's provisions.

1993   Charles Jacobs, Mohamed Athie, and David Chand break the story in the American press about widespread slavery in the African countries of Mauritania and Sudan. They then found the American Anti-Slavery Group.

1994   OECD Declaration and Decisions on International Investment and Multinational Enterprises is adopted. The document recommends that companies observe guidelines approved by the OECD that address investment policy and practice in non-industrialized countries. Trade unions note that these guidelines are not an alternative to obligations that all enterprises have under the OECD Guidelines for Multinational Enterprises adopted by governments.

1995   The United States government issues the Model Business Principles, a voluntary model business code (apparently to pacify human rights and labor activists in the United States who protest the renewal of China's trade status). The principles urge all businesses to adopt and implement voluntary codes of conduct, including the avoidance of child and forced labor as well as discrimination based on race, gender, national origin, or religious beliefs. The principles also promote respect for the right of association and the right to organize and bargain collectively.

Christian Solidarity International, a Swiss-based charity, begins a campaign to liberate Sudanese slaves by buying them back.

1996   After representatives from the American Anti-Slavery Group testify before the U.S. Congress about slavery in Mauritania, U.S. foreign aid to that country is cut.

The International Organization of Employers, a subsidiary of the ILO, calls on employers and employers' organizations immediately to end slave-like, bonded, and dangerous forms of child labor and simultaneously to develop formal policies with a view toward the eventual elimination of child labor in all sectors. The resolution notes, however, that "attempts to link the issue of working children with international trade and to use it to impose trade sanctions on countries where the problem of child labor exists are counter-productive and jeopardize the welfare of children."

The Rugmark campaign is established in Germany to ensure that handwoven rugs are not made with illegal (slave) labor. The Rugmark seal guarantees that the entire production of the rug was accomplished without slave or child labor.

The World Congress Against Commercial Sexual Exploitation of Children is held.

Barbara Vogel's fifth-grade class in Colorado launches STOP—Stop Slavery that Oppresses People. The children raise thousands of dollars to support the redemption of slaves in Sudan.

1997   The United Nations establishes a commission of in-
            quiry to investigate reports of widespread enslave-
            ment of people by the Myanmar (Burmese)
            government.

            A bill entitled the "International Child Labor Elim-
            ination Act" (H.R. 267) is introduced in the U.S.
            House of Representatives to prohibit U.S. assis-
            tance, except for humanitarian aid, to countries that
            utilize child labor.

            Imported goods made by child-bonded laborers are
            banned by the United States.

1998   The Myanmar (Burmese) government refuses to
            allow the United Nations Commission of Inquiry to
            enter its borders.

            The Global March Against Child Labor is estab-
            lished. This organization plans and coordinates
            demonstrations against child labor worldwide.
            One aim is a new Convention in the UN on the
            Worst Forms of Child Labor.

1999   A consortium of nongovernmental agencies calls
            for international aid and a cease-fire in Sudan to
            help end slavery there.

            Despite being barred from entering Myanmar
            (Burma), the United Nations collects sufficient evi-
            dence to condemn government-sponsored slavery
            there. The official report states that the Myanmar
            government "treat the civilian population as an un-
            limited pool of unpaid forced laborers and servants
            at their disposal as part of a political system built on
            the use of force and intimidation to deny the people
            of Myanmar democracy and the rule of law."

            The ILO passes the Convention Against the Worst
            Forms of Child Labor. This convention establishes
            widely recognized international standards protect-
            ing children against forced or indentured labor,
            child prostitution/pornography, use of children in

drug trafficking, and other work harmful to the health, safety, and morals of children.

2000   A new bill to address human trafficking is proposed in the U.S. Congress.

The government of Nepal bans all forms of debt bondage after a lengthy campaign by human rights organizations and freed bonded laborers.

2003   The year that the Pakistani government has assured the United Nations that "all bonded labor will stop" in its country.

3

Biographical Sketches

Who are the new abolitionists? Around the world men, women, and children are actively fighting slavery, liberating slaves, pressing governments for action, studying bondage, rehabilitating freed slaves, and developing strategies to end slavery. Most of these people are little known outside their own organizations and the networks that join these groups together. Many of them have firsthand knowledge of slavery, and many have faced and suffered threats, physical violence, political pressure, and defamation in their fight against slavery. Today most of us only know about the great antislavery figures of the past: everyone remembers Abraham Lincoln, and most know about Frederick Douglass and Harriet Tubman. Many of the great antislavery workers of the past inspire the abolitionists of today. For that reason, included here are the stories of just four of these historical figures whose lives are especially worth knowing, but the majority described are the abolitionists of today. Some are old, and some are very young. Some are widely known, and others are known only in their local areas. All are working to bring slaves into freedom.

Swami Agnivesh (1939–)

Coming from a well-off Hindu family in India, the young man named Shyam Vepa Rao—who would become Swami (Holy Man or Teacher) Agnivesh—studied in Calcutta and earned degrees in law and economics. He then renounced his family status and became a "priest" (taking vows of chastity and poverty) in a Hindu group dedicated to social justice. He started his career as a college teacher but in 1977 was elected as a representative to his state legislature. In 1979 he was made the state Minister for Education. In that year police shot down workers protesting bonded labor, and he felt compelled to meet the workers and grew to support their plight. When he confronted the state government about the terrible suffering of the bonded workers, he was told to "shut up and stick to education." Faced with government inaction he resigned his post and went to work on the problem of debt bondage.

Angering powerful interests, he was soon arrested and imprisoned as a "subversive." At the time the Bonded Labor Law was being passed in the Indian Congress, Agnivesh was in jail, reading the works of Ghandi and contemplating his role in the struggle for freedom. Upon his release he decided to devote himself to the poorest of the poor. Turning his attention to workers enslaved in stone quarries, he found extensive debt bondage and violence used against workers. Soon he was again persecuted for his work; a false charge of murder was made against him and he spent eight months in hiding before being acquitted. In 1981 he founded the Bonded Labor Liberation Front (BLLF) of India. The BLLF has liberated thousands of bonded laborers, including children, and trained hundreds of activists. It works through direct action and through the courts. After liberation, the freed workers are given basic education, skill training, and social and legal support.

In his saffron-colored robes, Swami Agnivesh is now a well-known representative for the poorest workers in debt bondage. He personifies an active religion that seeks to affirm human dignity for everyone. "I have never been able to compartmentalize religion, politics, and social action," he says. "They all exist together in the web of social realities." This social reality has included two assassination attempts on his life, but Agnivesh does not give up. He has been given numerous human rights awards and is now the chair of the United Nations Trust Fund on Contemporary Forms of Slavery. A tireless traveler, he has led mass campaigns against bonded labor, child labor, consumerism, ecological destruction, and racial and religious discrimination. Agnivesh is especially critical of religions that ignore human suffering. "What good," he once wrote, "is all of this great talk about simplicity, love, meekness, sharing and cooperation, if it cannot be applied in daily life because of an economic ideology that puts profit before human happiness?"

Jean-Robert Cadet (1955–)

Jean-Robert Cadet was born in Haiti, the son of a wealthy, white businessman and a black mother who died when Cadet was only four. His father sent the young Cadet to a former mistress to become a *restavec*, a child slave. *Restavec* is a French term that means "staying with," a term that disguises the reality of slavery. Under his master's control, Cadet was forced to perform a range of menial tasks; if he made any mistake, he was beaten severely. Unfortunately, this incident of slavery is not unique—there are more than 250,000 restavec child slaves in Haiti. For the most part, these are children of the very poor who are given to well-off families in the hope that they will be given an education and a chance at a better life. Once handed over, most of the children lose all contact with their families and, like the slaves of the past, are sometimes given new names. In many ways the restavec children are treated worse than the slaves of the past since they cost nothing and their supply is inexhaustible. They receive very little food or food of poor quality. Their health is usually poor and their growth stunted. Girl restavecs are worse off because they are sometimes forced to have sex with the teenage sons of their owners. If they become pregnant, they are thrown into the street. At maturity, most restavec children are thrown out and have to make a living any way they can, shining shoes, gardening, or as prostitutes.

As a restavec, Cadet served the family but was not part of it. He slept under the kitchen table or on a back porch. Though a small child, he received no affection or care from his owner. His sole possessions were a tin cup, an aluminum plate, a spoon, and the rags he was given to wear. In the stress and abuse of his situation, Cadet became a regular bed-wetter, which only increased the punishments he was given. Once Cadet's only friend, another restavec child named Rene, stole two dollars and bought food that he shared with Cadet. When he was found out, he was whipped severely and then forced to kneel on hot rocks so that he would confess with whom he shared the food. When he did not implicate Cadet, he was sent to the police station for a beating; he returned terribly injured and then disappeared.

Cadet's salvation was the occasional chances he had to attend a charity school. Showing a native intelligence, he learned to read and write quickly, even in the small amount of time he had managed to keep up with schoolwork. His life changed dramatically at the age of fourteen when he was taken to the United States to continue serving his owner there. Upon arrival in the United States, his owner discovered that minors had to attend school, so Cadet was sent to junior high in spite of speaking no English. Before and after school he was still a full-time servant and cleaner.

By the age of sixteen he was required to work at cleaning jobs before and after school. Finally, he was thrown out, but with the help of the school guidance counselor Cadet attained welfare benefits and was able to finish high school. After graduation he joined the army, and while there became a U.S. citizen.

In the army and afterwards, as he pursued a college degree, he had to confront the racism of the United States. When he received his bachelor's degree he confronted the woman who had enslaved him, showing her his degree and what he had made of his life. This confrontation was the first of many steps in the recovery of his confidence and self-esteem. With more study, he became a teacher and met the woman he would marry. But the psychological burden of his childhood in slavery still had a damaging impact on his life and relationships. In 1993 he began to write a letter to his newborn son explaining his past. This letter turned into the book *Restavec: From Haitian Slave Child to Middle-Class American;* the book deeply moved many readers, generating several television reports about slavery in Haiti. In 2000 he left his job as a teacher to devote himself full-time to the cause of restavec slave children.

Thomas Clarkson (1760–1846)

If there was one person most responsible for the abolition of legal slavery in the West, it was Thomas Clarkson. Abraham Lincoln, William Wilberforce, and others followed the lead of the man the poet Samuel Coleridge called "the moral steam engine—a Giant with one idea." Clarkson's "one idea" was to end slavery. In the 1780s Great Britain was the world's preeminent slave trader. Its empire was held together by slavery, and vast fortunes were being made from slaves and slave products like sugar and cotton. The British government took in a large part of its taxes from slave owners and slave-made products. Even those who thought slavery to be wrong tended to believe that it was too important for the national economy to be abolished.

While at university Clarkson entered an essay contest; the question to be answered was, "Is it lawful to make slaves of others against their will?" As the young student researched the subject, he was shocked and absorbed by what he learned. After winning first prize, he developed the work further, publishing it as a book in 1786. Though trained to be a minister, Clarkson, aged twenty-five, decided to devote his life to ending slavery. Through this work he came into contact with a committee set up by the Quakers in 1783 to seek abolition of the slave trade. Joining this committee and gaining the promise of William Wilberforce to bring the matter to Parliament, Clarkson became the campaigner who rallied people to the cause. Traveling by horseback he covered thirty-five thousand miles in the next seven years. He studied the slave trade firsthand in ports like Liverpool, England, and organized antislavery groups wherever he went. Within a few years, the government was being bombarded by petitions and letters urging an end to slavery.

When Parliament in 1791 defeated a law that would abolish the slave trade, Clarkson increased his efforts, crisscrossing the country again and again to speak publicly and organize local groups. A national boycott of slave-made sugar was mounted, resulting in a reduction of sugar consumption by up to one-half in parts of the country. In 1794 Clarkson, exhausted by the work, retired temporarily from his campaign and spent the next few years living in the countryside and writing a book about the Quakers. He returned to the fight in 1804, supplying evidence to the government and organizing support for abolition. In February 1807, after many delays, Parliament passed a law abolishing the slave trade throughout the British Empire. This law stopped the trade in slaves, not slavery itself, so Clarkson turned his attention to full emancipation. By the 1820s a full antislavery campaign was underway. Now in his sixties, Clarkson embarked on another grueling tour of speaking and organizing, and thousands of petitions rained down on the government. In 1833 slavery itself was abolished in the British Empire. In the 1840s the now grand old man of the antislavery movement presided over the first world antislavery convention and pressed for an end to slavery in the United States. He continued campaigning until days before his death.

Caroline Cox (1937–)

Caroline Cox was born in England and worked as a nurse for some time before marrying and starting a family. While her three children were still young she returned to school to study sociology and economics. After earning a degree with honors, she took a job teaching at one of the local universities in London and found herself in a troubling web of ideological struggle as her academic department tore itself apart in political leftist infighting. The experience was an important one for Cox and reinforced her conservative viewpoint. Writing a book about her experiences led to a widening of her efforts to act as a "voice for the voiceless." In this work she has become the special friend of the Armenian Christian community in Azerbaijan, a group little known in the West that was terribly persecuted by Azeri troops after the breakup of the Soviet Union. Although most governments ignore the plight of the Azerbaijan Armenians—remaining silent because of their dealings with Azerbaijan for oil—Cox has raised their case repeatedly and delivered large amounts of aid to the troubled region.

This led her to an interest in the civil war in Sudan, where southern tribes of Christians and Animists suffer under genocidal attacks from the Muslim government. Joining Christian Solidarity International (CSI) in 1990, she became president of its British office. A central figure in the "redemptionist" movement, Cox has made many trips to Sudan to deliver aid and to purchase and free tribespeople captured and enslaved by northern militias. In October 1999 she led a group that liberated more than five hundred slaves in Sudan. Her research into the impact of the civil war and the policies of the Sudanese government has helped bring the terrible suffering there into plain view. Her aim is to serve those who "are bereft of aid and advocacy; who are among the most isolated, outcast, and deprived in the world, the ones forgotten by the world," she says. In honor of her work she was made Baroness Cox of Queensbury and became the deputy speaker of the British House of Lords. In the late 1990s her organization separated from CSI to become Christian Solidarity Worldwide.

Frederick Douglass (1817–1895)

Born a slave in Maryland, Douglass spent his childhood as a domestic servant in Baltimore. In spite of the laws against slave literacy, he began to secretly teach himself to read using old newspapers and any other printed matter he could find. At about the age of thirteen he found a discarded book on rhetoric (public speaking) and carefully worked through all of the exercises, becoming a skilled speaker in the process. When he was fifteen he was sent to work on a plantation. There he organized a secret slave school, which was discovered by slaveholders; he was punished and sent to another plantation. Upon returning to Baltimore, he escaped from slavery at age twenty using the papers of a free black sailor. He settled in Massachusetts, changing his last name to Douglass from Bailey, his master's name, to conceal his background and confuse slave catchers.

Soon after coming to Massachusetts he got involved with the emerging antislavery movement. His talk at an Abolitionist convention in 1841 impressed the Abolitionist organization so much that he was hired to be a traveling lecturer. From that time he gave hundreds of speeches around the country, though he was often met with assaults, rotten vegetables, and mob violence. His public profile meant he was in constant danger of recapture. At age twenty-six he wrote the story of his life, *Narrative of the Life of Frederick Douglass,* which sold more than thirty thousand copies and was translated into several other languages. *Narrative* made him the most famous black person in the world and increased the danger he was in. After he toured Great Britain, antislavery activists purchased his freedom from his original owners, giving him more security. He started his own antislavery journal, then began to drift away from many of the more conservative abolitionists with his calls for public resistance and slave revolts. With the coming of the Civil War he pushed hard for blacks to be armed and included in the military. After the war he campaigned for equal treatment and citizenship for ex-slaves and worked with select politicians to carry forward civil rights. Shortly after the death of his wife, he married his white former secretary, alienating some blacks and whites but not lessening his influence. The most influential African American of the nineteenth century, Douglass spent his life confronting the public conscience with the facts of slavery and discrimination. Less than a month before his death, when a young black man asked his advice on how to move ahead, he replied "Agitate, agitate, agitate!"

Charles Jacobs (1943–)

Born in Newark, New Jersey, Jacobs studied psychology and English at Rutgers University and spent a year in Spain at the University of Madrid. A formative moment as a young man came when his uncle, a labor union organizer, took him to the March on Washington, and Jacobs heard Martin Luther King Jr. give his "I Have a Dream" speech. He began work toward a Ph.D. in psychology but dropped out to work full-time in the peace movement during the Vietnam War. When the war ended he became an eighth-grade English teacher and later worked in Mexico. By the late 1980s he had returned to the United States to study for a Ph.D. in education at Harvard University. Concurrently he worked part-time as a management consultant to government agencies, nonprofit organizations, and private businesses.

In the early 1990s Jacobs saw a short article in the *Economist* magazine about slavery in Sudan. A short time later, when he was doing a management workshop for a child sponsorship agency, he happened to talk with the agency's worker from Senegal. The worker confirmed that slavery was widespread in the region. "I began to just feel furious," Jacobs says. "Here was real slavery, including children for sale, and the information just seemed buried; no one seemed to care!" Moved to take action, he contacted his congressman, who recommended careful research on which to build a case and a coalition. After spending weeks on the research, "I was stunned," Jacobs relates. "I found that everyone who should have known about this injustice *did* know, so why was it being ignored?"

Joined by activists from Sudan and Mauritania, Jacobs set up the American Anti-Slavery Group (AASG) in 1993. An article about the issue in the *New York Times* provided the AASG with initial publicity, and the group began to organize abolitionist conferences. In the early years Jacobs supported the AASG from his own pocket and was the main worker, but the organization grew as he worked to break the silence about slavery. Television programs and extensive coverage in newspapers followed. Most important, the AASG gave the victims of slavery a chance to speak out for themselves. Joining with Christian Solidarity International, the AASG was soon involved in directly freeing slaves in Sudan. The growth in coverage and interest helped to raise the AASG's profile, and by 1997 it was hiring workers and forming important alliances like that with the STOP campaign. Jacobs remains committed: "What is America about," he asks, "except a belief in freedom? We know in our hearts and minds the higher truth, that slavery must end and that each of us must take responsibility for ending it."

Cheikh Saad Bouh Kamara (1944–)

Born in the West African country of Mauritania in 1944 and educated there and in France, Kamara is a leading human rights and antislavery activist. For standing up for human rights, this teacher was put into prison by his own government. Slavery exists across Mauritania on a very large scale. One of the last places on earth where chattel slavery is practiced, slaves can be inherited, hired, or lent out. Slavery is often passed down through generations of a family. In Mauritania ethnic differences are also important in slavery, most slaveholders being Arab Berbers and most slaves being the descendants of black Africans. Slavery has been legally abolished several times—the latest in 1981—but no law has been put in place for the prosecution of slaveholders, for the rehabilitation of freed slaves, or for setting up the law enforcement necessary to free slaves.

Kamara, a professor of sociology at the main university in Mauritania, was a founding member of the Mauritanian Human Rights Association (MHRA). This association was set up in the wake of mass killings and the expulsion from the country of thousands of black Mauritanians in the early 1990s. At first the association had to operate in secret, and when it went public most of its initiatives were blocked by the government—especially research into secret executions and the "disappearance" of political prisoners. Though never allowed to be a legal association in Mauritania, the MHRA was recognized by outside bodies like the Organization of African Unity. Speaking out around the world about the slavery in Mauritania, Kamara was asked to join the United Nations Trust Fund on Contemporary Forms of Slavery.

In 1998, the president of an antislavery organization in Mauritania gave an interview to a French TV program. The bad publicity angered the Mauritanian government, which responded by arresting several human rights workers, including Kamara, even though he had nothing to do with the interview. Charged with running an unlawful organization (the MHRA), he was held in jail for two months and put on trial. All of the activists were convicted and sentenced to thirteen months in prison. A few days later they were set free on the orders of the Mauritanian president, but their convictions were still in place, which meant that they could be rearrested at any time and that their organizations were permanently banned from operating or doing any more human rights activity. Upon his release, Kamara left Mauritania and continues to work for human rights. In late 1998 he was presented with Anti-Slavery International's Anti-Slavery Award.

Craig Kielburger (1982–)

Craig Kielburger was just twelve years old when he and other students founded Free the Children (FTC), an international children's organization now active in more than twenty countries, whose mission is to free children from poverty and exploitation and to empower young people to become leaders in their communities. Kielburger first became an advocate for children's rights when he read about the murder of child labor activist Iqbal

Masih in April 1995 (see Masih's biography below). Moved by Masih's story, he worked with fellow students to start the campaign that became Free the Children. At first they found that no one, especially adults, would take a group of twelve-year-olds seriously, but they learned that by assembling the facts and making clear presentations they could gain the attention of the public. Since then, Kielburger has traveled to more than thirty countries around the world visiting street children and child laborers and speaking out in defense of children's rights. He gained international recognition from his appearances on television in North and South America and Europe. His efforts on behalf of working, poor, and marginalized youth have been featured in many newspapers, and he has received many awards for his work. Kielburger's first book, *Free the Children,* written with Kevin Major, was published in 1998.

Free the Children has initiated projects all over the world, including the opening of schools and rehabilitation centers for children, the creation of alternative sources of revenue for poor families to free children from hazardous work, leadership programs for youth, and projects linking children on an international level. Young people affiliated with the organization have helped to convince members of business communities to adopt codes of conduct with regard to child labor, and governments to change laws to better protect children from sexual exploitation. Free the Children also initiated a "Friendship Schools Campaign." To date, students taking part in this campaign have raised funds to build twenty schools in Latin America. They have put together and shipped more than five thousand school kits to South Africa, the Philippines, Latin America, and India. Because they believe that education is the key to breaking the cycle of poverty and eliminating child labor, their Millennium Challenge is to build one hundred schools and to ship 100,000 school kits to children by the year 2001.

Young people from FTC have also raised money to set up a pipe-and-reservoir system to bring clean water from the mountains into two villages in Nicaragua and to build a medical clinic. FTC raised over $100,000 to build a rehabilitation and education center for freed bonded child laborers in India. The center, which accommodates up to one hundred children at any given time, provides counseling, education, medical aid, and vocational training and thereby facilitates the reintegration of these children into society. The rehabilitation center was completed in the fall of 1998 and is operated by the South Asian Coalition on Child Servitude (SACCS). During the Kosovo crisis, students in more than one hundred schools put together ten thousand health care and hygiene kits, eight thousand stuffed animals, two thousand baby kits, fifty thousand items of clothes, and thousands of other items for the Balkan refugees. The health kits and other necessities were distributed to children in camps in Kosovo, Belgrade, and North America. In 2000, Free the Children joined with international development agencies representing 180 countries to launch the Campaign for Education. This campaign aims to have basic education provided for all children by 2015 and to get western governments to forgive the heavy international debt that prevents poor countries from spending more on education.

Dona Pureza Lopez Loyola (1943–)

When her son disappeared in 1993, Pureza Lopez Loyola set off to find him. She left her youngest daughter at home to go in search of her youngest son, Abel, who had disappeared after going to work on an estate in Para state, Brazil. "No matter how many children there are," she said, "the mother's heart is so big and her love so strong that she goes looking for the one that is lost, no matter where he or she may be." A poor woman with relatively little education, she sold most of her possessions to fund her trip, and with a camera and a tape recorder she traveled thousands of miles, often risking her life, but sustained by her faith. "When I was in the middle of the jungle, I used to say, 'Jesus, hold that jaguar so that I can pass.' And he did it. No animals did me harm, and even the gunmen let me go."

She sought out isolated and heavily guarded estates where she found hundreds of enslaved workers but not her son. "Many were beaten or starved," she said, "and on one estate I heard how workers who were too exhausted to work further were hung up on trees and used by gunmen for target practice." Despite her efforts, she had to return home without Abel. But in May 1996 she suddenly received a telephone call from her son, and shortly afterward Abel escaped from his forced labor and returned to her. "I had encountered hundreds of slave laborers, hidden away from prying eyes. Many were beaten or starved," she said. Assisted by the Pastoral Land Commission (an agency of the Catholic Church), she began registering official complaints, leading to the release of many enslaved laborers. After her son was located and freed from slavery, she also began to confront politicians over the lack of enforcement of antislavery laws. "After two years on the road, I had already seen enough suffering. I had seen how my son would have died. I was desperate and I began to cry out in newspapers, radio, and TV stations so that the problem was widely publicized. I have no doubts that the majority of Brazilians know about it nowadays. . . . There is labor and human rights legislation, but they don't use it." Now in her fifties, she has become a fearless advocate for the enslaved and in 1997 was given Anti-Slavery International's Anti-Slavery Award.

Iqbal Masih (1982–1995)

At the age of four, Iqbal Masih was placed in debt bondage to a carpet maker in rural Pakistan. His parents, poor laborers, received the equivalent of $12 for Iqbal. For the next six years he worked at a carpet loom for twelve or more hours per day. Sometimes chained to the loom, regularly beaten, he was fed little and worked in terrible conditions, leaving him stunted and underdeveloped for his age. In 1992, when he was ten years old, Iqbal escaped from his slaveholder and attended a meeting organized by a Pakistani human rights group that was pressing the government to enforce its laws against bonded labor. Learning of his rights, he refused to return to the loom despite pressure from the slaveholder. He enrolled in a school, learned to read and write, and became active in campaigns to free other child workers.

Over the next two years he helped to liberate hundreds of children from bonded labor. His youth and activism inspired people around the world and gained international attention. In 1994 he was given the Human Rights Youth in Action Award by the Reebok Foundation and was named "Person of the Week" by ABC News. Around the world he visited schools and spoke to students about the problem of child labor and bondage. After his call for a boycott of Pakistani carpets, exports from that country fell.

On April 16, 1995, a few months after his return to Pakistan from the United States, Iqbal was gunned down while riding a bicycle with a friend near his grandmother's village. Some Pakistani human rights workers claim that his murder was the work of the "carpet mafia," angry loom owners whose ability to enslave children had been hampered by Iqbal's work. The Pakistani government says there is no evidence of this, but the government has also jailed or persecuted those people who have called for an investigation of Iqbal's murder.

While in the United States, Iqbal had visited the Broadmeadows Middle School in Quincy, Massachusetts, and talked to the children there about debt bondage and child labor. Shocked by his murder, the students there organized the "School for Iqbal" campaign in order to build a school in his home village of Muridke. They raised thousands of dollars over the next two years; the school was built, equipped, and opened in 1998. Broadmeadows students have been honored for their campaign with many awards, and in 1998 they joined the Global March Against Child Labor. You can visit their campaign on-line at www.mirrorimage.com/iqbal.

Keshav Nankar (c. 1961–)

Keshav Nankar was born into a debt-bonded family in Maharashtra state, India. When Nankar was two years old his father died, thereby transferring his debt to Nankar and his mother. When he was six he attended school and was considered a bright student, but the moneylender demanded that he leave school in his second year and work full-time grazing animals. At age sixteen Nankar became a bonded laborer in his own right, and his decision to marry further bound him to his landlord. Despite having worked for ten years, he had no money because his labor supposedly went to repaying his father's debt, and he had to borrow 700 rupees (about $20) from his master to pay the "bride price." There was no written agreement for the loan, and he was only given food for his work.

Seven years later, Vivek and Vidyullata Pandit visited Nankar's district, where they identified forty bonded workers in his village (see the Pandits' biography below). In July 1983 the Pandits were able to secure Nankar's release. In revenge, local landlords organized a labor boycott in the area and refused to employ any of the former bonded laborers. The Pandits arranged to provide food for them and their families so they would not have to reenter the cycle of bonded labor. Nankar organized a campaign in his village demanding work for all of the ex-bonded laborers at minimum wage. His success led him to become a labor activist organizing the people in his area, and he set up a cooperative growing watermelons that is still operating. Thanks to his activism, the workers in his area are receiving a fair wage and a meal in return for their labor. He is currently the chairman of the labor union and an executive member of organizations that campaign against bonded labor. He has ensured that his children, who are now in school, do not return to a life in debt bondage. When Vivek and Vidyullata Pandit received the 1999 Anti-Slavery

Award from Anti-Slavery International, they immediately presented it to Keshav Nankar, who received it on behalf of bonded laborers in India.

Vivek (1957–) and Vidyullata (1957–) Pandit

Vivek and Vidyullata Pandit are a husband-and-wife team who have touched and changed the lives of thousands of bonded laborers. Vivek was born in 1957 in Maharashtra, India, Vidyullata in Bombay the same year. Vivek's uncle had bonded laborers who served him food as a child, but he did not realize until later that they were enslaved. The two met in a political youth movement in Bombay, where Vivek was studying sociology and Vidyullata was studying science at a university. In 1975 Vidyulatta went to jail for two and a half months in protest of government actions. Soon disillusioned with India's political parties and standard answers, the couple decided to start out on their own. They left their jobs and moved to a small village in the countryside.

Working with like-minded friends, they established medical camps and preschool classes and organized a leprosy detection campaign. Getting to know the young people of the village, they realized that there was a widespread problem with debt bondage. Together they decided to devote their energies to bonded laborers, and ever since they have put their lives at stake to help people out of bondage and into freedom. More than fifteen hundred people have been liberated through their efforts.

The Pandits have set up three integrated organizations based in Thane District that operate throughout Maharashtra, creating a framework that first liberates bonded laborers and then ensures that they can lead a free life: Vidhayak Sansad, set up in 1979, identifies and releases bonded laborers; Shramajeevi Sanghatana, a trade union for former bonded laborers and other marginalized groups founded in 1982, secures equal and fair wages for men and women; and Samarthan, formed in 1993, lobbies state officials for the development and implementation of legislation against this system of enslavement.

The Pandits believe that in order for bonded laborers to be truly free, they must be released from the psychological bonds as well as the physical. They must be made to believe that it is possible to stand up to their former landlords and to adjust to a life of freedom. As Vidyullata Pandit says, "the three most important things people need to fight bonded labor are knowledge of the law, self-confidence to bring about change, and . . . conviction to ensure they don't go back to bonded labor once they are released." The Pandits have devised a program of education that prepares the former bonded laborers for a life of freedom. They are taught basic science to increase their curiosity and attention for detail, role-playing to stimulate problem solving, and games to develop strategic thinking and teamwork. Those who want to become active in the trade union receive further training, and former bonded laborers work in all three organizations. The Pandits' philosophy is based on self-worth. They teach bonded laborers that they have the same value as any other member of society, that no human being deserves to be exploited and oppressed. By providing these structures, the Pandits have enabled former bonded laborers to break free from the cycle of bonded labor.

Father Edwin Paraison (1962–)

Father Paraison, a Haitian Episcopal priest, braved armed guards to rescue and repatriate over a hundred children separated from their families and forced to work on sugar plantations in the Dominican Republic. Haitian workers, including children, are lured with offers of work and then enslaved in the sugar harvest. Haiti and the Dominican Republic are located on the same island and share a border. Traditionally rivals, poor Haitians are treated badly in the Dominican Republic.

Edwin Paraison was born in Haiti in 1962, and studied theology at seminary. His first church was in Romana, Haiti, where he developed a strong relationship with the sugar workers at the local sugar processing plant. A change of bishops and some political friction meant that Paraison was transferred to Barahona, in the Dominican Republic, to establish a local church. Here he became more involved in the plight of Haitians enslaved to work on the sugar harvest in the Dominican Republic. Since the Haitian government was receiving a payment for every worker provided and the Dominican government was keen to avoid any exposure of the use of slave labor that would threaten their market for sugar in the United States, Paraison faced deadly opposition. To counter the abuse, Paraison set up programs to help Haitian workers with their basic needs and to educate them about their rights. With other priests he monitored the movement of people, especially children, into the Dominican Republic, and set up a 24-hour helpline. The work immediately generated many cases of enslaved workers and children, who Paraison freed. After more than sixty-five cases had been resolved, an armed attack killed one of Paraison's coworkers, and a wounded coworker who was taken into police custody after the attack "committed suicide" while in jail. Threatening phone calls explained that Paraison was next.

Paraison conducted research at this time to discover how many Haitians were being held in Dominican prisons, often without having been charged. These prisoners he then sought to free. When the Haitian government was overthrown in 1991, very large numbers of Haitians fled into the Dominican Republic, and Paraison found himself the key spokesperson for this refugee community. His work there brought to light the serious violations of human rights suffered by the refugees even after the Dominican Republic passed laws to protect them. After U.S. network news broadcast a report on his work, he was called to testify before the U.S. Congress, but in Haiti a foreign coworker was expelled for helping him carry out research. In 1992 he received a special award from the City of Boston and was asked to advise the European Community. In 1994 he received the Anti-Slavery Award from Anti-Slavery International. He still lives in the border region between Haiti and the Dominican Republic, helping migrants and refugees.

Shakil Patan (1956–1998)

Born in Hyderabad, Pakistan, Shakil Patan was the child of refugees from India at the time of the division of India and Pakistan. He was born with the last name Khan but changed it as a protection for his family when he got involved in human rights work. He received a master's degree in political science and was active in student campaigns for democracy and rights, becoming a leader in the fight to restore democracy in Pakistan during the military dictatorship of the 1970s. While still a teenager he was jailed by the government for a month, then later for two months; then in his twenties he spent twenty-one consecutive months in jail. His crime was calling for democracy and civil rights.

In 1986 he was one of the cofounders of the Human Rights Commission of Pakistan (HRCP); in 1991 he organized the HRCP Task Force on the Sindh. The Sindh is a rural state within Pakistan that has large amounts of slavery through debt bondage. Patan collected documentary evidence in Sindh of debt bondage, imprisonment of workers, buying and selling of people, rape of women in bonded families, and terror and torture committed by landlords. This evidence was submitted to the government according to Pakistan's law against bonded labor, but the corruption of local officials is such that no action has been taken. More often, exposed landlords have just made threats and sold their bonded families to get rid of the evidence. Patan worked closely with one village inhabited by oppressed minority families, leading raids that freed more than two thousand people in all. Television coverage of these raids resulted in Patan becoming well known, and death threats began to follow him. In 1998 he was killed in a car accident. His widow, Nasreen Patan, has taken over the leadership of the HRCP Sindh Task Force.

Father Ricardo Rizende (1952–)

Rizende is a Roman Catholic priest who fought for human rights in the Para state of Brazil. Despite repeated threats to his life from well-known killers in Para's lawless frontier, Father Rizende persistently denounced the enslavement of workers in mining and ranching since his arrival in the Amazon. The Brazilian-born Rizende took a course in religious studies and philosophy and then earned a master's degree in agricultural and social development. He moved to the town of Rio de Maria in Para to take his first job as a priest in 1977. Working with trade unions and lawyers, he has freed and helped to rehabilitate hundreds of slaves. The cost has been high—since the mid-1980s seven of the activists in the local rural workers' union have been killed, other priests and lawyers have been gunned down, and several attempts have been made on Rizende's life. Rio de Maria became known as the "town of death foretold" because the published threats were so often followed by murder.

In 1996 Rizende left Para when his colleagues convinced him that the danger had become severe and that his death was next. He moved to Rio de Janeiro and gained a doctorate degree with research into human rights. From Rio he has continued to campaign and speak out against the enslavement of workers in Brazil. Author of several books, he has grown from a local parish priest into an international expert on human rights and slavery. He was given the Anti-Slavery Award in 1992.

Amar Saran (1954–)

Amar Saran comes from the city of Allahabad in India. He studied sociology at a university in New Delhi, then later earned a law degree, following in the footsteps of his father and grandfather. For many years he practiced law, mostly criminal law, and had nothing to do with questions of slavery. But in 1995 he was asked to join the state Vigilance Committee on Debt Bondage. These committees are supposed to watch for and prosecute cases of bondage, but the committee in the state of Uttar Pradesh had become quiet and the state government had announced that Uttar Pradesh was free of bondage. Not long after he joined the vigilance committee, a local human rights activist told Saran he could show him some bonded labor. Not far into the countryside they discovered entire villages bonded and working at making gravel and quarrying.

Shocked by what he found, Amar Saran began to press a case for their release and soon discovered that the moneylenders and landlords had powerful friends. He found that the raja (or prince) of Shankargarh, which included the local area, had secured perpetual leases for the minerals in the land under more than forty villages. Because the land is poor for farming, mining is the only way that local people can make a living. The local people were threatened with expulsion by the raja's middlemen and then led into bondage to work the gravel pits and quarries. The little money gained by the adults was not enough to support their families, and all the children of the villages were also pressed into the work. When Saran brought legal cases to abolish the debts and bondage, the courts delayed taking action. Gaining no help from the courts, Saran began working with a local group to organize the villagers into small-scale credit unions. Although it seems hard to imagine that bonded laborers could benefit from a credit union, they managed to put tiny amounts into the "bank" each week and slowly built up a sum that could be borrowed without terrible interest or false accounting. Even greater than the amount of pooled savings was the sense of empowerment gained by the credit union members. After a portion of the savings had been used to buy some members out of their bondage, most of the other members simply freed themselves, refusing to work any longer unless it was for a decent wage, thus canceling their own debts.

Faced with united workers, the middlemen backed down, and soon villages were building schools and taking their children out of the quarries. But being freed of debt did not always mean that the villagers could earn a good living. Soon it became clear that to gain any security the workers would need to lease their own quarries and work for themselves. But here they collided again with the raja, who controlled all of the mineral rights and would only give leases for huge sums. Since it is Indian government policy to support poor people with grants of mineral leases, to make rehabilitation payments to freed bonded workers, and to support credit unions, and given that little of this had happened, Saran filed a major lawsuit. The lawsuit asked that the existing laws be enforced and that the question of leases be resolved. The families in the one village that has been able to get a lease to some government land have seen their lives transformed and their incomes greatly increased. The lawsuit is still not resolved, for delaying tactics are being used by the landlords. Saran continues to press the case and to work with local groups to help them free themselves from bondage.

Suman (1961–)

This remarkable young woman has guided almost two thousand children freed from slavery into their new lives. Suman was born in New Delhi, India, the daughter of a government employee. While attending university she volunteered to help when a flood destroyed many homes nearby. Many of the victims were poor migrants, whose temporary shelters and few possessions had been swept away. She was struck both by their resilience and by the lack of interest shown by the government in their condition. The experience made her reconsider her plan to enter government service.

One day in 1982 Suman was waiting for a bus and began to talk with two little boys. The boys were wearing ragged clothes and carrying bundles. When she asked where they lived they replied, "In the garbage dump." Forgetting about the bus, she went with them to see their "home" and found more children working in the dump sorting the rubbish and picking out any sort of material that could be sold. She discovered that because they were illiterate they were regularly cheated when they sold their goods. Raising some funds through grants and loans, Suman bought gloves and shoes for the children and began to teach them to read and write.

After a few years Suman learned about the release of children from slavery in the carpet industry. While attending a conference, she met others concerned about children in slavery as well as released bonded laborers. In 1989 she cofounded the South Asian Coalition on Child Servitude (SACCS) and led the development of Mukti Ashram, a rehabilitation center for freed child slaves. Since then she has managed the center, developing the techniques for helping child slaves reclaim their place in the world. As they grow the children take much of the responsibility for maintaining the center.

Suman uses only one name because the caste system in India is sometimes used to justify the enslavement of people from so-called "lower" castes. Since a person's last name usually indicates his or her caste position, she has given up her last name in order to demonstrate the equality of all people. When asked about her plans for the future, she responds, "I will work until child labor is abolished and all the kids are in school. My dream is that the children here at the center will become natural leaders, participating in all levels of decision making." Her advice to any young person who wants to make a difference is this: "Have confidence and clarity in your desire to do the right thing; get experience by helping others. You don't have to be special—anyone can do it!"

Moctar Teyeb (1959–)

Moctar Teyeb was born an *abd*, or slave, in Mauritania. As a child one of his duties was to take his master's children to school each morning; if he tried to listen to the lessons through the window of the school, he was driven away. When he tried to attend the local Koranic (religious) school, he was beaten. During most of his youth Teyeb lived a nomadic life, traveling with his master's livestock, walking long distances and doing the hardest work. As he grew older his interest in education increased, and he began to clash with his master. Then, in the early 1970s Teyeb's father escaped to Senegal. Like Frederick Douglass, Teyeb continued to educate himself in any way he could, secretly teaching himself to read. When he told his master in 1977 that he wanted to become a teacher, he was ridiculed and sent away to the capital city to work there. Slave life in the city was less controlled than in the countryside, and in 1978 Teyeb took the opportunity to follow his father and escape to Senegal.

After reuniting with his father, they set off together for the Ivory Coast, where they believed there would a chance for Teyeb to attend school. After a harrowing trip across country, they reached their destination. At the age of twenty-two, Teyeb attended school for the first time in his life. He learned French and then persuaded the French Embassy to give him papers that stated he was Mauritanian (Mauritania was once a French colony). His academic skills were so good that he was soon awarded a scholarship to study in Libya and then Morocco. Though overjoyed at the chance to learn, his time in Libya and Morocco was made difficult by the fact that Arab classmates resented having an ex-slave in class and condemned him for his antislavery activism. Ultimately earning a law degree, he returned to Mauritania and found himself in a strange situation: Though he was regularly picked up and questioned by the police, he was not imprisoned. His old master did not attempt to reclaim him, but he found he did not fit into any community. He was able to continue contact with the underground antislavery movement.

Finally receiving a Mauritanian passport, he gained a visa to the United States and came to live with a relative in New York. Taking any sort of job, he devoted himself to studying toward an American law degree and improving his English. He also began speaking out and educating others about slavery in Mauritania. Before high school and university audiences as well as in various public gatherings, Teyeb discusses the deep-rooted slavery system from the unique perspective of an ex-slave. He often works with the American Anti-Slavery Group. Speaking out in this way takes courage—the Mauritanian government is already trying to silence him. But every opportunity to tell his story brings more support for the antislavery movement. He continues to live in New York where he works and studies.

Harriet Tubman (1820–1913)

Harriet Tubman was the most courageous and daring of the "conductors" on the Underground Railway, which brought American slaves to freedom in the early nineteenth century. She was born Araminta Ross, a slave, in Maryland. Physically abused and starved as a child, she was partially disabled. Her life almost ended at fifteen when she blocked an overseer pursuing an escaping slave and received a terrible blow to the head. For years she was dull-witted and unproductive, but family support and a strong will guided her to a slow but miraculous recovery. In the 1840s she was angered to learn that her mother had been freed by a previous owner's will, but her mother had never been told, and that her family was about to be sold again. In 1849 she escaped to Philadelphia and took her mother's name, Harriet.

Within two years she had joined with William Still, the black abolitionist and organizer of the Underground Railway in Pennsylvania. In 1851 she sneaked back into the slave states and came back with a group of escaped slaves; it was the first of many such trips. Though illiterate, she was a superb strategist and planned her trips carefully, carrying them through with rigid determination. Making at least nineteen trips, she freed hundreds of slaves, including her own parents and other relatives. More than $40,000 was offered for her capture, the equivalent of $4 million in today's money. While taking slaves to the North she met and worked with Frederick Douglass as well as Susan B. Anthony and Elizabeth Cady Stanton. During the Civil War she organized a group of black spies and scouts who carried out espionage and gained valuable information for the Union forces. She personally guided a group of black soldiers into a Confederate-held town and disabled the rebel supply line. After the war Tubman worked to get women the right to vote. She was buried in 1913 with military honors.

John Woolman (1720–1772)

John Woolman was a Quaker and pioneer abolitionist born in colonial New Jersey. He has been described as having been an odd young man. During his youth he tried to find simplicity and an ethical way of life that often led him to curious decisions, such as choosing to wear only clothes that had not been dyed with colors. After some time as a shopkeeper, he gave it up in order to travel more among the Quakers in colonial America. He took up "conveyancing"—the writing up of bills of sale, deeds, and leases—as a way to support himself. When his first employer asked him to draw up a bill of sale for a slave, Woolman did so but was very troubled at the time and afterward. From that point he refused to write up any legal document regarding slavery, and he would take every opportunity to convince his clients of the immorality of slavery and urge them to free their slaves.

In 1746 he traveled in the southern colonies, where slavery was more prominent, and stayed with slaveholding Quaker families. He was so disturbed by what he saw that he wrote a pamphlet against slavery that was published, then followed it with a call to all Quakers to renounce slavery. By 1758 his quiet but urgent campaigning among Quakers paid off with a general rule against keeping slaves or participating in the slave trade. By this action, the Quakers became the first organized body to oppose slavery in North America. Woolman also campaigned for equal treatment for Native Americans and for living simply so that a person's resources could be better put to helping others. "The business of our lives," he wrote, is "to turn all the treasures we possess into the channel of universal love." Though a quiet and simple person, Woolman's example led the Quakers to become the mainstay of the coming abolitionist movement. Quakers are still active today in anti-slavery work.

4

Facts and Documents

The material included here aims to give the reader a sense of the scale and diversity of slavery in the modern world—and some insight into its inhumanity—at the beginning of the twenty-first century. This chapter offers an overview of the main forms of slavery old and new that exist around the globe. It draws on a wide range of documents, including book extracts, reports to United Nations committees, interviews with modern-day slaves, speeches from antislavery campaigners and their supporters, press stories, and briefings prepared by nongovernmental organizations.

The chapter begins with some key facts and figures, followed by a summary of the most important documents in international law and conventions that define and condemn slavery. This helps provide the context for the individual and collective stories of slaves and antislavery activists that follow.

These stories and evidence are divided into different kinds of slavery, although in practice there is much crossover between them. Traditional-style slave ownership in Mauritania, bonded labor in rural Asian societies, forced labor in Bosnia or Burma, the trafficking and sexual slavery of young girls from Thailand to the United States, domestic slavery in countries as diverse as the Philippines, Haiti, and the United Kingdom—all these variations on contemporary slavery have much in common. But in their different ways, they show the many forms that slavery as a social and economic relationship can take.

The chapter concludes with a brief examination of the complex issue of child labor and two recent campaigns aimed at ending the use of young children in the production of goods sold to consumers. Not all child labor is slavery. But children enslaved in

bonded labor or forced prostitution are two particularly perni-
cious kinds of slavery that have received a significant amount of
attention worldwide.

Facts and Figures

The Slavery Index

- Number of slaves thought to be taken from Africa in
  the 400-year-long Atlantic slave trade: 13 million.[1]
- Number of slaves conservatively estimated to be in
  bondage in 1999: 27 million.[2]
- Maximum estimated number of slaves transported
  from Africa by British slave traders at the height
  of the Atlantic trade (1730s–1740s), per year:
  23,000.[3]
- United Nations estimate of number of persons illegally
  trafficked across borders and enslaved in 1990s, per
  year: 2 million.[4]
- Number of international treaties enacted between
  1815 and 1957 "for the suppression of the slave trade":
  300.[5]
- Average price of an agricultural slave in Mississippi in
  1850, in 1999 dollars: $40,000.[6]
- Average price of an agricultural slave in debt bondage
  in India today, in 1999 dollars: $80.[7]
- Average profit of the British slave trade, 1761 to 1807:
  9.5 percent.[8]
- Average profit of Thai brothel using enslaved prostitutes, 1997: 856 percent.[9]
- Estimated number of slaves in debt bondage in Pakistan today: 20 million.[10]
- Year the law banning debt bondage came into effect in
  Pakistan: 1992.[11]
- Number of convictions of slaveholders under that law
  from 1992 to 1998: 0.[12]
- Year that Pakistan has assured the United Nations that
  "all bonded labor will stop": 2003.[13]

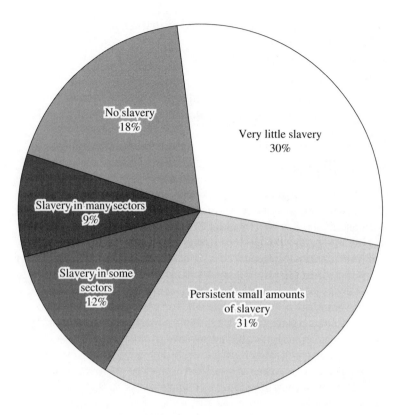

Figure 4.1   Percentage of Countries with Different Levels of Slavery
(192 countries total), 1990s

The Spread of Slavery

Figure 4.1 shows the percentage of countries in the world having
different amounts of slavery. Less than one country in five has no
reported slavery, and a little under a third of all countries have
very little or rare slavery. Slavery is a regular and persistent feature of life in just over half of all countries. Just under one country in ten has slavery regularly contributing to many sectors of
their economy. About two-fifths of all countries have smaller
amounts of slavery that are, nonetheless, constant features in
their national economy.

But why do some countries have more slavery than others?
Why do some countries have persistent regular slavery and
some countries have none at all? If we look at all the countries
around the world and ask what things most strongly predict

whether or not slavery exists in a country, a statistical test gives this answer:

Strongest Predictors of Slavery in a Country (in this order):

- Government and police corruption
- High level of infant mortality
- Population has high proportion of young people and children
- Country has low gross domestic product (GDP) per capita

What this points to are the very factors discussed in Chapter 1 that have led to the emergence of new forms of slavery and an increase in slavery worldwide. Countries with a high proportion of children under the age of fourteen are experiencing the bulk of the population explosion. For those countries that also suffer from extremes in poverty and a lack of welfare services (measured by GDP and infant mortality), economic and social vulnerability become a regular part of life. When this large, poor, vulnerable population lacks protection from government and police corruption, one result can be slavery.

Another pressure that seems to push countries toward higher levels of slavery is international debt. Many countries in the developing world must carry large debts to the World Bank or other lenders and so must put most of their national income toward paying the interest on these debts. If we look at those countries that are named by the World Bank as having a heavy debt load and compare them with countries that do not have big international debts, there is a marked difference with regard to slavery. Half of the countries with a heavy debt load have slavery as a regular feature in their economies, compared to only 12 percent of those countries with a small amount of international debt. Almost three-quarters of countries with a large international debt find that their citizens are regularly trafficked into slavery in other countries, compared with less than a third of those with low international debt. Figure 4.2 shows how international debt and slavery are related.

With slavery so widespread, it is fair to ask what laws and international agreements have been passed against it and to wonder whether they are, in fact, effective. The next section reviews the many, and often confused, laws and conventions that exist concerning slavery.

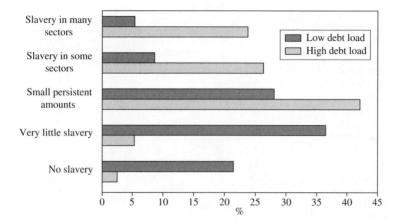

Figure 4.2   Amount of Slavery in Countries with High and Low International Debt, 1990s

Table 4.1.
Summary of the Evolution of Slavery Conventions

Slavery Convention	Definition/Declaration Regarding Slavery
Slavery Convention (1926)	**Slavery defined:** Slavery is the "status or condition of a person over whom all of the powers attaching to the right of ownership are exercised." **Forced labor added:** States should "prevent compulsory or forced labor from developing into conditions analogous to slavery."
Universal Declaration (1948)	**Servitude added:** "No one shall be held in slavery or servitude; slavery and the slave trade should be abolished in all their forms."
Supplementary Convention (1956)	**Servile status added:** Practices referred to as servile status should be abolished: (a) debt bondage (b) serfdom (c) unfree marriages (d) the exploitation of young people for their labor
Economic, Social, and Cultural Covenant (1966)	**Freedom to choose work added:** Recognizes "the right of everyone to the opportunity to gain his living by work which he freely chooses or accepts."
Rome Final Act (1998)	**Trafficking added:** Slavery defined as "the exercise of any or all of the powers attaching to the right of ownership over a person and includes the exercise of such power in the course of trafficking in persons, in particular women and children."

Table 4.2.
Practices Defined as Forms of Slavery in International Conventions

Practice/Criteria Y = Yes, N = No	Totally Controlled (Y/N)	Paid Nothing Economically Used (Y/N)	Violence or Threat of Violence (Y/N)
Chattel Slavery	Y	Y	Y
"White Slavery"	Y	Y	Y
Forced Labor	Y	Y	Y
Debt Bondage	Y	Y	Y
Child Prostitution	Y	Y	Y
Forced Prostitution	Y	Y	Y
Sexual Slavery	Y	Y	Y
Migrant Work	Y/N	Y/N	Y/N
Prostitution	Y/N	Y/N	Y/N
Forced Marriage	Y/N	Y/N	Y
Apartheid	Y/N	N	Y
Incest	Y/N	N	Y
Organ Harvesting	Y/N	N	Y/N
Caste	N	N	Y
Prison Labor	N	Y/N	Y

Key International Laws and Conventions on Slavery

Slavery has not always been defined in the same way in international conventions. Table 4.1 shows how the definition of slavery has changed over time.

These different definitions and the naming of other activities as "slavery" means that a lot of things have been called slavery that you may or may not think actually constitute slavery. Table 4.2 shows most of the activities that have been called "slavery" by international agencies and compares them to our definition of slavery as a social and economic relationship in which a person is controlled through violence or its threat, is paid nothing, and is economically exploited.

Literally hundreds of international laws and conventions variously define, condemn, and outlaw slavery in its various past and present forms. The following selected extracts mark key moments in the evolution of international law on slavery.

Slavery Convention of the League of Nations (1926)

Article 1 For the purpose of the present Convention, the following definitions are agreed upon:

(1) Slavery is the status or condition of a person over whom any or all of the powers attaching to the right of ownership are exercised.

(2) The slave trade includes all acts involved in the capture,

acquisition or disposal of a person with intent to reduce him to slavery; all acts involved in the acquisition of a slave with a view to selling or exchanging him; all acts of disposal by sale or exchange of a slave acquired with a view to being sold or exchanged, and, in general, every act of trade or transport in slaves.

Article 2 The High Contracting Parties undertake, each in respect of the territories placed under its sovereignty, jurisdiction, protection, suzerainty or tutelage, so far as they have not already taken the necessary steps:

(a) To prevent and suppress the slave trade;

(b) To bring about, progressively and as soon as possible, the complete abolition of slavery in all its forms.

Article 3 The High Contracting Parties undertake to adopt all appropriate measures with a view to preventing and suppressing the embarkation, disembarkation and transport of slaves in their territorial waters and upon all vessels flying their respective flags.

(The 1926 Convention was adopted with slight amendments by the United Nations in 1953.)

The Universal Declaration of Human Rights, G.A. Res. 217A (III) (1948) (Excerpts)

Article 1 All human beings are born free and equal in dignity and rights.

Article 4 No one shall be held in slavery or servitude; slavery and the slave trade shall be prohibited in all their forms.

Article 13(I) Everyone has the right to freedom of movement and residence within the borders of each state.

Article 23(I) Everyone has the right to the free choice of employment, to just and favourable conditions of work and to protection against unemployment.

Supplementary Convention on the Abolition of Slavery, the Slave Trade, and Institutions and Practices Similar to Slavery, G.A. Res. 794 (VIII) (1956)

Section 1—Institutions and Practices Similar to Slavery

Article 1 Each of the States Parties to this Convention shall take all practicable and necessary legislative and other measures to bring about progressively and as soon as possible the complete abolition or abandonment of the following institutions and practices, where they still exist and whether or not they are covered by the definition of slavery contained in article 1 of the Slavery Convention signed at Geneva on 25 September, 1926:

(a) Debt bondage, that is to say, the status or condition arising from a pledge by a debtor of his personal services or of those of a person under his control as security for a debt, if the value of those services as reasonably assessed is not applied towards the liquidation of the debt or the length and nature of those services are not respectively limited and defined;

(b) Serfdom, that is to say, the condition or status of a tenant who is by law, custom or agreement bound to live and labor on land belonging to another person and to render some determinate service to such other person, whether for reward or not, and is not free to change his status;

(c) Any institution or practice whereby:

(i) A woman, without the right to refuse, is promised or given in marriage on payment of a consideration in money or in kind to her parents, guardian, family or any other person or group; or

(ii) The husband of a woman, his family, or his clan, has the right to transfer her to another person for value received or otherwise; or

(iii) A woman on the death of her husband is liable to be inherited by another person;

(d) Any institution or practice whereby a child or young person under the age of 18 years is delivered by either or both of his natural parents or by his guardian to another person, whether for reward or not, with a view to the exploitation of the child or young person or of his labor.

Article 2 With a view to bringing to an end the institutions and practices mentioned in article 1 (c) of this Convention, the States Parties undertake to prescribe, where appropriate, suitable minimum ages of marriage, to encourage the use of facilities whereby the consent of both parties to a marriage may be freely expressed in the presence of a competent civil or religious authority, and to encourage the registration of marriages.

Section II—The Slave Trade

Article 3 1. The act of conveying or attempting to convey slaves from one country to another by whatever means of transport, or of being accessory thereto, shall be a criminal offence under the laws of the States Parties to this Convention, and persons convicted thereof shall be liable to very severe penalties.

2. (a) The States Parties shall take all effective measures to prevent ships and aircraft authorised to fly their flags from conveying slaves and to punish persons guilty of such acts or of using national flags for that purpose.

(b) The States Parties shall take all effective measures to ensure that their ports, airfields and coasts are not used for the conveyance of slaves.

3. The States Parties to this Convention shall exchange information in order to ensure the practical coordination of the measures taken by them in combating the slave trade and shall inform each other of every case of the slave trade, and of every attempt to commit this criminal offence, which comes to their notice.

Article 4 Any slave who takes refuge on board any vessel of a State Party to this Convention shall ipso facto be free.

Section III—Slavery and Institutions and Practices Similar to Slavery

Article 5 In a country where the abolition or abandonment of slavery, or of the institutions or practices mentioned in article 1 of this Convention, is not yet complete, the act of mutilating, branding or otherwise marking a slave or a person of servile status in order to indicate his status, or as a punishment, or for any other reason, or of being accessory thereto, shall be a criminal offence under the laws of the States Parties to this Convention and persons convicted thereof shall be liable to punishment.

Article 6 1. The act of enslaving another person or of inducing another person to give himself or a person dependent upon him into slavery, or of attempting these acts, or being accessory thereto, or being a party to a conspiracy to accomplish any such acts, shall be a criminal offence under the laws of the States Parties to this Convention and persons convicted thereof shall be liable to punishment.

2. Subject to the provisions of the introductory paragraph of article 1 of this Convention, the provisions of paragraph 1 of the

present article shall also apply to the act of inducing another person to place himself or a person dependent upon him into the servile status resulting from any of the institutions or practices mentioned in article 1, to any attempt to perform such acts, to being accessory thereto, and to being a party to a conspiracy to accomplish such acts.

Section IV—Definitions

Article 7 For the purposes of the present Convention:

(a) "slavery" means, as defined in the Slavery Convention of 1926, the status or condition of a person over whom any or all of the powers attaching to the right of ownership are exercised, and "slave" means a person in such condition or status;

(b) "A person of servile status" means a person in the condition or status resulting from any of the institutions or practices mentioned in article 1 of this Convention;

(c) "Slave trade" means and includes all acts involved in the capture, acquisition or disposal of a person with intent to reduce him to slavery; all acts involved in the acquisition of a slave with a view to selling or exchanging him; all acts of disposal by sale or exchange of a person acquired with a view to being sold or exchanged; and, in general, every act of trade or transport in slaves by whatever means of conveyance.

Convention on the Rights of the Child, G.A. Res. 44/25 (1989) (Excerpts)

Article 27 1. States Parties recognize the right of every child to a standard of living adequate for the child's physical, mental, spiritual, moral and social development.

Article 28 1. States Parties recognize the right of the child to education, and with a view to achieving this right progressively and on a basis of equal opportunity, they shall, in particular: (a) Make primary education compulsory and available free to all. . . .

Article 32 1. States Parties recognize the right of the child to be protected from economic exploitation and from performing any work that is likely to be hazardous or to interfere with the child's education, or to be harmful to the child's health or physical, mental, spiritual, moral or social development.

ILO Convention Concerning the Prohibition and Immediate Action for the Elimination of the Worst Forms of Child Labour, ILO 87/C182 (1999) (Excerpts)

Article 1 Each Member which ratifies this Convention shall take immediate and effective measures to secure the prohibition and elimination of the worst forms of child labor as a matter of urgency.

Article 2 For the purposes of this Convention, the term *child* shall apply to all persons under the age of 18.

Article 3 For the purposes of this Convention, the term *the worst forms of child labor* comprises:

(a) all forms of slavery or practices similar to slavery, such as the sale and trafficking of children, debt bondage and serfdom and forced or compulsory labor, including forced or compulsory recruitment of children for use in armed conflict;

(b) the use, procuring or offering of a child for prostitution, for the production of pornography or for pornographic performances;

(c) the use, procuring or offering of a child for illicit activities, in particular for the production and trafficking of drugs as defined in the relevant international treaties;

(d) work which, by its nature or the circumstances in which it is carried out, is likely to harm the health, safety or morals of children.

Reports, Evidence, and Testimony about the Different Types of Slavery

Bonded Labor

Bonded labor is the most common form of slavery in the modern world. A person pledges him or herself against a loan of money, but the length and nature of the service is not defined and the labor does not reduce the original debt. The debt can be passed down through generations, and "defaulting" can be punished by seizing or selling children into further debt bonds. It is most common in India and Pakistan.

Testimony about Bonded Labor in India

Keshav Nankar is an ex-bonded laborer who now works to liberate others from such slavery. Vivek Pandit works with bonded laborers in the Thane district of India (see also their biographical sketches in Chapter 3). They made the following speeches to an audience in London on jointly receiving Anti-Slavery International's annual Anti-Slavery Award for 1999.

Keshar Nankar Today, I am here in front of you, speaking to you, after travelling thousands of miles. This is unbelievable considering who I was in 1983. Today, I have the capacity and the confidence to address thousands of brothers and sisters. I am proud that today I can deal with government officials at various levels. And, if they do not pay attention to my community's genuine demands, we will protest and demand our rights. Furthermore, I have become actively involved in the political process. I contested the elections for the State Assembly. I teach my fellow farmers the latest, modern techniques of farming practices. Looking back at my past I cannot believe my present today. It seems unreal but it's not a dream, it is a reality born out of a lot of pain, a lot of struggle and a lot of dreams put together.

I remember as a child, when I was six or seven years old, my father enrolled me in the village school. I used to like my school very much. I especially loved the singing, dancing, and playing. But my father needed some money. He asked his landlord—for whom he had worked his entire life—for some money. The landlord gave him the money but took me in return. He asked my father, "What would your child do in school?" and "How will he feed himself?" He said, "Remove him from school, send him here to look after my cattle and I will give him one meal a day." That is how I was taken out of school when I was seven years old and I was not allowed to study beyond my first standard.

I continued working with the landlord. I got married and my wife and I worked in the fields and at home. Through marrying me, my wife also became a bonded laborer to my landlord. From dawn to midnight, we used to fetch water, clean the utensils, wash clothes, collect firewood and remove cow dung. We also had to prepare the ground for sowing the seeds, transplanting the saplings, nurturing the plants, harvesting the field, and finally husking the grains. The other agricultural laborers, who were lucky not to be bonded, worked much less and earned much more than me.

Once, to earn a bit more, I went to work with another landlord. This angered my landlord. He sent his henchmen to fetch me. They brutally assaulted me and verbally abused me during the journey back to my landlord.

My wages were not sufficient to feed my family even once. My debt kept increasing. I was getting sucked into a whirlpool. As a result, I became suppressed, with no voice of my own. I wanted to break the shackles and get out of this misery but I could not see any way out. In 1983, I met a few workers of Shramjeevi Sanghatana, a trade union that had started mobilizing bonded laborers, agricultural laborers and small farmers in the neighboring areas. They built our confidence and our powers. They taught us to say NO and not to bow to any injustice. They gave us the strength to fight against all sorts of atrocities that have been committed against us for generations. The landlords troubled us in many ways but the Sanghatana members remained with us through all our sufferings and hardships. When we were beaten severely, they were there getting beaten with us. When we had no food, they starved with us. This is how our struggle continued.

Today, in our area nobody dares to keep a bonded laborer. We proudly run the village Gram Panchayat (Council). I contested the assembly elections based on the credibility of Sanghatana, not on the power of money. I lost the elections but it is not the result, but the process that is important. I proved that a poor person once without any rights, suppressed beyond imagination, could also emerge stronger and exercise his democratic rights to the fullest.

Today, I also do collective farming, along with the

other freed bonded and agricultural laborers. The landlords who were keepers of bonded labor now come to me for advice on farming. This is not my story alone but a story of thousands of changed lives.

Source: Acceptance speech given at the 1999 Anti-Slavery Awards Ceremony, London, England, 27 October 1999. Reprinted by permission of Anti-Slavery International.

Vivek Pandit When I went to get my visa before coming here I was interviewed by a lady at the Consulate who asked me in wonder, "Are there still slaves in India?" Perhaps some of you would ask the same question. The answer, my friends, is yes. Even after fifty years of freedom from colonial rule there are still millions of men, women, and children who live lives of bondage. When we went to work in the rural areas in the late seventies we knew nothing of bonded labor or slavery, what we saw in the villages was that they were not a homogeneous community. We saw that the landlord belonging to the upper caste, with more money and political connections, owned the tribals who were landless, abjectly poor and belonged to the lowest stratum of the caste system. The power was literally concentrated at the core even geographically. All resources came to villages where the landlords lived, while the tribals (indigenous people) were pushed to the far-flung hamlets, in the interior and inaccessible forests.

We learned from the people how they took small sums of money from the landlord during illness or marriage and then were bonded to him for generations. The bonded laborer was less than an animal. The landowner's bullocks were better taken care of than the human beings. After the season transplantation of paddy rice the bullocks were rested for a month or more and all this time the bonded laborer was expected to gather the green fodder for the cattle. I remember that the tribals would work without respite till their feet rotted by being continuously in the water. Ironically, the owners would beat the tribals who could not work.

These were the slave citizens of a free country. This was the irony in the largest democracy in the world. When we began working for the release of bonded laborers we realized we were challenging the vested interests in the area. The release of bonded labor is a process from slavery to freedom, and freedom is never gifted away. Freedom can only be won through struggle, by building the strength of the people. We realized that those in bondage have to be prepared to overthrow their chains at any cost, even at the cost of their lives. My advice to those who say they want to free bonded laborers but are unable to do so because of police cases or threats by landlords, I ask them, "What else did you expect?" It is only natural that the powerful will react to keep their interests intact. Dr. Martin Luther King had said, "Freedom has always been an expensive thing." Indeed we have to prepare to pay the highest price for it.

The essential condition of bondage is in the minds of the people. While recording the statements of the hundreds of bonded laborers, whenever we asked, "What is your problem?" invariably they replied, "Nothing." A bonded laborer has no dreams and torture is the way of life. They have been conditioned to accept that their place is at the periphery of society. The process of release and rehabilitation of bonded labor is to restore the personhood of the person, to restore self-esteem, confidence, and the feeling that they too can win. Until yesterday we had nothing, but we can build for a better tomorrow for our children. Release from bondage can only come through collective action saying "no" to an inhuman system. Thus, there were uniting slogans that brought together the bonded laborers: "Tribals are human beings, not cattle"; "We are demanding our rights as human beings."

Slogans and songs like these are helpful in reinforcing the feeling of dignity in the bonded labor. When the landlords attacked them, a tribal woman said, "We will eat bitter roots and crabs, but we will not bow down before the landlords." That became another powerful slogan in the struggle against bonded labor. The system of bonded labor could not be fought in isolation. The struggle against bonded labor was linked to the larger struggle for rights of agricultural laborers, for minimum and equal wages, for the restoration of tribal land grabbed by the landlords, and so on. The movement grew; not strength in members, but strength in feeling, belief, and solidarity. More and more marginalized people joined it and strengthened it. We learned that bonded laborers do not become free because they are not convinced that they can remain in freedom. The message that goes across to the bonded laborer is that the entire system is against them.

The landlords are obviously exploiting them, but the law enforcement agencies do not help them either. They know that they are being tortured, but there is no one to listen to their plight. They are not even convinced that social workers or NGOs [nongovernmental organizations] will listen to them. I remember when we first came across the issue of bonded labor, we spent nearly two whole years trying to convince the tribals to become free. The landlords were angry that we were campaigning against them, and the tribals ran away whenever they saw us because my uncle was a bonded labor keeper. They thought we were the agents of the landlords. A bonded laborer does not become free overnight. In this period of transition we have to help them in every possible way. Once they are free, the bonded laborers become part of the larger community of the workforce and are free to sell their labor to any person. The issues of the larger community become theirs. The poverty, illiteracy, disease, and exploitation that are the lot of the free labor also become their lot.

Another lesson we learned was that social legislation by itself cannot destroy slavery. While powerful laws are important and useful, without an insistent and equally powerful voice to demand their implementation, laws have remained on paper. Similarly, any other tool like using the media, public interest litigation, or using legislative devices have to be linked to collective action if they are to bring long-lasting change in the lives of the people. Releasing bonded laborers is not a project. It is entering into the politics of tilting the balance of power in favor of the marginalized. This requires knowing the various democratic institutions, the laws, and the pulse of the people, the mind of the opponent. But once bonded laborers are free, the sky is the limit. They do not wait for alternative employment or rehabilitation packages. Freed bonded laborers in Thane (our district in Maharashtra) have helped other bonded laborers all over the country in their struggle for freedom. They have even collected one Rupee each as a token contribution in the freedom struggle of Nelson Mandela and the African National Congress. They have truly understood in their hearts that no one is free till every one is free.

Source: Acceptance speech given at the 1999 Anti-Slavery Awards Ceremony, London, England, 27 October 1999. Reprinted by permission of Anti-Slavery International.

Evidence about Bonded Labor in Pakistan

In Pakistan debt bondage operates under the *peshgi* system. Offers to lend money to poor families trap them, often for generations, due to high interest rates and manipulation of the books. Bonded labor exists in agriculture as well as trades such as carpet weaving and brick making. This newspaper article from Pakistan illustrates the problem.

Karachi: Pakistani authorities on Sunday rescued a group of former slaves who were abducted by their previous masters from a town in Sindh, officials said. "After three days of hectic efforts we have recovered these persons from the fields in far-flung areas," senior police official Sain Rakhio Mirani told reporters. The attackers abducted more than 100 peasants, including women and children, from the town of Matil, 220 kilometers (136 miles) northeast of here on Wednesday. Police said those recovered included 42 children and 17 women. The recovery came after a series of protests by activists from the private Human Rights Commission of Pakistan (HRCP) and political parties over the attack which left at least 32 people injured, including two Roman Catholic priests which had given land and shelter to the peasants. An old woman died of her injuries on Saturday.

The liberated peasants said they were denied food and badly beaten by their captors. Master Laiji, an HCRP activist, said he was happy at their release but added they needed proper security. "We fear about the lives of these people and need proper security arrangements. They are already terrorised," Laiji said. Thousands of poor farmers have been forced into bonded labor in southern Sindh and Punjab provinces despite a ban on such practices introduced in 1992. Over the past four years human rights activists have secured the freedom of 3,500 peasants from slavery camps allegedly run by landlords.

They were made slaves by feudal lords after they failed to return petty debts, activists said. The HRCP activists said they had sent lists of 4,500 such peasants, 70 percent of whom were children and women, to Prime Minister Nawaz Sharif's government. However there were so far no signs of securing their release, they said.

Source: "Pakistan Police Recover Abducted 'Slave Laborers,'" *News International,* London, translated from the *Daily Jang,* September 15, 1998. Reprinted by permission.

Contract Slavery

Contract slavery shows how modern labor relations are used to hide slavery. Contracts are offered that guarantee employment, but when the workers are taken to the place of work they find themselves enslaved. This is the second largest but also the most rapidly growing form of slavery today.

Contract Slavery in Brazil

The main form of slavery found in modern-day Brazil is contract slavery based on debt bondage. In a country where an estimated one in five of the population lives in absolute poverty, workers from areas hit by recession or natural disasters such as drought are enticed into accepting verbal contracts on the basis of false promises of well-paid work. They are then transported thousands of miles in trucks to work on estates in isolated parts of the Amazon states. Recruitment is carried out by a *gato* (cat). The workers are then told they are in debt for their transportation, tools, food, and other inflated living costs while working and are thus forced into a cycle of bonded labor. In 1995 the Brazilian government formed an interministerial task force known as the Executive Group for the Repression of Forced Labor and set up mobile teams to carry out inspections wherever slavery is reported.

Evidence and Testimony from Brazil about Contract Slavery

From the early 1980s, as the wave of development swept into Mato Grosso do Sul, recruiters began to appear in the slums of Minas Gerais seeking workers with some experience in charcoal making. These recruiters are called *Gatos* (cats) and are key players in the process of enslavement. When they drive into the slums with their cattle trucks and announce that they are hiring men or even whole families, the desperate residents immediately respond. The *Gatos* will go from door to door or use loudspeakers to call people into the street. Sometimes the local politicians, even local churches, will let them use public buildings and help them to recruit workers. The *Gatos* explain that they need workers in the ranches and forests of Mato Grosso. Like good salesmen they lay out the many advantages of regular work and good conditions. They offer to provide transport to Mato Grosso, good food on site, a regular salary, provision of tools, and a free trip home every month to see the family. For a hungry family it seems a miraculous offer of a new beginning. In a charcoal camp in Mato Grosso do Sul I spoke with a man named Renaldo who told me about being recruited by the *Gato:*

"My parents lived in a very dry rural area and when I got older there was no work, no work at all there. So I decided to go to the city. I went to Sao Paulo but that was even worse, no work and everything was very expensive, and the place was dangerous—so much crime! So then I went up to Minas Gerais because I heard that there was work there. If there was I didn't find it, but one day a Gato came and began to recruit people to work out here in Mato Grosso. The

Gato said that we would be given good food everyday, and we would have good wages besides. He promised that every month his truck would bring people back to Minas Gerais so that they could visit their families and bring them their pay. He even gave money to some men to give to their families before they left and to buy food to bring with them on the trip. He was able to fill up his truck with workers very easily and we started on the trip west. Along the way, when we would stop for fuel, the Gato would say 'Go on into the cafe and eat as much as you like, I'll pay for it.' We had been hungry for a long time, so you can imagine how we ate! When we got to Mato Grosso we kept driving further and further into the country. This camp is almost fifty miles from anything, it is just raw cerrado for fifty miles before you get to even a ranch, and there is just the one road. When we reached the camp we could see it was terrible: the conditions were not good enough for animals. Standing around the camp were men with guns. And then the Gato said, 'You each owe me a lot of money, there is the cost of the trip, and all that food you ate, and the money I gave you for your families—so don't even think about leaving.'"

Renaldo was trapped. With the other workers he found he could not leave the camp or have any say in the work he was given to do. After two months, when the workers asked about going home for a visit they were told they were still too deeply in debt to be allowed to go.

Source: Kevin Bales, *Disposable People: New Slavery in the Global Economy* (Berkeley: University of California Press, 1999), copyright © The Regents of the University of California. Reprinted by permission.

Chattel Slavery

This is the form of slavery closest to the old slavery. A person is completely owned by a master or mistress. He or she is sold, captured, or born into a lifetime of slavery. The slaves' children are usually also treated as property and can be traded like cattle between owners. Modern chattel slavery is most commonly found in parts of northern and western Africa and in some Arab countries. It represents a small portion of today's slaves.

Evidence of Chattel Slavery in Mauritania

Mauritanian society is made up of three groups: the Arab Moors from the north, slaves and ex-slaves called Haratines, and the Afro-Mauritanians in the south. Slavery has been abolished many times in Mauritania, most recently in 1980, when perhaps as many as one-third of the country's population of two million became ex-slaves on paper. But many remain enslaved, either unaware of their rights or unable to translate legal freedom into practical action. Moctar Teyeb is a former Mauritanian slave; his biographical sketch appears in Chapter 3.

Translation of Bill of Sale for Two Slaves (from Arabic)

In the name of Allah, most gracious and most merciful, salutation and peace upon him:

Mohamed Vall Ould Nema, son of Sidiba, bought from Mohamed Lemine Ould Sidi Mohamed, son of Taleb Ibrahim, a slave with her daughter named Kneiba in the price of 50,000 [$30] *Ouguiya* received entirely by the seller from the buyer. Therefore, it becomes effective: his ownership of the two slaves listed. The two parties did receive my witness and the buyer before accepted the hidden defects of the slaves. The contract was made at the end of the month of Hija of the year 1412 [1992] by Abedrabou Montali Ould Mohamed Abderrahmane, son of Berrou. God forgive me and my father and all the believers.

Here is the finger[print] of the buyer's left hand.

Source: Unpublished bill of sale dated 1992, reprinted by permission of Anti-Slavery International.

Testimony about Chattel Slavery in Mauritania

Aichana Mint Abeid Boilil was a slave in Mauritania until 1995. Her testimony was to be published in a newspaper in March 1997, but it was censored.

My name is Aichana Mint Abeid Boilil. Like my mother and grandmother, I was born a slave to Mr Abdallahi Salem. I am 23 years old. From the age of three or four onwards, from dawn until night I ran errands between the various tents of my master's family. As I grew up I was given domestic work to do. When I was about 13 Ould Weddou [my master] lent me to his cousin for whom I worked for several years. I grew up under the yoke of this family. Later on I learned the reasons for this "loan": my master was in debt to his cousin, and my period working there was to pay back the debt. I had to take care of everything all the time.

Around 1989 I was sent to work for the master's half-brother in Nouakchott hired out to herd the animals of all the neighbors in village and my master. I fell out with his wife who asked me to separate from my second husband. When I refused, she sent for the police, telling him that my husband had been encouraging me to be rebellious."

Aichana Mint Abeid Boilil escaped in 1995 and asked *SOS Slaves*, a Mauritanian antislavery organization, to help her recover her five children whom she had been forced to leave behind. In the affidavit prepared for the case, Aichana was able to list, in addition to her own children, the names and ages of twenty-four other slaves owned by her master. With legal representatives from *SOS Slaves*, Aichana visited the government prosecutor's office again and again. When the human rights organization threatened to take the case to international aid agencies, the Mauritanian minister for justice asked a court to rule on the case. In order to avoid international embarrassment the government pressed the court to return her children, and, in time, her master, Mohamed Ould Moissa, returned four of her five children. The fifth child (a twelve-year-old girl), he explained, had been given to his daughter, Boika, and was no longer his concern. Ould Moissa argued that he had a right to all the children because Aichana was his wife and he had fathered some (he didn't say which) of the children. Aichana denied she was his wife and insisted that she had never had sex with him. No fine or punishment was levied against the slaveholder, and Aichana is still pressing for the recovery of her fifth child.

Source: Unpublished account included in statement made to the United Nations Working Group on Contemporary Forms of Slavery, June 1997. Reprinted by permission of Anti-Slavery International, London.

The following article from the *Christian Science Monitor* presents another view of slavery in Mauritania:

Slavery obsesses this desert nation. In parliament, in mosques, lying in tents sipping sweet, green tea, people discuss—and often argue—over whether the Haratin, meaning "former slaves," are in fact free.

Officially, slavery has been illegal in this West African nation almost as long as it has in the United States. Yet many Haratin still provide unpaid services, such as tending livestock and cleaning house. In return, their masters feed and clothe them and are expected to treat them like their own children.

In a society where bartering is still common, is this slavery?

The US Congress says it is. In September, it imposed a ban on all economic and military assistance to the government of Mauritania until the practice is "eliminated." But according to the US State Department and the US Embassy in Mauritania, slavery has "virtually disappeared."

US antislavery lobbyists, many of whom had never been to Mauritania, testified before two congressional subcommittees, telling of Arab slave raids, women and children being sold for about $15 a head, and exotic tortures for disobedient slaves.

Evidence included a receipt for a sale that stated that the buyer "accepts the slave in spite of her insubmissiveness."

But Principal Deputy Assistant Secretary for African Affairs William Twaddel disputed this, and much of the testimony. Embassy staff in Mauritania investigated allegations of the slave sale, he told Congress, and concluded that the signatures on the receipt were forged. And his staff couldn't confirm a single case of "involuntary servitude," he said.

Arab-Berber Maurs enslaved black Africans in the 8th century. But Mohammed ould Hamidy, Mauritania's former representative to the UN and himself a Haratin, claims slavery was never like it was in the US. "Intermarriage [between slaves and other classes] has always been common and acceptable," Mr. Hamidy says. "The enslaved are a class with mobility." His own father was the chief of a powerful Maurish clan.

But other Haratin argue that thousands of their people are not yet free. Messoud ould Boulkheir, head of Action pour le Changement, a political party for the Haratin, says that "many [illiterate slaves] don't even know that slavery has been abolished."

In the "slave section" of Boutilimit, a town in the south-west Sahara desert, Haratin complain that they do not have control over their own lives. Imetha mint Sidaty says her master decided whom she married. Gargayte ould Meyssa says he divorced his wife, a fellow slave, because her master would not let their children go to school. "I did not want to be reproducing slaves," he says.

When Kariya mint Mahomoud's father died, their master inherited everything. Conflict over the inheritance of a slave's property is common, and cases often go before the courts.

Not all Haratin, however, seem oppressed. On Boutilimit's main street, a black man walks hand in hand with an Arab-Berber. Dressed in matching blue tunics, they say they are slave and master as well as best friends.

Some who call themselves slaves admit they have no masters, while others say their masters have little power over them.

Hanna mint Souleymine is one of her master's 25 slaves. But he is destitute, she says, and her family takes care of him.

Increasingly, masters are worse off than their slaves. With recurring drought, many herders have lost their cattle and had to move to the towns with their families and slaves. Urbanization grew from 14 percent in 1970 to 50 percent in 1992, and slaves have often adapted to city life better than their masters.

"Drought and no industry add up to no-wage labor," says Habib Ould Nahfoudh, executive secretary of SOS Enclave, an advocacy group for slaves. "How else are freed slaves and impoverished masters meant to survive?"

Bad economic planning after independence from France in 1960 left Mauritanians among the most in-debted people in the world. And while the World Bank says restructuring has been effective in the 1990s, statistics show that the average Mauritanian's purchasing power has declined.

Though the country does not agree on whether real slavery still exists, most Mauritanians admit that some aspects remain.

For Hindou mint Ainina, editor of *Le Calame*, an independent newspaper, the problem is mostly psychological. "There is the slave mentality and the master mentality. And they both need to change," she says. Although a critic of the government, she does not hold it responsible for slavery. She also questions whether, with US sanctions, the US is pointing its finger at Mauritania or its own past.

Source: David Hecht, "Where Slavery Still Exists in the Eyes of Many," *Christian Science Monitor,* February 13, 1997. Reprinted by permission.

War Slavery

Slavery has been a feature of war for thousands of years. A special form of slavery exists in southern Sudan—a chattel slavery revived from the past and reborn to serve a war economy. The civil war in Sudan between the Muslim North and the Christian and Animist South (particularly the Nuer and Dinka peoples) began in 1955, a year before the country gained its independence. A peace accord in the early 1970s led to a ten-year cessation in fighting; it collapsed in 1983. In the current round of the civil war, slavery emerged as a weapon used by Northern militias against Southern villages. It was a new factor in the war but also the revival of one of the most ancient processes of enslavement. During assaults on "enemy" villages, government-supported militias attack and kill people, destroy crops, take livestock, and capture and enslave some of the inhabitants as a strategy of war.

Testimony about Slave Raids in Sudan

Murahliin are militiamen fighters armed by the Khartoum-based Sudanese government drawn from semi-Nomadic cattle herding communities in the Darfur and Kordofan regions. They carry out violent raids on Dinka villages in the South, sometimes with members of the Popular Defense Force militias as well as some regular army officers. During these raids, slaves are often captured. The new master has absolute control over the captured person, who may be sold, exchanged, or bartered. He or she may be used as forced labor in agriculture, cattle herding, or domestic servitude. Women and girls are often kept as concubines. Boy captives are commonly sexually abused as well. The following is the testimony of a Dinka woman captured in a slave raid.

My name is Angelina Adut. I am a Dinka from Aweil. My home village is Nyamlel. I don't know how old I am because I was born in the village where there are no birth certificates. I am not married.

I was a virgin and had remained so for several years after my customary initiation into womanhood, although I was looking forward to getting engaged to a young man from the village.

My hopes were dashed overnight in 1991. That night our village was woken from sleep by violent sounds of gunshots. The Arab Murahliin had attacked the village. My father's household was gripped with panic and confusion. The Arabs rode on horse-back and fired bullets on people and burned the grass huts. Many villagers were killed while trying to escape. I saw four men gunned down and I froze with fear.

I was among five women captured, in addition to the children whose mothers had abandoned them while escaping the killing. The Murahliin looted cattle and goats.

We walked at gunpoint for four days up to Daein. We were beaten and called many bad names. At the outskirts of Daein, we were ordered to settle at a big camp full of rough-looking Murahliin.

That night the other women were raped. There was this man called Hussein who wanted to rape me too. I put up a fight. He beat me using a hide whip.

He thought he would beat me into submission but I resisted. The other women saw something sinister in our struggle, so they advised me to give in lest I be killed, because the Murahliin are renowned for ruthlessness. And so Hussein broke my virginity.

I stayed with Hussein for eight months and was already pregnant. Although we stayed together and shared one bed, I was not happy because he was not husband but a brute who treated me like an animal, and he often forced me.

One day I made up my mind, I stole some of Hussein's money and ran away. I bought a train ticket and came to Khartoum, where I found my mother and brothers in the Al Salama camp for the displaced people. This was a family reunion since we were separated on that unforgettable night at Nyamlei, when the Murahliin attacked.

One month after my arrival to the camp in 1992 I gave birth to a baby boy with big red ears—a real Arab Murahliin. I was not happy with the baby because it was a boy. When I remembered how Hussein raped me and mistreated me I could not stomach the idea of bringing up a son of a Murahliin, because sons take after their fathers. I wouldn't have cared if it had been a girl because girls take after their mothers—and after all, they get married anyway.

On the third night after I had delivered I made up my mind. I boldly gripped the sleeping baby by the neck and squeezed and squeezed and squeezed until life went out of it. In the morning we buried it and that was all. I don't feel guilty because I have done away with that thing which would otherwise be a living memory of my rape and days in bondage. I am happy now because I ran away from the torturing Murahliin.

Source: Peter Verney, *Slavery in Sudan,* London: Sudan Update and Anti-Slavery International, 1997, p. 19. Reprinted by permission.

Evidence about Slavery in Sudan

Not everyone has accepted that slavery continues in southern Sudan. The following transcript from the Voice of America radio network reports on a challenge to prove its existence:

UN organizations have reported for years that children are sold into slavery in Sudan. But African leader Louis Farrakan charged that the reports were false. The *Baltimore Sun* recently decided to investigate, sending two reporters to Sudan. Their report of a transaction proves beyond doubt the existence of slavery.

Two reporters from the *Baltimore Sun* newspaper traveled to [Southern Sudan] to see the situation for themselves and even went through the process of buying slaves. Publicity about this is creating greater awareness in the United States about slavery in Sudan.

The State Department, international human rights organizations and Sudanese opposition groups have long been saying that slavery exists in Sudan. But many Americans, including politicians, ignored the story, refusing to believe it was true. Then last March, Nation of Islam Minister Louis Farrakhan was asked about the issue at a news conference in Washington. He had recently concluded a tour of Africa that included visits to Sudan, Libya and other countries opposed to the United States. Mr. Farrakhan challenged the person asking the question to go to Sudan and get the proof that slavery exists.

The *Baltimore Sun* decided it would take up the challenge and send two reporters—one black and one white—to a remote, dangerous area where slave trading was reportedly taking place. They were flown in by the Swiss-based human rights group Christian Solidarity International (CSI). In a three-part newspaper series based on their findings the reporters accused the Sudanese government of involvement in the slave trade. They say unpaid Arab militia are directly helping the Islamic government in its 13-year war against the rebels in the mostly Christian and animist south. The reporters spoke to locals who told them the militia raid villages with the consent of the government and take whatever booty they want—including humans, who are traded in the north and elsewhere as household slaves and concubines.

To prove to Minister Farrakhan that slavery was indeed real in Sudan, an editor at the *Baltimore Sun* told the reporters to try and buy a slave. Reporter Gilbert Lewthwaite explains what happened:

"We had learned during our research of a system that had been established between the chiefs of a local Arab tribe in the region we were in and the local Dinka tribe. In return for getting grazing rights in the Dinka land, [the Arab tribe] have undertaken to try to facilitate the return of enslaved women and children but for a price. The price is five cows each or $500, and that's the price we paid. The day after we arrived we heard in the nearby market town that an Arab trader

had arrived with a group of young children to return them for the asking price of their parents. We met him under a mango tree and he agreed to sell us one of the slaves."
Source: Voice of America, June 26, 1996.

Evidence about American Student Involvement in the Liberation of Slaves in Sudan

The liberation of slaves in Sudan has exerted a strong appeal on many people in the United States. Several organizations have joined in this "redemption" movement, including the fifth-grade class profiled in the following article.

Barb Vogel's fifth-graders had just been through the Civil War. She had led her 27 pupils through tales of slavery and oppression, struggle and emancipation and how all of it changed America so long ago. But on a February day earlier this year, the class at Highline Community School in Aurora, Colorado, listened in shock as their teacher read a newspaper story about a country in Africa called Sudan and the thousands and thousands of people, mostly women and children, who were being traded as slaves there. Recalls Vogel: "There was terror and disbelief in their little eyes." Says Brad Morris, 11, who was in class that day: "No one had any idea that slavery could still be going on anywhere in the world. We decided to do something so it wouldn't go on and on."

And so the kids wrote letters. They wrote to the President and the First Lady, to Oprah Winfrey, Bill Cosby, Steven Spielberg and other famous names. Laura Christopher, 11, wrote Colorado Senator Wayne Allard, saying, "We would like to know if you could contact the United States Government and let them know what is going on, so they can take action and put a stop to slavery!" To Hillary Clinton the kids and their teacher wrote, "You once said that it takes a village to raise a child. Now we would like you to know that it takes the whole world to save the village that will raise that child." The Clintons failed to respond. Oprah said the issue was too complex to deal with, simply urging the youngsters to keep up their grades.

Says Laura: "She answered us like she hadn't even read our letter."

But Vogel had also got her kids to explore the issue on the Internet. They found the American Anti-Slavery Group and through it the website of a Swiss-based human-rights group, Christian Solidarity International, which specializes in redeeming victims of religious oppression held in bondage. The children learned that for $50 to $100, they could, through Christian Solidarity, buy the freedom of a Sudanese slave. The group has kept meticulous records and case histories of the 4,016 people, mostly of the Dinka tribe, it has rescued so far. It takes advantage of the market to free the people taken by bandits, tribal leaders and professional slave traders. Says Gunnar Wiebalck, who is in charge of disaster aid for Christian Solidarity: "Arab traders know that we buy them back." The ex-slaves, many uprooted by the country's civil war, are then re-established in society by other Christian Solidarity programs.

The class launched a fund-raising drive, pouring dimes and quarters from their allowances and the proceeds from lemonade, toy and T-shirt sales into an old water-cooler bottle. "It makes me really angry that these people could be traded just like pets," said Doni Taipalus, 9, who chipped in $6 he earned from household chores. Each time the children raised enough to free one person, a brown-paper cutout was pasted on the classroom wall.

And then, one of the recipients of their letter-writing campaign responded. Sumner Redstone, chairman of Viacom, put the kids and their message on his Nickelodeon Channel. News of the crusade spread everywhere—and outside contributions began streaming in. A Texas company kicked in $5,000; a homeless Alaskan scraped together $100; a destitute elderly woman mailed in a dollar, calling it "all I can afford." When Casey Reed, a Wisconsin trucker, heard about the kids on his radio, he sent $200 and spread the message on his travels. The developments stunned the kids' parents. Says Sandy Morris, Brad's mom: "Our first response was, 'Oh, yes, isn't that nice.' But the kids kicked us in the behind and taught us something. Adults get complacent and think tragedies like Sudan are too far off to do anything about. But children don't get overwhelmed by the big picture. They just say, 'Go for it!'" Says Alphonso Mc-Donald, 9, who emptied his penny jar regularly: "I was shocked that the grownups weren't doing anything about this."

Donations and pledges now approach $50,000, and Vogel's wall has long since run out of space for the cutouts. She also has a new class—fourth-graders—to help carry out the campaign. By Christmas, she and her new charges hope to send enough money to Christian Solidarity to have freed 1,000 Sudanese. While that is but a small number of those believed held in bondage (and the spotlight may raise the price of freedom), it doesn't diminish the spirit of the kids. Says Joshua Hook, 10: "This is a big wrong, and we're helping make it a right." Says classmate Lindy deSpain, 9: "It feels good to know that more people will be coming home for Christmas."

Source: "The Children's Crusade: How Fourth- and Fifth-Graders in Colorado Are Buying the Freedom of Slaves in a Faraway Land," Richard Woodbury in Aurora, with reporting by Clive Mutiso in Nairobi and Helena Bachmann in Geneva, "Philanthropy/Charity Watch," *Time* 152, 25 (December 21, 1998). Reprinted by permission.

Slavery Linked to Religious Practice

Evidence and Testimony about the *Trokosi* System in Ghana

Slavery can be linked to religion, as in the case of the young girls given by their families as slaves to local fetish priests in southeastern Ghana, Togo, Benin, and southwestern Nigeria. *Trokosi* is a religious system and a traditional form of "justice" whereby young girls in Ghana are dedicated to a shrine—and its priest—to atone for offences usually committed by men in their family, often rape. The girl, who must be a virgin, may herself be the product of the rape, and the slavery is seen as a way of atoning the gods and society. In other cases the crime is trivial, but the girl often remains a fetish slave for the rest of her life, cooking, cleaning, farming, and serving the priest sexually until he frees her, usually after she has born children. At that point the girl's family must provide another slave to take her place. Ghana's constitution forbids slavery, but the practice continues to be justified at village level on religious grounds.

The following three case testimonies involve women from the Volta region in eastern Ghana who have all been released by International Needs, a local nongovernmental organization (NGO) based in Accra that has joined forces with other organizations to oppose the abuse of women and children through harmful culture practices or religious beliefs.

Enyoham Akorli, twenty-six and the daughter of a Trokosi slave union, was born and raised in the Koloe Trokosi shrine. Julie Daobadri, twenty-four, was sent to the Tsaduma Trokosi shrine. Mercy, twenty-three years old, spent twelve years at the Avakpe shrine. She is now training to be a dressmaker. All three accounts were published in the *Anti-Slavery Reporter*, July 1998.

Enyoham Akorli

My mother was sent to the Koloe shrine when she was only 12. She was neglected by her family, who sent her there. She gave birth to me a few years later in the shrine. My father, the priest, never did anything to merit being called a father. I was treated as one of the fetish slaves at the shrine. I ate very little. The little food that my mother managed to lay her hands on was very poor, mainly carbohydrates. I was not sent to school and whenever I asked to go I was beaten mercilessly. When my mother came to my rescue she was also beaten.

My mother collected oysters for a living. But when she sold the oysters in the nearby market, the priest took two thirds of the earnings and gave only a third to my poor mother who was saddled with feeding, clothing and protecting me from the rigors of shrine life. When I was 20, I told my mother that if we stayed in the shrine we would die of hunger, disease and maltreatment. Sending an innocent girl to the shrine is like burying her alive.

Julie Daobadri

I was only seven when I was sent to the shrine because my grandfather, who I had never met, had allegedly stolen four *cedis* (about 1 pence) from a

Trokosi slave. I was taken to the shrine to prevent my family being killed. Between the age of 10 and 12, I labored in the fields for the priest. Then the priest started to sexually abuse me. If I refused his almost daily sexual demands, I was beaten mercilessly.

There was no food for me in the shrine. I was left in tattered clothes and my parents, who promised to visit me regularly with essential items, abandoned me. It dawned on me that if I didn't try and change the situation, I would die in slavery. So I escaped to a nearby village where a young man made me pregnant. He accepted me into his house and fed and clothed me.

The priest sent young men after me and I was taken back to the shrine where I was beaten until I collapsed. I still have the scars that remind me of those evil days. I wish I could erase those terrible years from my mind. The young man was summoned to the shrine, fined and warned to stay away from me or die. At the age of 21, after more than 14 years in the shrine I escaped and sought refuge at the International Needs Vocational Training Center.

Mercy Senahe

I was sent to the shrine when I was nine years old because my grandmother stole a pair of earrings. I was made to work from dawn until dusk in the fields and when I came home there was no food for me to eat. When I was 11, the priest made his first attempt to sleep with me. I refused and was beaten. The other girls in the shrine told me it was going to keep happening, and if I refused I would be beaten to death and so the next time he tried I gave in. The suffering was too much so I tried to escape to my parents but they wouldn't accept me and sent me back to the shrine. I couldn't understand how my parents could be so wicked.

Source: Anti-Slavery Reporter, July 1998, a publication of Anti-Slavery International, London. Reprinted by permission.

Forced Labor

Forced labor is practiced by governments, often in times of armed conflict. In Burma, for example, tens of thousands of men, women, and children are used as laborers or bearers in military campaigns against indigenous people or on government construction projects. Here violence is used to enslave people whom the regime wishes to punish or eliminate for the economic benefit of the state. When a state is democratic and just and an individual commits a crime with knowledge of possible imprisonment, he has taken on the risk of incarceration of his own free will. If, however, a state is neither democratic nor just, then incarceration may well be enforced enslavement, often for political ends.

Evidence of Forced Labor in Myanmar (Burma)

On June 17, 1999, the United Nations International Labor Organization virtually expelled Myanmar (Burma), banning it from receiving aid or attending meetings until it halts widespread forced labor. A resolution—adopted by an overwhelming majority, including the United States—condemned the Burmese military dictatorship of inflicting "nothing but a contemporary form of slavery" on some of its people. The move was unprecedented in the ILO and came after years of trying to stop forced labor there. The government of Burma, which is now also known as Myanmar, signed the ILO Convention Against Forced Labor in 1955. The following are excerpts from the official United Nations investigation report:

> A United Nations Commission of Inquiry into forced labor in Myanmar (Burma) was established in March 1997, which visited the region early in 1998. The military regime could have participated in the hearings and presented its own witnesses. It could have cooperated with the Commission of Inquiry when it travelled to the region, but it had chose not to and barred the Commission from even entering the country.
>
> Despite this total lack of cooperation, the Commission of Inquiry completed its work and submitted a document of almost 400 pages. The Commission of Inquiry considered that "the impunity with which government officials, in particular the military, treat the civilian population as an unlimited pool of unpaid forced laborers and servants at their disposal is part of a political system built on the use of force and intimidation to deny the people of Myanmar democracy and the rule of law. The experience of the past years tends to prove that the establishment of a government freely

chosen by the people and the submission of all public authorities to the rule of law are, in practice, indispensable prerequisites for the suppression of forced labor in Myanmar." The Commission of Inquiry had hoped and trusted that in the near future the old order would change, yielding place to the new, where everyone in Myanmar would have an opportunity to live with human dignity and to develop his or her full potential in a freely chosen manner, and that there would be no subjection or enslavement of anyone by others. It had concluded that this could only happen if democracy were restored, so that the people as a whole could wield power for their common good. The Worker members [representatives from trade unions around the world] reaffirmed that, until such fundamental change occurred, the challenge of ridding the country of decades of forced labor could not even begin.

There is abundant evidence showing the pervasive use of forced labor imposed on the civilian population throughout Myanmar by the authorities and the military for portering, the construction, maintenance and servicing of military camps, other work in support of the military, work on agriculture, logging and other production projects undertaken by the authorities or the military, sometimes for the profit of private individuals, the construction and maintenance of roads, railways and bridges, other infrastructure work and a range of other tasks. . . . Forced labor in Myanmar is widely performed by women, children and elderly persons as well as other persons otherwise unfit to work. . . . All the information and evidence before the Commission shows utter disregard by the authorities for the safety and health as well as the basic needs of the people performing forced or compulsory labor . . . and many are killed or injured.

Source: International Labor Conference Eighty-Seventh Session, Geneva, *Report of the Committee on the Application of Standards, Discussion in Plenary, General Report, Part Two—Observations and Information Concerning Particular Countries,* June 1999.

The UN remarked that a Commission of Inquiry seldom uses such forceful terms as those found in its report on forced labor in

Myanmar, which referred to the "widespread and systematic" use of forced or compulsory labor "with total disregard for the human dignity, safety and health and basic needs of the people of Myanmar."

Evidence of Forced Labor in Bosnia

The following is a report made to the United Nations by Anti-Slavery International concerning forced labor in Bosnia. The "Roma" mentioned in the article are the people sometimes called "gypsies." The report was made in 1995.

> Forced labor has been used by all sides in the Bosnian conflict and at different stages in the war abuses have occurred. The nature of the abuse varies in degree according to fluctuations in the fortunes of the warring parties, the character of the local power structures and the whim of individuals concerned. Most impartial observers however agree that the most systematic violations are occurring in the Serb-held areas of Northern Bosnia. There the use of forced labor is not limited to front line areas or crisis situations, but encompasses the whole territory including towns such as Banja Luka, that have seen no armed conflict and whose populations are under no threat of attack.
>
> Forced labor is used for a variety of purposes. The most dangerous use is at the front lines, to dig trenches, chop wood in land-mined fields or evacuate the dead and wounded. However, it is also widely used in other sectors. There is evidence of its use in agriculture, mining, manufacturing and services, cleaning and road widening.
>
> The Bosnian Serb Authorities maintain that what they call the "Work Obligation" is a justifiable call for all members of the civilian population of military age to serve the State in which they are living, by meeting essential labor shortfalls in a time of crisis. There is, however, evidence to show that in this region forced labor is applied in a highly discriminatory way against the minority groups. Serb civilians do not appear to be subject to the same criteria to which the minority groups are exposed. The work gangs are made up more or less exclusively of Moslems, Croats or Roma, while the supervisors are more or less exclusively Serb.

Exemptions on grounds of poor health or essential positions within the community are widely ignored in the case of the minority groups. Workers do not receive any form of remuneration, usually work excessive hours, are not provided with protective equipment or training and often are not given rest days. There do not appear to be any restrictions on the number of days per year those on the "obligation" are ordered to work. . . .

In Northern Bosnia violations of the use of forced labor do not occur purely as a result of individual excess, but in fact are the founding principles behind its administration. It is implemented in a sophisticated way, is highly organized and involves the processing and movement of large numbers of individuals. Many are held in camps and are away from their dependents for weeks and months at a time. In short, it is an increasingly significant part of a policy by the Bosnian Serb Authorities designed to oppress and humiliate the minority civilian population under its control.

The problem is worsening: women and children above 15 years of age since the end of July 1994 have also become officially subject to the work obligation. The systems by which the work obligation is administered are becoming sophisticated and evasion more and more difficult. The fears are that with a dwindling minority population the situation for those Moslems, Croats and Roma that still remain will continue to deteriorate further as less people are available to carry out the work. The margins will thus be increasingly squeezed in that those currently not directly affected will also become subject to forced labor. Furthermore there are strong indications that reverses suffered by the Serbs on the battlefield fuel an increased level of violence against those on the work obligation. The recent upsurge in fighting within the theatre therefore puts those on the working obligation in an increasingly vulnerable position. The use of forced labor in these circumstances is clearly in breach of International Humanitarian Law. The Common Article 3 of the Geneva Conventions provides for minimum human treatment of persons who are taking no part in hostile activities.

Source: United Nations Working Group on Contemporary Forms of Slavery, Twentieth Session, *Report by Anti-Slavery International to the United Nations Economic and Social Council Commission on Human Rights, Subcommission on Prevention of Discrimination and Protection of Minorities,* Geneva, 1995. Reprinted by permission.

Evidence and Testimony of Forced Labor in China
Chinese *Laogai* Survivors

Forced labor began in China after 1949 and was based on the Soviet system, with an emphasis on work as a means of reeducation. Today, following economic reforms, the *laogai* system is increasingly used to make huge profits for the state. The number of "reeducation" camps estimated to exist ranges from 3,000 to 5,500, holding up to twenty million people, many of them political prisoners. Larger camps may have as many as eighty thousand inmates. Almost 90 percent of those convicted by courts are sent to these camps as opposed to prison. The ILO Conventions on Forced Labor state that political prisoners should not be forced to work and that it is illegal to use forced labor for economic development. In 2000 the use of forced labor in China became an important issue in the United States. President Clinton was urging the U.S. Congress to grant full trade status to China. Human rights organizations and labor unions pointed out that it would be very difficult to determine if goods imported from China had been made by slave labor, thus violating U.S. import laws. In spite of this concern, Congress chose to approve full trade status for China. The following are testimonies given by people who have survived the laogai system:

Palden Gyatso

I have spent 33 years in my 64-year-old life in Chinese *laogai* camps in Tibet. I have been a monk since I was ten years old. In 1959, at the climax of the Chinese military invasion of Tibet, I was arrested, accused of being a "reactionary element" and sentenced to a seven year prison term.

In the prison, I was made to do hard labor, ordinarily for nine hours a day, and sometimes more. We were yoked to plows like animals to till prison land. When we became too exhausted to pull the plow we were kicked and whipped. We were not given enough food to eat so were forced to steal food meant for pigs.

We also ate things like used leather items, bones, dead animals, mice, worms and grass.

Ill-treatment included being lashed with a leather belt and beaten with an electric cattle prod or iron bar. Our feet were fettered with iron manacles and hand-cuffs and thumb-cuffs were used to tie our hands and thumbs.

Catherine Ho

I was born into a well-educated family in Shanghai. I became a Christian while at high school, and was arrested before I was 18 years old. I was kept in a *laogai* camp for 21 years.

Physically we were tired, hungry and filthy. The women were forced to do heavy labor like plowing the desert, raising cattle or running a tea farm. We were forced to produce high level products, for instance, tea, silk and cloth.

Today I often wonder if the tea I drink or the silk I wear comes from a *laogai* camp and is made by all those poor *laogai* slaves still suffering in China.

Hongda Harry Wu

I spent 19 years in the *laogai* at 12 different forced labor camps. I was forced to do slave labor at agricultural farms, a chemical factory, a steel plant and a coal mine. I was regularly denied food and during one period, nearly starved to death. Torture permanently damaged my back. I had my arm broken during a beating. . . . There are millions still fighting to survive the *laogai*.

Source: Testimonies to the Subcommittee on International Operations and Human Rights, United States House of Representatives, April 4, 1995, quoted in *Cause to Communicate*, London: Anti-Slavery International/Volunteer Service Overseas, 1998, p. 64.

Commercial Sexual Slavery and Trafficking of People

Women and young girls are held in slavery and forced into prostitution for the financial gain of others in brothels in the United States, Europe, and many developing countries such as Thailand and the Philippines. The following newspaper articles are typical accounts of this type of enslavement in America.

Evidence of Sexual Slavery in the United States

Trafficking in teenage girls for the sex industry is occurring throughout the US. For example, from February 1996 to about March 1998, some 25 to 40 Mexican women and girls—some as young as 14 years old—were trafficked to Florida and South Carolina for prostitution. The traffickers had promised the girls good jobs in landscaping, childcare, and elder care, and worked to convince their parents that the jobs were legitimate. In a different investigation, an INS agent in New York reports that Mexicans are trafficking Mexican teenagers into California and bringing them to New York for prostitution. Some of the teens know they will be prostitutes, while others are duped.

The FBI reports that Asian girls have also been discovered in forced prostitution cases. In August [1999], an organized crime task force in Atlanta indicted 13 members of an Asian smuggling ring for trafficking up to 1,000 Asian women and girls, between the ages of 13 and 25 to Atlanta and other US cities for prostitution. The women and girls were held in bondage until their $30,000 to $40,000 contracts were paid off. One brothel was described by law enforcement as a "prison compound" with barbed wire, fences, chained dogs, and gang members who served as guards.

In Vancouver, British Columbia, an INS investigator in Vancouver reports that a group of American Canadian pimps, calling themselves the West Coast Players, are actively involved in trafficking Canadian teenagers to Los Angeles for the sex industry. There are indications that the West Coast Players are establishing links with Asian organized crime groups in British Columbia. Canadian law enforcement officials also believe that American girls are also being trafficked from the US to Canada. In 1998, a pimp and his co-defendants were convicted in Washington DC on eight counts of transporting minors from Canada across the US-Canadian border and across state lines for prostitution.

Source: Amy O'Neill Richard, "International Trafficking in Women to the United States: A Contemporary Manifestation of Slavery and Organized Crime." Center for the Study of Intelligence, U.S. Dept. of State.

Evidence of Sexual Slavery in Thailand

Thailand is well known as a destination for "sex tourism," which exploits large numbers of women and children. What is less known is the widespread use of prostitutes by working-class Thai men, and the way that young women are enslaved to work in the working-class brothels. The following excerpt details the economics of a brothel using enslaved prostitutes in a provincial city in Thailand:

> Forced prostitution is a great business. The overheads are low, the turnover high, and the profits immense. In this research I have tried to detail for the first time the business side of this form of slavery and to expose the scale of exploitation and its rewards. It is far, far different from the capital intensive slavery of the past which required long-term investments and made solid but small profits. The disposability of the women, the special profits to be made from children, all ensure a low risk, high return enterprise. For all its dilapidation and filth the brothel is a highly efficient machine that in destroying young girls turns them into gold.
>
> To set up a brothel requires a relatively small outlay. About 80,000 baht ($3,200) will buy all the furniture, equipment, and fixtures that are needed. The building itself will be rented for anywhere from 4,000 to 15,000 baht per month ($160 to $600). In addition to the prostitutes the brothels need a pimp (who often has a helper), a cashier/book-keeper, and sometimes employs a cook as well. Pimps will get from 5,000 to 10,000 baht per month in salary ($200 to $400), cashiers about 7,000 baht ($280) and the cook about 5,000 baht ($200) or less. For electricity and other utilities about 2,000 baht ($80) is needed each month. Beer and whisky must be bought, which is resold to clients. This leaves only two other outgoings—food and bribes.
>
> Feeding a prostitute costs 50 to 80 baht per day ($1.50 to $3.20). Slaveholders do not skimp on food since men want healthy looking girls with full figures. Healthy looks are important in a country suffering an HIV epidemic, and young healthy girls are thought to be the safest. Bribes are not exorbitant or unpredictable; in most brothels a policeman stops by once a

day to pick up 200 to 400 baht ($8–$16), a monthly expenditure of about 6,000 baht ($240), which is topped up by giving the policeman a girl for an hour if he seems interested. The police are interested in the stability of the brothels: a short side-street generates $32,000 to $64,000 each year in relatively effortless income. The higher priced massage parlors and nightclubs pay much larger bribes and will usually require a significant start-up payment as well. Bribe income is the key reason that senior police officials are happy to buy their positions and compete for the most lucrative.

Income far exceeds expenses. Each of the twenty girls makes about 125 baht ($5) for the brothel with each client she has, and each day she has between ten and eighteen clients, making 1,250 to 2,250 baht ($48 to $104). A single day's return is 25,000 to 45,000 baht ($1,000 to $1,800) just on sex. And as can be seen from the table below, there are a number of other ways for the brothel to turn a penny.

Monthly Income & Expenditures (in baht) for the Always Prospering Brothel

Outgoings (per month)	Income (per month)
Rent, 5,000	Commercial sex,* 1,050,000
Utilities & bills, 2,000	Rent paid by prostitutes, 600,000
Food & drink, 45,000	Sale of condoms, 70,000
Pimp's salary, 7,000	Sale of drinks, 672,000
Cashier, 7,000	Virgin premium, 50,000
Cook, 5,000	"Interest" on debt-bond, 15,000
Bribes, 6,000	
Payments to taxis etc., 12,000	
Beer & whisky, 168,000	
TOTAL, 257,000	TOTAL, 2,457,000

(in U.S. dollars, $10,280)
MONTHLY PROFIT, 2,200,000 (in U.S. dollars, $88,000)
*average 14 clients per day at 125 baht per client for 20 prostitutes for 30 days

The amount made on drinks, mostly the sale of beer and whisky, is difficult to measure. In the table above the 672,000 baht is a conservative estimate based on each client buying a single beer, which has been bought by the brothel for 20 baht and sold for 80 baht. The prostitute's rent averages 30,000 baht per month for their rooms, and if half the girls are repaying a debt-bond the amount made by the brothel each month on the "interest" would be at least 15,000 baht. The sale of condoms is pure profit. Condoms are provided free of charge to brothels by the Ministry of Health in an attempt to slow the spread of HIV. Clients are charged 10 baht for a condom and most clients are required to use one. Siri [a prostitute] explained that she got through three to four boxes of condoms each month; there are 100 condoms in each box.

The income shown as the virgin premium requires some explanation. Some customers, especially Chinese and Sino-Thais, are willing to pay very large amounts to have sex with a virgin. There are two reasons for this. The first is the ancient Chinese belief that sex with a virgin will reawaken sexual virility and prolong life. According to this belief, a girl's virginity is a strong source of yang (or coolness) and it quenches and slows the yin (or heat) of the aging process. Wealthy Chinese and Sino-Thais (as well as Chinese sex tourists from Taiwan, Singapore, Malaysia, and Hong Kong) will try to have sex with virgins as regularly as possible and will pay well for the opportunity. When a new girl is brought to the brothel she will not be placed out in the selection room with the other prostitutes, but kept back in another room, the *hong bud boree sut*, the "room to unveil virgins." Here she will be displayed, possibly with other children, and her price will be negotiated with the pimp. To deflower a virgin these men pay between 5,000 and 50,000 baht ($200 to $2,000). Deflowering often takes place away from the brothel in a hotel room rented for the occasion. The pimp or his assistant will often attend as well since it is usually necessary to beat the girl into submission.

The second reason the brothel can make a virgin premium is the general fear of HIV/AIDS. While Thai men or other non-Chinese customers do not hold the same beliefs about yin and yang, they do fear HIV infection. It is assumed that virgins cannot carry the virus, and even after a girl has lost her virginity, she can be sold at a higher price as pure or fresh. One Burmese girl reported being sold as a virgin to four different clients. The younger the girl, or the younger looking she is, the higher her price can be, as in Siri's case. The premium might also be paid to a brothel by another, higher class, commercial sex business. Special "Members Clubs" or massage parlors might take an order from a customer for a virgin, a pure girl, or a child. If the brothel doesn't have a suitable young girl on hand, it might arrange with a broker for one to be recruited, or if time is pressing, kidnapped. The more expensive establishments don't normally want to get involved in procurement and are willing to pay the brothels to find the young girls. Once used in this way, the girl is put to work with the other prostitutes in the brothel to feed the normal profit stream.

This profit stream makes sex slavery very lucrative. The Always Prospering Brothel nets something like 26,400,000 baht a year ($1,056,000), a return of 856 percent on outgoings. Key to this level of profit is the low cost of each girl. A new girl, at a cost of 100,000 baht, requires a capital outlay of less than 5 percent of one month's profit. Just counting the sale of her body and the rent she must pay, a brothel recovers the cost of buying a girl within two or three months. Within the sex industry it is the slaveholder that makes the highest profits. Voluntary prostitutes in night-clubs and massage parlors charge higher prices, but have only three to five clients a day. Escort girls may have only one client a night. Voluntary sex workers also keep a much larger proportion of the money they make, and exercise some discretion over which clients they will take. By contrast, for the slaveholder, total control of the prostitute, over the volume of clients she must take, over the money she makes, means vast profits. There is no good estimate of the part the sex industry plays in the Thai economy, and the total number of sex workers is hotly debated. But if we look just at the estimated 35,000 young women held in debt bondage, the annual profits they generate are enormous. If their brothels follow the same scheme as Always Prospering, the annual profit made on these girls is over 46 billion baht ($1.84 billion). There is one other cost to be laid against this profit; the price the girls pay with their bodies, minds, and health.

Source: Kevin Bales, *Disposable People: New Slavery in the Global Economy* (Berkeley: University of California Press, 1999), copyright © The Trustees of the University of California. Reprinted by permission.

Testimony about Sexual Slavery in Cambodia

A member of the Sex Workers Union of Cambodia, Dina Chan, gave the following speech, published in the local press, to the First National Conference on Gender and Development in Cambodia, held in Phnom Penh in September 1999.

I came here today as a woman, a Khmer woman. I came here today to tell you my story, in the hope that after you listen to me you can understand my situation and the situation of thousands of Khmer women and other women around the world.

It is very difficult for me to come here and speak to you; but I am doing this because I want you to listen, to me the real person; and I want you to remember me and what I say to you today when you are in your offices talking about policies and strategies that affect me and my sisters.

I want you to remember we are not "problems," we are not animals, we are not viruses, we are not garbage.

We are flesh, skin and bones, we have a heart, and we have feelings, we are a sister to someone, a daughter, a granddaughter. We are people, we are women and we want to be treated with respect, dignity and we want rights like the rest of you enjoy.

I was trafficked, I was raped, beaten, and forced to accept men. I was humiliated and forced to be an object so men, yes, men, could take their pleasure, I brought profit to many and brought pleasure to others. And for myself I brought shame, pain and humiliation.

But worst of all I receive demeaning comments from you: you discriminate against me, you give yourselves a job because of me and you are busy thinking about the best way to protect the community from me.

The police come to Toul Kork [an area where prostitution is common] almost every day. They always have a reason to come, but they come more frequently before festivals like Pchum Ben, because we are an easy target to extract money from.

In a public forum the chief of these police stands up and states "We do not arrest the girls": lies and more lies. They arrest us and take our money, our jewelry, sometimes even our few possessions we have in our room like our bed covers.

If we cannot pay then they detain us for a day or two, they give us no water. When they are convinced we simply have no money to pay they take us to another brothel and sell us to a new *maebon* (pimp), usually for US$100 for one girl. Then we become indebted once again and have to pay off that debt to the new *maebon*.

This is trafficking. The police, yes, the police sell us for another cycle of slavery. Do you think it is in their interests to see my occupation decriminalized? Of course not: then they lose their share of the money.

In one day we pay almost 15,000 riel in bribes to the district police, to the municipal authorities and the local authorities. Then another group of police come and arrest us. If we do not run and hide we are resold to slavery.

Your solution is to ask these people to protect us. Think again. They live off our blood. Money is too important to everyone, money and more money. It is not enough to eat: people demand more because they want nice things.

I come from a poor family; they sent me to study at a cultural school in Phnom Penh. I was living with a family but I could not contribute to my living, so they helped me find a job in a nearby hotel washing dishes. This hotel had many sex workers. But I just washed dishes and went to school.

One night a man followed me when I was on my way home and raped me. I was only 17 years of age. You cannot imagine how I felt and what impact this had on me. But after that, I was lured to becoming a sex worker under false promises.

I was sent to Stung Treng; I was beaten when I refused to accept men. Shortly after I was taken to Stung Treng a man came to pay for me to go with him. He paid my *maebon.*

He took me to the pig slaughter house where he worked and locked me in a dirty smelly cell. Then he came back with six other men. They all, one by one, raped me; one man raped me twice. After a whole night of gang rape I was faint with pain.

When the morning came I heard the workers preparing to start their work. I heard the pigs being pushed into the pens, they were screaming. I knew what that feeling was like: I was no better than the pigs to these men; they could have killed me. Something inside me did die, and I will never be the same.

I am 24 years old and my life has been like this since 1993. I did not know the Khmer Rouge years but I have heard the stories of suffering. People say they were slaves.

Compared to my life for the last five years I think I and my sisters have suffered and are suffering more than you have. I know starvation, I know slavery, I know being forced to work all day. But I also know physical violation and torture every day, I know discrimination and hatred from my country-people, I know not being wanted and accepted from my society, the society that put me in this condition. I know fear, I feel it every day, even now that I dare speak my life is in danger.

This is a crime, but no one is punished. I fought the Khmer Rouge [the communist dictatorship that controlled Cambodia in the past], I was a soldier fighting to protect you from the Khmer Rouge and risking my life. I fought for the freedom of the Cambodian people, this is what the commander told us we were to do and I was proud I was fighting for freedom. I fought for your freedom—only to become enslaved and abused by you.

After all these years I now work as a sex worker. I also run a union to unite sex workers to fight for basic rights and for freedom. We bring our voices to forums like this to educate people like you, with the hope you can learn from us. Many of my sisters are scared to join our struggle because they live in constant fear of abuse and threats.

Some of you think that I am bad because I choose

to remain a sex worker. My answer to those people is: I think your society, my society, my motherland Cambodia, is bad because it does not give girls like me choices; choices that I see are better for me.

I think it is bad that my country allows men to rape young women like me and my sisters and go unpunished. I think it is bad that my society lets men seek and demand the services of women like me. I think it is criminal that we are enslaved to make money for the powerful.

I think it is bad that my family are so poor and getting poorer because they can not survive as farmers with little resources which are getting smaller because more powerful people move them off their land.

I think it is bad the police treat me and my sisters like we are criminals but those who exploit us and take our dignity, our money and sometimes our lives live in freedom, enjoying their lives with their families. Because why? Because they have a powerful relative, because they have money.

Is this right? Is this justice? My sisters and I do not create the demand, we are the objects; the demand comes from the men, the men come to us. We are cheated, deceived, trafficked, humiliated and tortured. Why? Because men want us and we bring money to the powerful. But we are the powerless.

You give us AIDS; when we are no longer profitable you leave us to die, but we do not die in peace: you point your finger and you blame us. You, the development organizations, give us condoms and teach us all the time about AIDS. We do not want your words, we do not want your judgment, we do not want you to tell us what is better for us. We know about AIDs; we watch our sisters die from the disease.

Ask us if we have the power to demand condom use from our clients. Look at me: you see a woman, but my boss sees dollars. An extra payment to my boss and the client does not wear a condom. If I protest I receive a beating. If I die tomorrow no one cares: there are many other girls who will be tricked and trafficked like me, because we feed many people.

I do not want to go to your shelter and learn to

sew so you can get me work in a factory. This is not what I want. If I tell you that you will call me a prostitute. But those words are easy for you because you have easy solutions to difficult problems you do not understand, and you do not understand because you do not listen.

My life has become this way now; for me there is no turning back, so let me continue to practice my occupation, but recognize my occupation and give me my rights, so I am protected and I can have power to demand justice.

Source: *Phnom Penh Post*, September 17–30, 1999. Translation provided by CamClips and the NGO Forum on Camboda. Reprinted by permission.

Evidence of Sex Slavery in Cambodia

Given the powerful speech by the young woman forced into prostitution in Cambodia, it is useful to read an American journalist's report on how the Cambodian government has dealt with prostitution.

Meas's recent experience has been hard, but her future looks brighter.

Three months ago, the 16-year-old orphan from Vietnam, whose wisps of long black hair frame a narrow face with slight, plaintive eyes, was sold by her neighbor for $400 and brought to Phnom Penh, Cambodia, to join the teeming number of young girls who work unwillingly in the sex industry.

After being beaten and denied food for three days, Meas gave in to her brothel owner's demands to submit to customers, as many as eight men a day.

Now, however, Meas's life has taken a turn for the better, thanks in part to the Phnom Penh police she had been taught to fear. Meas had been rescued and the brothel owner arrested as part of a crackdown on forced prostitution.

Police sweeps are the way Cambodia's capital city is coping with the growing problem. They are viewed as encouraging by social groups who are fighting to end child trafficking and slavery.

Attitudes in Cambodia toward prostitution differ from those in most Western nations. Sex workers and their clients cannot be arrested for solicitation.

"If they want to be prostitutes, they can do it," says Chhuth Sok, director of the women's section of the Cambodian Human Rights and Development Association. "But nobody should force them to do it."

With this in mind, Phnom Penh officials resurrected a two-year-old law that makes anything offensive to Cambodian culture illegal. The measure was designed specifically to capture sex traffickers and brothel owners.

"Prostitution leaves a bad image on Cambodian culture and society," says Man Chhoeurn, chief of Phnom Penh's municipal cabinet. "Prostitution is the biggest problem in society, and it's helping the spread of AIDS."

Officials in Phnom Penh would not release current figures, but interviews with police and social organizations indicate they have rescued more than 500 prostitutes and arrested about 20 traffickers since November. This figure does not include the hundreds of sex slaves in provincial towns that police claim to have rescued.

On New Year's Eve, police and human rights workers in the port town of Sihanoukville announced the capture of trafficker Chay Heang. They also rescued 14 Cambodians, many of them children, who officials say Mr. Heang planned to send into sexual servitude in Thailand. Heang is a minor criminal, but police say he is connected to Chea Sarith, an alleged major trafficker, who lives in Koh Kong Province near the Thai border. Police are also investigating two men who may have kidnapped the 14 for Heang.

The police, however, also have allegedly served as a help to traffickers. Prostitutes said brothel owners scare young women into submission with the help of stories about police raping, robbing, and beating captured prostitutes.

"The brothel owner told me to run [from the police] and not get caught," says Chanchanda, a 17-year-old from Cambodia's northern provinces who was rescued eight days after being sold into sexual servitude.

Often, the fears of corruption and brutality are realized. Sex workers and social service groups say police take the more attractive prostitutes, keep them for a week, and sell them back to the brothel owners.

There also are reports of police brutalizing women until they relinquish their life savings.

Meas said the police took her life savings of 30,000 riel, roughly $8.50, when she was captured.

"They need morality training," Chanthol Oun, executive director of the Cambodian Women's Crisis Center, says of the police. Police rarely tell sex workers where they are being taken and rarely let them even gather their belongings, Ms. Oun says. Robbed or not, most rescued prostitutes leave their servitude with no money, she says.

Deputy Police Chief Hor Sokha, who oversees Tuol Kok district, Phnom Penh's most infamous red-light district, says the only time his officers have had to get rough was when prostitutes have tried to flee. Then, policemen only pushed the women into pickup trucks to take them to various social organizations, Deputy Chief Sokha says.

"The accusations of abuse, bribes, and theft are unfounded and not true," Sokha says. "Our policemen have discipline."

While some traffickers, like Heang, are captured, others are protected from on high. The governor of Koh Kong Province recently banned human rights investigators who raided a trafficking ring without his permission. Some 45 kidnapped sex workers were freed. On the same day, members of Cambodia's National Assembly were calling for the governor's resignation and accusing him of supporting the brothel rings there. "There are members of the government who are behind the brothel owners," human rights worker Sok says.

And there are other barriers. Child sex workers are ordered to lie about their age to avoid the special attention underage prostitutes get. Social workers and investigators say Cambodians are apathetic because many of the prostitutes are from Vietnam. Centuries of fighting between the two nations have left each numb to the other's problems.

Also, the sheer number of sex workers in Phnom

Penh—estimates range from 10,000 to more than 20,000 in the city of 1 million—makes the problem seem almost insurmountable. Prostitution can be found from the infamous red-light districts to the karaoke bars and 24-hour massage parlors along main streets.

"If they arrested all the prostitutes," social worker Oun says, "we couldn't take them."

Mr. Chhoeurn, the municipal cabinet chief, agrees. "We cannot successfully crack down 100 percent; other countries have a little prostitution" too, he says. "But we will try our utmost."

As for Meas, she was taken to a women's crisis center, where she says she will learn a more promising trade—sewing.

Source: Chris Seper, with contributions from Van Roeun, "Police Sweeps Help Clean Up Child Prostitution," *Christian Science Monitor,* January 8, 1998. Reprinted by permission.

Evidence of Trafficking of People in Kosovo

Slavery linked to armed conflict often becomes enslavement for sexual exploitation. In the chaos and breakdown of law and order that come with war, slavery can emerge quickly. The following demonstrates how this can happen.

Kosovar refugees have made repeated complaints about gangsters who kidnap girls and sell them to pimps. Last week, five armed men burst into a house rented by refugees on the outskirts of Vlora and tried to grab a 16 year old Kosovar girl, named by police as Josa Spasolli. Her father held onto the girl and refused to let her go. "When they failed to separate them they shot him and the girl," said police chief Ali Hajdini. Jola died in hospital. Her father is in a critical condition.

The smuggling gangs in Vlora use a fleet of speedboats varying in size from rigid inflatable dingies with powerful outboard motors to big open boats similar to light landing craft used by commando units. The high speed night crossings have become vastly more expensive in the past few weeks. The Italian government has questioned customs and immigration officials in Vlora, but they have been unable to stop the trade in people. The Tirana-based business magazine *Albanian Observer* recently described Albania as "one of the most corrupt countries in the world." It is a disturbing thought for the European powers, like Britain, which has become Albania's possible future sponsor in NATO and the European Union.

Source: Keith Dovkants, *Yorkshire Post* (a U.K. regional weekly paper), June 4, 1999. Reprinted by permission.

Domestic Slavery

Evidence of Domestic Slavery in the United States

Enslaved domestic workers have escaped or been freed from rich households in the United States, United Kingdom, and France, as well as in other countries. Domestic slavery is one of the most common types of slavery around the world. Children are especially vulnerable to being made domestic slaves. In some parts of the Caribbean and West Africa children are given or sold into domestic service and organizations have grown up to free them and provide them with an education. In Haiti and the Dominican Republic these children are called *restavecs*. Ownership is not asserted as such, but strict control, usually enforced by violence, is used. The domestic services performed by the child provide a good return on the upkeep costs. When slavery is discovered in the United States, it is often domestic slavery.

At the age of 14 Deborah was tricked into leaving her native Cameroon and coming to the US to work for a couple in the Washington DC area. The husband and wife showed Deborah the jobs they wanted her to do. Soon the jobs filled her day completely and they rapidly took complete control of her life. Up at six in the morning, Deborah would be working long past midnight. When she began to question her treatment, the beatings began. "They used to hit me," Deborah told me, "I couldn't go for three days without them beating me up." The smallest accident would lead to violence. "Sometimes I might spill a drink on the floor by mistake, they would hit me for that," she said. In a strange country, locked up in a strange house far from home, Deborah was cut off from help. If she tried to use the phone she was beaten, if she tried to write anything it was taken away from her.

Under complete violent control, paid nothing, working all hours, this fourteen-year-old schoolgirl had become a slave. The promises to help her go to school in America were just the bait used to hook her. In Cameroon her parents received no word from her, but had occasional reassuring messages from the family that had enslaved her. The beatings and constant verbal abuse broke the will of this young girl for a time, and her life dissolved into a blur of pain, exhaustion, work, denigration, and fear. In this state of permanent exploitation Deborah lived for another four years.

Source: Kevin Bales, *Even Slaves Shall Prophesy*, unpublished manuscript, July 2000.

Evidence of Domestic Slavery in the Philippines and Worldwide

The use of slaves as domestic servants is one of the most widespread, yet hidden, forms of contemporary slavery. As the previous excerpt shows, domestic slavery is to be found in the richest countries in the world. Domestic slavery is also found in poor countries, as the following articles about the Philippines and Haiti make clear.

Len Len, 15, crawled her way round her last employers' house. She was so badly beaten she couldn't stand, so she carried out her domestic chores on her hands and knees. She says: "My whole body was in pain. I couldn't walk anymore. I would rather have died than suffer there like an animal. I wanted to kill myself."

Len Len managed to escape on her third attempt and now works as a live-in domestic for a better employer. She receives no wages and still works very long hours in return for a roof over her head and food. But now her mother and sister live with her too so she is not separated from her family. They are all allowed out on the rare occasions when their work is done.

Others among the estimated one million child domestics in the Philippines are not always so fortunate. One 14 year old girl died last year after being forced to drink drain cleaner which burnt her stomach. Some are tortured. Child domestics make up more than a third of the estimated 250 million child laborers around the globe—the largest but least visible group of working children. Most are girls, some sold into domestic slavery at the age of five, but the majority are adolescents vulnerable to sexual assault and exploitation.

In the Indonesian capital of Jakarta there are 700,000 domestic workers under the age of 18. In Venezuela, 60 percent of working girls aged 10–14 are employed in domestic service. In West Africa, cross-border trafficking of such girls is on the increase.

Such girls are the "silent cindarellas" of the labor market, according to Maggie Black, coauthor of a new report on child domestic work published by the United Nations Children's Fund. The report, *Child Domestic Labor*, concludes that lack of education is one of the worst deprivations such children suffer.

Source: Sally Ramsden, "1 Million Child Domestics in Philippines," *Times Educational Supplement*, July 11, 1999. Reprinted by permission.

Evidence of Domestic Slavery in Haiti

In Haiti children as young as 6 are given into slavery as "restavecs." The term comes from the French "rester avec" meaning "to stay with." The Foyers Maurice Sixto (children's refuge project) grew out of a shelter for child domestic servants opened on the outskirts of the capital Port-au-Prince in 1989. Such shelters provide educational activities for children every afternoon. Those involved in this issue will agree that child domestic servitude in Haiti is a dominant institution whose roots go back to the time of slavery. It exposes minors of both sexes to a form of bondage that profits the adults to whom they have been entrusted.

The total number of child domestic servants fluctuates constantly. They come from rural families facing great hardship. They do not have the opportunity to go to school or acquire a practical trade. They number between 200,000 and 300,000 which is 14 percent of Haiti's young population; 85 percent of them are young girls between 6 and 18 years.

The "restavec" as they are commonly called are typically treated like young slaves. They are used as beasts of burden to perform various household tasks: cleaning, frequent trips to shop at the market and to fetch water from the well, taking care of the children at home, carrying rubbish and excrement produced by people and animals in the house, etc. They are the first members of the house to get up in the morning and the last to go to bed at night. For food, they are usually given the leftovers of the family's meals. According to a survey conducted by the Institut-Psycho-Social de la Famille (IPSOFA) for UNICEF, 30 percent of these children say they only receive one meal a day. All this for little or no pay. One meal a day and the promise of being sent to school are their only reward for the hard work, beatings and humiliating insults they suffer.

Source: Contribution by Father Miguel of the Foyers Maurice Sixto, Haiti, to the UN Economic and Social Council Commission on Human Rights, Subcommission on Prevention, Discrimination and Protection of Minorities, Working Group on Contemporary Forms of Slavery Twenty-Third Session, Geneva, May 1998.

Child Labor and Slavery

Child labor becomes slavery in the officially recognized sense when it involves debt bondage or the child is sold into prostitution or given into domestic service. The most vulnerable children, as with adults, are those who come from indigenous and migrant communities. The new ILO Convention on the Worst Forms of Child Labor calls on states to take swift and effective measures to prevent the most damaging exploitation of children, including child slavery, prostitution, and pornography. But how should governments go about stopping child labor and child slavery? When the United States began to act against child labor, the situation of some children was actually made worse.

Experience shows that blanket policies of banning all child labor led by rich countries does not work. At the beginning of the 1990s U.S. Senator Tom Harkin of Iowa introduced a draft law, or bill, calling for a ban on the import of any goods that were manufactured wholly or in part by children under the age of fifteen. The U.S. Child Labor Deterrence Bill has not yet become law. However, while it was under discussion, fifty thousand children in Bangladesh lost their jobs as employers fired them rather than risk having their products, mostly clothing, banned from the United States. Desperate for money, many of these children took even more exploitative and abusive jobs in other industries or were forced into prostitution. The Harkin Bill has since been overtaken by the Sanders Amendment, which passed in Congress in 1997, banning import of bonded child labor products. It also provided funds for the United Nations Commission on Human Rights and for the ILO for activities relating to child bonded labor.

Evidence of Child Slavery in India
The Sanders Amendment played a part in the following example that concerns the beedi cigarettes discussed in Chapter 1.

> At a time when the United States is set to revise its list of Indian firms facing sanctions, one company has been added to the taboo list—Ganesh Beedis—which stops the company from marketing its hand-rolled, unfiltered cigarettes (beedi) in the US for reason that it employs child labor.
>
> The "detention" order came into effect last week following a feature on *Tobacco Slaves in India* on the CBS television network exposing the use of child labor in India's beedi industry.
>
> The feature apparently included indentured children working for slave wages and being exploited in the Mangalore Ganesh beedi industry in Tamil Nadu (India). The film showed plenty of raw footage of children toiling for up to 12 hours in abject conditions.
>
> US Customs Commissioner Raymond Kelly said that it is morally, ethically and legally wrong to import goods made with forced or bonded labor, especially the forced labor of children, into the US.
>
> The order against the company will continue pending the final results of an investigation. The agency however has been investigating allegations of forced child labor in the beedi industry in India even before the feature surfaced. The estimated value of all imported beedis, including those made by Mangalore Ganesh, in fiscal year 1999 was $1.28 million, up from $915,000 the year before, said Customs spokeswoman Layne Lathram.
>
> Mangalore Ganesh Beedis spokesman Priya Das,

denying the charges of employing child labor for manufacturing beedis, has threatened legal action against CBS. Mr. Das argues that "beedi rolling is a skilled or semiskilled job. A child cannot roll a beedi. It has to be rolled by an adult."

Mr. Das also points out that beedi rolling work was given on contract and the company checks the quality when they are returned to roll. "Morally we ensure that no such irregularity like employment of child labor takes place," he said. "Ever since the company began in 1940, there was no complaint about child labor," he added.

Source: Child Labor News Service, "Citing Child Labor, US Stubs out Bindi Beedis," December 1, 1999. Reprinted by permission.

The Worst Forms of Child Labor

The International Labor Organization's Convention on the Worst Forms of Child Labor—1999 (excerpts given earlier in this chapter) bans all forms of slavery or practices similar to it, such as the sale and trafficking of children. President Bill Clinton made the following speech at the signing of the ILO Convention in Seattle on December 2, 1999.

I would like to begin this day by thanking all the members of the Senate. Thank you, Senator Murray, for being here. And I want to thank the Republicans, as well as the Democrats, who voted on this together. But I would be remiss if I did not say that the first person who ever discussed this issue with me in 1992 when we were both running for the office I am privileged to hold was Senator Tom Harkin of Iowa. And for more than seven years now, at every occasion, he has talked to me about this issue. It has been truly one of the driving passions of his life and without him, we would not be here doing this today. And I would like to ask him to stand.

Thank you, Senator Harkin. Thank you. (Applause.)

I also want to thank Secretary Herman and Gene Sperling and Karen Tramontano for what they did in our administration to spearhead the effort. Perhaps there is no better way to conclude my visit here, because what we celebrate this morning symbolizes in many ways what we're seeking in the launch of a new round of trade talks: not just to lower barriers, but to raise living standards, to help ensure that people everywhere feel they have a positive stake in global trade that gives them and their children a chance for a better life.

We are here in Seattle to continue our efforts to help establish a new consensus on international trade—that leads to jobs that are secure, development that is sustainable, prosperity that is broadly shared. We seek to widen the circle of opportunity, deepen our commitments to human rights and human freedom, and put a human face on the global economy.

Some say that it is not possible, that the interests of nations, businesses and labor within and across national borders, are too divergent. This Child Labor Convention proves that, at least on this profoundly important issue, it is possible. It is a living example of how we can together come to level up global standards, and lift up core labor values.

The step we take today affirms fundamental human rights. Ultimately, that's what core labor standards are all about—not an instrument of protectionism, or a vehicle to impose one nation's values on another, but about our shared values: about the dignity of work, the decency of life, the fragility and importance of childhood.

In my State of the Union address almost two years ago, I asked Congress to help make the United States a world leader in this cause, and to start by working to end abusive child labor. We are making good on that effort. Together—again, across party lines—we secured the largest investment in American history to end abusive child labor around the globe.

We're establishing the first-ever United States government purchasing ban on goods made by forced or indentured child labor. And we've beefed up enforcement to stop the importation of goods made by such labor. Just last week, the Customs Service banned the importation of certain hand-rolled cigarettes, known as bidis, because of evidence that one firm was making them with bonded child labor.

Today, we build on our achievements and our common commitment. This convention is truly a victory for labor, for business and for government—for all those who worked long and hard for two years to reach a consensus; a victory for the nations of the world who joined together in the ILO this summer to adopt this convention on a unanimous vote. Today we say with one clear voice: abusive child labor is wrong and must end.

Above all, of course, this is a victory for the children of the world, and especially for the tens of millions of them who are still forced to work in conditions that shock the conscience and haunt the soul; children brutalized by the nightmare of prostitution; children indentured to manufacturers working against debt for wages so low they will never be repaid; children who must handle dangerous chemicals or who are forced to sell illegal drugs; children who crawl deep into unsafe mines; children who are forcibly recruited into armed conflicts and then spend the rest of their entire lives bearing the scars of committing murder when they were eight or nine or 10 years old.

For the first time, this convention calls on the international community to take immediate and effective steps to stop the worst forms of child labor. This convention enables the world to say, no more. We recognize, of course, that no treaty or convention is enough and that to end abusive child labor once and for all we must untangle the pathology of grinding poverty and hopelessness that lies at its root. If we want to slam the door shut on abusive child labor, we must open the door wide to education and opportunity. After all, nations can only reach their potential when their children can fulfill theirs.

John Sweeney put it best when he said economic development is based in education, and school is the best place for children. That's why this convention places a priority on basic education, and we are trying to honor that priority.

Around the world, we are investing in creative solutions to get children out of abusive workrooms and into classrooms. We are giving them a way out of the soccer ball industry in Pakistan, the shoe industry in Brazil, the fireworks industry in Guatemala. We are giving them back the most precious gift of all, their childhood.

And as we work to provide both boys and girls access to schools, we are also working to provide their parents with viable economic alternatives and access to jobs. In Pakistan, for example, when 7,000 children moved out of the soccer ball manufacturing plant into the schools, 7,000 parents moved into jobs they didn't have before, at better incomes.

Microcredit loans help people in developing countries, and women in particular, to start businesses, raise their standard of living, build a better life for their children. I am proud that through the Agency for International Development, the United States financed 2 million such loans last year. So we have here not only the Secretary of Labor, but the Secretary of Commerce. We see this not only as a labor issue, but a business and an economic issue. We believe that everyone will be better off when children are given back their childhoods.

We are working to integrate the agenda, also, as all of you know, of the World Trade Organization, the IMF and the World Bank with the agenda of the ILO. That is key to making sure that the issues of child labor—and core labor standards more generally—are on the international economic agenda and they don't become either/or conflicts. That's why ensuring the rights, the basic rights of labor, is central to our mission here in Seattle.

This is a good day for the children of the world, but we can make tomorrow even a better day. We can do it by seeing that other nations also ratify this treaty and join in our cause, and we can do it by building on the solid foundation of this convention, and the common ground forged by leaders here, in the work of the WTO, the IMF, the World Bank and other international institutions. We have to harness the spirit of progress and the sense of possibility that this noble document embodies. We can light the way out of the darkness of abusive child labor into the dawn of a new century of promise for all the children of the world.

Thank you very much. (Applause.)

Let me just say this. I would like to ask Mr. Sweeney and Ambassador Niles and all of the members of the Congress, the Governor and Secretary Daley, Secretary Slater, to come up and join us as we do this signing, please.

Source: U.S. Department of Labor, International Child Labor Program Website: www.dol.gov/dol/ilab/public/programs/iclp/.

Notes

1. Hugh Thomas, *The Slave Trade: The History of the Atlantic Slave Trade 1440–1870,* London: Macmillan, 1998, p. 806.

2. Kevin Bales, *Disposable People: New Slavery in the Global Economy,* Berkeley: University of California Press, 1999, p. 9.

3. Thomas, p. 246.

4. Kevin Bales and Peter Robbins, "No One Shall Be Held in Slavery or Servitude: A Critical Analysis of International Slavery Agreements," *Human Rights Review,* forthcoming, p. 12.

5. Ibid., p. 1.

6. Bales, *Disposable People,* p. 16.

7. Ibid.

8. Thomas, p. 443.

9. Bales, *Disposable People,* p. 55.

10. Ibid., p. 192.

11. Ibid., p. 191.

12. Ibid., p. 191.

13. Kevin Bales, notes made during the 24th Working Group on Contemporary Forms of Slavery, United Nations, Geneva, Switzerland, June 1999.

5

Directory of Organizations

If you wish to contact any of the following organizations by telephone from the United States, first dial the international access code 011, then the country code, then the city code, then the local phone number. To make the listings more clear, I have put the country code in square brackets and the city code in parentheses.

Anti-Slavery International
Thomas Clarkson House
The Stableyard
Broomgrove Road
London SW9 9TL UK
Phone: [44] (0207) 501-8920
Fax: [44] (0207) 738-4110
E-mail: antislavery@antislavery.org
Or:
Anti-Slavery International
1755 Massachusetts Avenue NW, Suite 312
Washington, DC 20036-2102 USA
Phone: (202) 232-3317
E-mail: info@stopslavery.org

Anti-Slavery International is the key organization concerned with contemporary slavery. Anti-Slavery is the oldest human rights organization in the world. It was responsible for the abolition of slavery within the British Empire in 1833 and was set up in its present form in 1839 to carry the fight to other parts of the world. It gave inspiration to the Abolitionist movement in the United States and Brazil and has contributed to the formulation of all the relevant international standards on slavery.

Throughout its history, it has campaigned relentlessly and intervened effectively on behalf of enslaved people. Generally, the most marginalized and dispossessed groups fall victim to slavery, and the antislavery movement has always been closely allied with the struggle of indigenous people.

Anti-Slavery promotes the eradication of slavery and slavery-like practices and supports freedom for everyone who is subjected to such practices. The abuses that Anti-Slavery opposes include slavery and the buying and selling of people as objects, trafficking of women and the predicament of migrant workers who are trapped into servitude, debt bondage and other traditions that force people into low-status work, forced labor, forced prostitution, abusive forms of child labor, and early or forced marriage and other forms of servile marriage. Anti-Slavery focuses on the rights of people who are particularly vulnerable to exploitation of their labor, notably women, children, migrant workers, and indigenous peoples.

Anti-Slavery pursues its objectives by

- collecting information about these abuses, bringing them to the attention of the public, and promoting public action to end them;
- identifying ways in which these abuses can be brought to an end and influencing policymakers in governments or other institutions at national and international levels to take action accordingly; and
- supporting victims of the abuses that Anti-Slavery opposes in their struggle for freedom, in particular by working with organizations they establish and other organizations campaigning on their behalf.

Publications: Anti-Slavery publishes more works on contemporary slavery than any other organization. Many of its publications are listed in Chapter 6. The organization also has the most complete archive of materials concerned with the historical antislavery movement.

Website: www.antislavery.org; www.stopslavery.org

The Anti-Slavery International website provides access to its publications (an extensive catalog of books, research reports, exhibitions, videos, and other materials), news of ongoing campaigns and recent successes, an explanation of policies, links to other groups, and a sound introduction to antislavery work around the world.

Africa

**African Network for the Prevention and the Protection
Against Child Abuse and Neglect (ANPPCAN)**
P.O. Box 71420
Nairobi, Kenya
Phone: [254] (2) 573-990
Fax: [254] (2) 576-502
E-mail: anppcan@arcc.or.ke

ANPPCAN is a Pan-African organization that advocates the protective rights of children and facilitates research and the exchange of scientific information about them.
Website: None

International Needs (IN)
P.O. Box 690 Dansoman Est.
Accra, Ghana
Phone: [233] (21) 226-620
E-mail: intneeds@ncs.com.gh

Founded in 1974, International Needs is a Christian organization that works to eradicate poverty, disease, and oppression worldwide. It also aims to uplift the standing of women and children. IN-Ghana's work includes a Trokosi liberation project that aims to free ritual slave girls and support them to build new lives.
Publications: The organization publishes press releases regarding current projects and events. These press releases are available on the website.
Website: www.africaexpress.com/internationalneedsghana
This website provides the mission statement of the organization, contact information, an extensive news page, a description of IN services, and a search page for the IN website.

WAO-Afrique
399, 168 Rue Tokoin Solidarité
B.P. 80242
Lomé, Togo
Phone: [228] 214-113
Fax: [228] 217-345
E-mail: wao-afrique@bibway.com

Founded by a former child domestic, WAO Afrique works for the protection and prevention of all forms of abuse, exploitation, and trafficking of children. Preventative initiatives include campaigning, education, and awareness at the community and gov-

ernment levels. The organization runs education and training projects for the police and other human rights organizations to help them respond better to the increasing incidents of child labor, exploitation, and trafficking of children into and within Togo and other West African countries.
Website: None

Asia

Anti-Slavery Society of Australia
G.P.O. Box 483 C
Melbourne, Victoria 3001 Australia
Phone: [61] (3) 964-2101
Fax: [61] (3) 9601-6437
E-mail: info@anti-slaverysociety.org

The Anti-Slavery Society is dedicated to ending slavery and the slave trade, as well as bonded labor, child labor, child prostitution, and the international trafficking of women and children for prostitution. The society not only investigates and campaigns against all forms of slavery but also organizes missions to rescue slaves, reintegrate them into their communities, and raise consumer awareness about goods produced by slave labor. The society receives no government funding; it relies on private contributions to pay for its activities.
Website: www.anti-slaverysociety.org
The website contains an extensive hierarchical table of contents describing current slavery practices and countermethods.

Asian Migrant Center (AMC)
4 Jordan Road
Kowloon, Hong Kong
Phone: [852] 2312-0031
Fax: [852] 2992-0111
E-mail: amc@hk.supr.net

The Asian Migrant Center was established in 1989 to help develop alternatives to migrant work and to empower migrants in Asia. It researches the conditions of migrant workers throughout the continent and investigates the political and social movements within their groups. The AMC supports a number of migrant worker organizations to foster reintegration of migrants and raise political awareness of their situation.
Publications: The organization's major publication is the annual

Asian Migrant Yearbook ($55), a reference book on Asian migrant workers and migration issues. The most recent edition of the resource contains full-color maps of Asian labor migration; photographs, charts, and country statistics; analytical reports from sixteen Asian countries; and special articles on the impact of the 1997 Asian financial crisis on migrant workers, violence against women migrants, and globalization and migration.
Website: iswww.pacific.net.hk/~amc
The AMC website provides a resource list, information for ordering the *Asian Migrant Yearbook,* descriptions of organization activities, and links to like-minded organizations.

Asia Monitor Resource Center (AMRC)
444 Nathan Road, Flat 8B
Kowloon, Hong Kong
Phone: [852] 2332-1346
Fax: [852] 2385-5319
E-mail: amrc@hk.super.net

The Asia Monitor Resource Center (AMRC) is an independent NGO that focuses on Asian labor concerns. The center provides information, research, publishing, training, labor networking, and related services to trade unions, labor groups, and other development NGOs in the region. Its main goal is the support of democratic and independent labor movements in the Asian arena.
Publications: Publications include a quarterly report entitled *Asian Labor Update* and various articles pertaining to labor concerns.
Website: www.freeway.org.hk/~amrc
The AMRC website provides a description of the organization and a list of AMRC publications, but very little other information.

Europe

Burma Peace Foundation
777 United Nations Plaza, Sixth Floor
New York, NY 10017 USA
Phone: (212) 338-0048
Fax: (212) 692-9748
Or:
85 Rue de Montbrillant
1202 Geneva, Switzerland
Tel/Fax: [41] (22) 733-2040
E-mail: darnott@igc.org

The Burma Peace Foundation confronts many of the same prob-

lems that the Burma Project addresses, such as human rights and economic abuses.
Website: None

Burma Project
25/27 Bickerton Road, Third Floor
London N19 5JT UK
Phone: [44] (171) 281-7377
Fax: [44] (171) 272-3559
E-mail: bagp@gn.apc.org
Or: Burma Project
Open Society Institute
400 West 59th Street
New York, NY 10019 USA
Phone: (212) 548 0632
Fax: (212) 548 4655
E-mail: burma@sorosny.org

The Burma Project, established by the Open Society Institute in 1994, aims to increase international awareness of conditions in Burma (Myanmar) and to assist the country in making its transition from a closed to an open society.

Publications: Publications include a bimonthly magazine, *Burma Debate,* which serves as a forum for discussion of central issues concerning Burma; *Burma: Country in Crisis,* a report that provides background information on current events in Burma; *Burma News Update,* a newsflash report that delivers timely updates regarding current developments in Burma; and *BurmaNet News,* an electronic newspaper covering Burma and providing recent articles from newspapers, magazines, newsletters, the wire services, and the Internet. Subscriptions to *Burma News Update* and *BurmaNet News* are free and available by e-mail. Most publications are available on the website.

Website: www.soros.org/burma

The Burma Project website has links to a history of Burma, news reports, publications, current projects, grant/scholarship information, political and economic information, and thorough descriptions of the problems threatening the Burmese people.

Catholic Fund for Overseas Development (CAFOD)
Romero Close
Stockwell Road
London SW9 9TY UK

Phone: [44] (207) 733-7900
Fax: [44] (207) 274-9630
E-mail: hqcafod@cafod.org.uk

CAFOD is the official relief and development agency of the Catholic Church in England and Wales. It is committed to justice for the world's poor, regardless of religion; CAFOD funds more than one thousand projects worldwide. It has been active in publicizing and working against slavery and bonded labor in the developing world.

Publications: CAFOD issues policy briefings covering relief and development issues; online factsheets describing issues facing the developing world, such as racism, the environment, land mines, food, aid, poverty, and the role of women; and press articles regarding CAFOD activities.

Website: www.cafod.org.uk

The CAFOD website has links to news articles, campaigns for human rights, job opportunities, and a wealth of information for people interested in becoming part of the organization.

Christian Aid
P.O. Box 100
London SE1 7RT UK
Phone: [44] (207) 620-4444
Fax: [44] (207) 620-0719
35 Lower Marsh
Waterloo
London SE1 7RT UK
E-mail: info@christian-aid.org

Christian Aid is an organization dedicated to helping people worldwide overcome poverty and human rights abuses. Its has volunteers in more than sixty countries. A leader in overseas aid and development, it also provides in-depth research and has campaigned actively against bonded labor.

Publications: Christian Aid's publication program issues regular reports to support its advocacy, campaigning, and lobbying work. Recent reports have focused on the impact of debt on poor countries, proposals for rapid debt cancellation, and business ethics and ethical trading. Other areas of publication include globalization, aid, human rights and governance, gender, and participation.

Website: www.christian-aid.org.uk/main.htm

The Christian Aid website provides newsbriefs, reports, and information concerning human rights across the globe.

Child Rights Information Network (CRIN)
17 Grove Lane
London SE5 8RD UK
Phone: [44] (207) 703-5400
Fax: [44] (207) 793-7630
E-mail: crin@pro-net.co.uk

CRIN is a global network of children's rights organizations striving to improve the lives of children by exchanging information about child rights, promoting the UN Convention on the Rights of the Child, and developing capacity building and networking tools.

Publications: CRIN maintains a publications database of the publications (journals, newsletters, articles, and reports) of member organizations. Many of these publications are available on CRIN's website.

Website: www.crin.org

Besides the publication database of member organizations, the CRIN website offers extensive links to human rights organizations and articles on the rights of children.

Christian Solidarity Worldwide (CSW)
1 Arnellan House
144/146 Slough Lane
London NW9 8JX UK
Phone: [44] (208) 942-8810

Christian Solidarity Worldwide works to obtain religious liberty for all Christians. It also states as its goal the liberation of people from all forms of oppression and misfortune, especially needy children and disaster victims. CSW campaigns for its goals by lobbying the British and European Union parliaments as well as petitioning the UN for relief missions. CSW workers routinely go on fact-finding missions to countries in need, and they publicize their findings in regular reports.

Publications: Publications include a bimonthly magazine, regular newsletters, country profile reports, and accounts of trips taken by the organization.

Website: www.csworldwide.org

The CSW website offers a subscription to organization information, chronological news summaries covering 1998–2000, and links to the CSW magazine. The site also offers the country and trip reports, a photo gallery, and contact information.

Clean Clothes Campaign
P.O. Box 11584
1001 GN Amsterdam
The Netherlands
Phone: [31] (20) 412-2785
Fax: [31] (20) 412-2786
E-mail: ccc@xs4all.nl

The Clean Clothes Campaign works to improve working conditions in garment industries worldwide. The campaign works with consumer organizations, trade unions, and other groups to make sure that employers are responsible for providing safe and fair conditions for their employees.
Publications: Several reports related to the work of the Clean Clothes Campaign, including accounts of poor working conditions, discussions of labor and consumer issues, and analyses of independent monitoring models, are published on the organization's website.
Website: http://www.cleanclothes.org
The website has general news and current events sections, a list of reviewed companies, a proposed code of conduct for employers, and contact information for concerned consumers.

Comite Contre L'Esclavage Modern (CCEM)
4 Place de Valois
75001 Paris, France
Phone: [33] (1) 5535-3655
Fax: [33] (1) 5535-3656

The CCEM, known in English as the Committee Against Modern Slavery, fights the intolerable practice of slavery in France and abroad. Made up entirely of volunteers, the committee enlists journalists, lawyers, social workers, doctors and health professionals, students, and retired people to work toward its goal of ending slavery worldwide. Branches of this organization exist in France, Belgium, Spain, and Italy.
Publications: The CCEM publishes reports on topics related to the organization's activities and findings.
Website: www.ccem-antislavery.org
The CCEM website is offered in both French and English. It has sections for news, activity reports, information for people interested in joining the committee, and contact information.

Defense for Children International (DCI)
P.O. Box 881211
20 Geneva, Switzerland
E-mail: dci-hq@pingnet.ch

Defense for Children International is a nongovernmental organization working for the protection and promotion of children's rights. Set up during the International Year of the Child (1979), DCI encourages concerted international action toward promoting and protecting the rights of the child. It also seeks to foster awareness and solidarity about children's rights situations by conducting research and monitoring of potentially abusive areas. DCI suggests both preventive and curative protection of all children's rights.

Publications: A regular newsletter and other information on all aspects of children's rights, through regular and ad hoc publications.

Website: childhouse.uio.no/childrens_rights/dci_what.html
The DCI website is very limited in scope; it provides a mission statement and links to children's rights standards.

Foundation Against Trafficking in Women
P.O. Box 1455
3500 BL Utrecht
The Netherlands
Phone: [31] (302) 716-044
Fax: [31] (302) 716-084
E-mail: fe@stv.vx.xs4all.nl

The Foundation Against Trafficking in Women was founded in the early 1980s in response to growing "prostitution tourism." The organization works with NGOs, international action groups, and other women's organizations to develop legislation and litigation addressing the issue.

Website: None

Human Rights Information and Documentation Systems International (HURIDOCS)
48 Chemin du Grand-Montfleury
CH-1290 Versoix, Switzerland
Phone: [41] (22) 755-5252
Fax: [41] (22) 755-5260
E-mail: huridocs@comlink.org

HURIDOCS, established in 1982, is a global network of human

rights organizations. Its goal is to provide a "decentralized information network" to workers in the field of human rights. HURIDOCS offers the tools and techniques for information handling, training courses on documenting human rights studies, and advice and support on documentation centers and information systems.

Publications: Reference books and software on the tools for "Human Rights Information Handling," reports on HURIDOCS activities, and a regular newsletter. Publications must be ordered through the organization. Some selections from the newsletter and reports are available on the website.

Website: www.huridocs.org

The HURIDOCS website contains general information about the organization as well as guidelines and formats for human rights documentation.

International Confederation of Free Trade Unions (ICFTU)
155, Bld Emile Jaqmain
1210 Brussels, Belgium
Phone: [32] (2) 224-0211
Fax: [32] (2) 218-8415

Established in 1949, the ICFTU is made up of 215 organizations in 145 countries worldwide; it has over 125 million members, over a fourth of whom are women. The ICFTU is open to all democratic trade unions. It works together with the International Labor Organization (ILO), the United Nations Economic and Social Committee (ECOSOC), the International Monetary Fund (IMF), the World Bank, and the World Trade Organization (WTO). The confederation's main goals are to defend workers' rights, encourage equal rights for women, eradicate child labor, make education available for all, and support the environment.

Publications: The ICFTU publishes a monthly journal entitled *Trade Union World* and a number of other publications each year on particular themes. Additionally, it publishes the *Survey of Trade Union Rights* each June, which provides information on more than 115 countries violating basic trade union rights norms. An online bulletin is also available via E-mail.

Website: www.icftu.org

The ICFTU website contains a history of trade unions and milestones in workers rights. It also provides a mission statement, a calendar of workers' rights events, educational materials, labor rights resolutions, and links to associated trade union campaigns.

International Labor Organization (ILO)
Ms. Karen A. Lee
ILO
1828 L. St. NW
Washington, DC 20036
Phone: (202) 653-7652
Fax: (202) 653-7687
Email: burrylee@ilo.org

The ILO's main purpose is to promote and develop policies inspired by ideals of social justice aimed chiefly at improving the position of workers within member states. The International Labor Conference, which is the permanent secretariat of the ILO, meets once a year. Every three years it elects the Governing Body, which includes ten member states designated as "states of chief industrial importance."

Publications: The Publications Bureau of the ILO presents an extensive array of materials including books, CD-ROMS, journals, radiographs, and videos dealing with such areas as employment policy, developments in industrial relations, occupational health and safety, and labor statistics and methods, as well as information on child labor practices. The website has a fully searchable online shopping catalog for easy purchase.

Website: www.ilo.org/public/english/index.htm

The ILO website has links to news and contact information, as well as a large, scrolling menu of links to worldwide branches of the organization.

International Textile Garment and Leather Workers Federation
8 Rue Joseph Stevens
Brussels 1000, Belgium
Phone: [32] (2) 512-2833
Fax: [32] (2) 511-0904

This organization works to protect the rights of laborers in the textile and leather industries. It seeks regulations regarding child workers, overworking of laborers, and similar abuse in these industries.

Website: None

La Strada Ceska Republika
P.O. Box 18
Prague, Czech Republic

Phone: [420] (2) 5732-5617
E-mail: lastrada@ecn.cz.trafficking

La Strada's goal is to prevent the trafficking of women in Central and Eastern Europe. It provides aid for victims and works to raise awareness of the problem by lobbying government bodies and conducting research.

Publications: The organization publishes informational brochures for women regarding the problems of trafficking.

Website: www.ecn.cz/lastrada/indexA.htm

This website is available in both Czech and English. It provides information on preventing women trafficking, support of victims, and international politics involved in the matter.

NGO Group for the Convention on the Rights of the Child

c/o Defense for Children International
P.O. Box 88
1211 Geneva 20
Switzerland
Phone: [41] (22) 734-0558
Fax: [41] (22) 740-1145

A coalition of more than forty international NGOs working to facilitate implementation of the Convention on the Rights of the Child, this organization is a subsidiary of DCI. Though the organization does not call for all child labor to be banned, it does support positive changes for child workers and "best interest" treatment of children. The group's major goal is to prevent exploitative and abusive child labor and improve conditions for working children.

Publications: Brochures on combating the sale of children, child prostitution and child pornography; eliminating the exploitation of child labor, education on the Convention on the Rights of the Child, and a guide for NGOs reporting to the Committee on the Rights of the Child are only available from the organization.

Website: www.childhub.ch/webpub/dcihome/26a6.htm

The website contains background information about the group, contact addresses, a list of aims and objectives, a list of NGO members, and a mailing list.

Norwegian Institute of International Affairs (NUPI)

Gronlandsleiret 25
P.O. Box 8159 Dep.
N-0033 Oslo 1

Norway
Phone: [47] (2) 177050
Fax: [47] (2) 177015

The Norwegian Institute of International Affairs researches international political and economic issues. Major topics of research include the integration and sovereignty of Europe, collective security and peace operations, international economics, and development policy.
Publications: Within the field of international relations, NUPI researchers publish articles, books, and reports. Some materials are published directly by NUPI, whereas others are published by domestic or foreign publishing houses.
Website: www.nupi.no/default-e.htm
This website is offered in both Norwegian and English. It contains research information, news items, general publications and texts of working papers, transcripts of international affairs seminars, and contact information.

Rädda Barnen
Torsgatan 4
107 88 Stockholm, Sweden
Phone: [46] (8) 698-9000
Fax: [46] (8) 698-9014

Rädda Barnen is the Swedish division of Save the Children.
Publications: Rädda Barnen publishes books, reports, videos, and a magazine. A documentation database and a newsletter on child soldiers are also available.
Website: www.rb.se/engindex.htm
This website is similar to the Save the Children website but focuses on a Swedish audience. The site is available in Swedish and English.

Rugmark
Rugmark–German office
c/o TRANSFAIR e.V.
Remigiusstrasse 21
50937 Köln, Germany
Phone: [49] (221) 941-1253
Fax: [49] (221) 94-2040-40
E-mail: rugmark@transfair.org
Or:

Rugmark–USA
Nina Smith
733 15th Street NW, Suite 920
Washington, DC 20005 USA
Phone: (202) 347-4100
Fax: (202) 347-4885
E-mail: ninajs@erols.com
Or:
Rugmark–Great Britain
c/o Anti-Slavery International
Thomas Clarkson House
The Stableyard
Broomgrove Road
London SW9 9TL UK
Phone: [44] (207) 501-8920
Fax: [44] (207) 738-4110

The Rugmark campaign monitors the use of illegal child labor in the carpet industry. It also aims to fulfill consumer demands for socially responsible production conditions to avoid a consumer boycott of hand-knotted carpets. Rugmark has worldwide organizational support including divisions in Europe, North America, India, and Nepal.

Publications: Publications include organizational reports and information on the status of child labor in the carpet industries in India, Nepal, and Pakistan.

Website: www.rugmark.org

The Rugmark website is offered in both German and English. It provides general information about the campaign's goals, news, information for prospective licensees, and contact information.

Survival International
11-15 Emerald Street
London WC1N 3QL UK
Phone: [44] (207) 242-1441
Fax: [44] (207) 242-1771
E-mail: info@survival-international.org

Survival International is a worldwide organization providing support of tribal and indigenous peoples. It supports self-determination of all people in regard to life, land, and human rights. The organization also offers for sale tribal goods produced under socially responsible conditions.

Publications: Publications include country-specific urgent action

bulletins, press releases, and success stories. All of these are available on the website and are searchable by publication type and country.
Website: www.survival-international.org
This website describes the organization's campaigns and offers backgrounds of numerous tribes and countries. It also has sections for current news and events, application information, a catalog of goods, and links to similar organizations.

World Trade Organization (WTO)
154 Rue de Lausanne
1211 Geneva 21
Switzerland
Phone: [41] (22) 739-5111

Organized in 1995, the WTO grew from the General Agreement on Tariffs and Trade (GATT). The WTO is an international trade organization that deals with the global rules of trade between nations. It works to ensure that trade flows as "smoothly, predictably, and freely as possible." The general goal of the WTO is to improve the welfare of the peoples of the member countries.
Publications: The extensive list of WTO publications is conveniently divided into the following categories: free publications, recent publications, legal publications, annual reports, trade policy reviews, special studies, and videos. The official WTO newsletter *FOCUS* is available in back issues online, and an online bookshop is available for immediate purchase of materials.
Website: www.wto.org
The WTO website has a hierarchical list of links under the broad heading "General Information, Trade Topics, and Resources." The categories contain news texts, trade documents and agreements, and links to other organizations.

North America

American Anti-Slavery Group (AASG)
510 Commonwealth Avenue #285
Boston, MA 02215
Phone: (800) 884-0719
E-mail: info@anti-slavery.org

The American Anti-Slavery Group is devoted to abolishing slavery worldwide, with a special focus on what it calls "the worst and most ignored cases of human bondage: black chattel slavery in

North Africa." Founded in 1993, it held the first abolitionist conference since the Civil War, which became a national conference in 1999. The AASG aims to increase awareness of slavery in Africa, and it monitors, documents, campaigns, and lobbies on the plight of slaves in today's world. The organization works closely with Christian Solidarity International to raise money to buy the freedom of Sudanese slaves.

Publications: The AASG has no publications, though its website lists a large number of articles based on its work and a quarterly newsletter, and through its links with STOP, the students' campaign to stop slavery, has produced an Anti-Slavery School Curriculum and a teacher's packet available through its website.

Website: www.anti-slavery.org

Lists monthly updates about antislavery efforts and provides several links to antislavery articles and other documents.

Amnesty International USA
322 Eighth Avenue
New York, NY 10001
Phone: (212) 807-8400
Fax: (212) 463-9193

One of the world's largest human rights organizations, Amnesty International lists as its goals the liberation of prisoners of conscience; ensuring fair, speedy trials for political prisoners; abolition of cruel treatment of prisoners (including torture and the death penalty); and ending extrajudicial killings and disappearances.

Publications: As part of its campaign to protect fundamental human rights, Amnesty International regularly publishes country reports and other documents on human rights issues around the world. All published information is scrupulously analyzed and cross-checked by the research department and legal offices in London to ensure the integrity of the final reports. These reports are regarded by experts in various fields of study as one of the most reliable sources for information on human rights issues. The accuracy and strict impartiality with which the organization's research is conducted has made it a vital resource for many news organizations, government agencies, lawyers, professors, and students.

Websites: www.amnesty-usa.org; www.amnesty-volunteer.org/usa/education

The websites have an enormous amount of information about human rights abuses, current events, and organization activities. Links to other Amnesty International sites and other human rights organizations are also provided.

Asian-American Free Labor Institute (AAFLI)
1925 K Street NW, Suite 301
Washington, DC 20006
Phone: (202) 778-4500
Fax: (202) 778-4525

The AAFLI is the international component of the AFL-CIO. The institute works with Asian trade unions to enforce child labor standards, worker health and safety standards, and safe labor conditions.
Publications: The AAFLI publishes a quarterly newsletter, the *AAFLI News,* and other informational material.
Website: None

The Campaign for Migrant Domestic Workers Rights
733 15th St. NW, Suite 1020
Washington, DC 20005-2112
Phone: (202) 234-9382 ext.244
Fax: (202) 387-7915
E-mail: ipsps@igc.org

The Campaign for Migrant Domestic Workers Rights is a coalition of legal and social service agencies, ethnically based organizations, social action groups, and individuals devoted to protecting the rights of the migrant domestic working community. Specifically, it focuses on those domestic workers carrying A-3 or G-5 visas.
Publications: The Legal Rights and Resources Available to G-5 and A-3 Domestic Workers. A handbook for work with domestic workers, available from the campaign (No ISBN).
Website: www.BreakTheChainCampaign.org
The website covers the work of the campaign. It includes a contact for those who know of a case of G-5 or A-3 abuse. One section details the abuse and exploitation of G-5 and A-3 domestic workers. Information on how to contact the Campaign for Migrant Domestic Workers Rights is also given.

Child Labor Coalition (CLC)
Linda Golodner
c/o National Consumers League
1701 K Street NW, Suite 1200
Washington, D.C. 20006
Phone: (202) 835-3323
Fax: (202) 835-0747

Since 1989 the CLC has worked to end exploitation of child labor and to encourage education, health, safety, and general well-being for working children. The CLC researches child labor abuses and publishes its findings in order to influence policy concerning child workers.

Publications: No regular publications.

Website: www.natlconsumersleague.org/clc.htm

The CLC website offers advice of what consumers can do to combat child labor, other background information, and links to other child labor organizations.

Coalition Against Slavery in Sudan and Mauritania (CASMAS)
P.O. Box 3293
New York, NY 10027
Phone: (212) 774-4287
E-mail: CASMASALC@aol.com

This human rights organization brings together abolitionists and human rights activists from all races, creeds, and nationalities to collectively fight for the eradication of the chattel enslavement of black Africans. It is a response to the centuries-old practice of buying, selling, and breeding Africans by Arab Moors and North African Arabs that never stopped in the countries of Sudan and Mauritania.

Publications: Cotton, Samuel, 1998, *Silent Terror: A Journey into Contemporary African Slavery.* New York: Writers and Readers Publishing, Harlem River Press. ISBN 0-86316-259-2.

Website: members.aol.com/casmasalc

The website contains recent news about work against slavery in Mauritania and Sudan as well as an archive of articles on the subject.

ECPAT USA
475 Riverside Drive, Room 830
New York, NY 10115-0055
Phone: (212) 870-2427
Fax: (212) 870-2055
E-mail: ipequeno@worldnet.att.net

ECPAT is an international institution dedicated to eliminating child pornography, child prostitution, and "the trafficking of children for sexual purposes." ECPAT is nonpolitical and nonreligious; it works with other organizations and governments to support its goals.

Publications: ECPAT has a number of books that are basic and fundamental explanations of child prostitution and trafficking, particularly *The ECPAT Story,* by Ron O'Grady (1996); *The Rape of the Innocent,* also by Ron O'Grady (1994); *Enforcing the Law against the Commercial Sexual Exploitation of Children,* ECPAT (1996); *Child Prostitution and Sex Tourism: A Series of Research Reports,* by Dr Julia O'Connell Davidson and Jaqueline Sanchez-Taylor, 1996; *1996–1997 Commercial Sexual Exploitation of Children: A Report on the Implementation of the Agenda for Action Adopted at the First World Congress against Commercial Sexual Exploitation of Children, Stockholm, Sweden, 28 August 1996;* and *1997–1998 Moving to Action: A Second Report on the Implementation of the Agenda for Action Adopted at the First World Congress against Commercial Sexual Exploitation of Children. Stockholm, Sweden, 28 August 1996.*
Website: www.ecpat.net
The ECPAT website details current efforts to end child exploitation, including the International Young People's Participation Project, which aims to increase the level of young people's participation in the campaign against the commercial sexual exploitation of children. It intends to do this by collaborating with national partners in more than thirty countries.

Free the Children
1750 Steeles Avenue West, Suite 218
Concord, Ontario L4K 2L7
Canada
Phone: (905) 760-9382
Fax: (905) 760-9157
E-mail: freechild@clo.com

Set up by Canadian schoolchildren, Free the Children is dedicated to eliminating the exploitation of children around the world by encouraging youth to volunteer in, as well as to create, programs and activities that relieve the plight of underprivileged children. It is an organization run by children for children. It now employs adults to work in its central office, but only on the understanding that they are facilitators and administrators but do not take part in making policy for the organization. Free the Children funds schools, rehabilitation programs for ex-child laborers, and aid for children in situations of conflict or natural disaster around the world.
Publications: The book *Free the Children,* by organizer Craig Kielburger, is sold through the website, as are a video about the organization's work and a CD of songs.

Website: www.freethechildren.org
The website has a guide to projects run by Free the Children and an explanation of its history.

Human Rights Watch (HRW)
485 Fifth Avenue
New York, NY 10017
Phone: (212) 972-8405
Fax: (212) 972-0905

HRW is dedicated to protecting human rights around the world. It investigates and exposes human rights violations and holds abusers accountable. The Human Rights Watch organization established the Children's Rights Project in 1994. This division of HRW examines countries and organizations suspected of children's rights violations and publishes its findings in reports distributed to governments, institutions, and NGOs capable of ending the child abuse. Human Rights Watch's Women's Rights Project examines reports of women's rights abuses worldwide. It publishes its findings along with HRW's other articles. The Women's Rights Project also keeps track of current events in the field of women's rights.
Publications: The organization regularly publishes reports on such topics as slavery, child rights, child labor, bonded child labor, abduction, and the trafficking of women and girls.
Website: www.hrw.org
The main website details HRW's many divisions and has extensive links to HRW publications, campaigns, essays, country briefings, and research materials. The Children's Rights Project web page (www.hrw.org/about/projects/children.html) has links to some of its reports. The Women's Rights Project web page (www.hrw.org/about/projects/women.html) has links to news articles about women's rights abuses and transcripts of HRW's reports on the subject.

International Forum on Globalization (IFG)
950 Lombard Street
San Francisco, CA 94133
Phone: (415) 771-3394
Fax: (415) 771-1121
E-mail: ifg@ifg.org

Founded in 1994, the International Forum on Globalization is dedicated to examining the impacts of economic globalization. It organizes activities to inform the general public about the effects of globalization.

Publications: Publications include a newsletter for members and papers discussing such issues as corporate governance, the World Trade Organization, and the effects of globalization on the environment, citizenship, and commerce. Descriptions of published papers are available on the website.

Website: www.ifg.org

The IFG website has links to forum events and partner organizations.

International Labor Rights Fund
733 15th Street NW, Suite 920
Washington, D.C. 20005
Phone: (202) 347-4100
Fax: (202) 347-4885
E-mail: pharis.harvey@ilrf.org

The ILRF encourages the enforcement of international labor rights. It pursues legal and administrative action on behalf of working people, creates innovative programs and enforcement mechanisms to protect workers' rights, and advocates for better protection for workers. The ILRF focuses on linking trade expansion to enforcement of recognized worker rights in order to more broadly distribute the benefits of global trade. It has been especially active in campaigning to end child labor and forced labor in Burma (Myanmar).

Website: www.ilrf.org

The website updates current campaigns and is rich in information about child labor and forced labor.

Laogai Research Foundation (LRF)
P.O. Box 361375
Milpitas, CA 95036-1375
Phone: (408) 262-0219
Fax: (408) 263-8477

LRF was established by ex-laogai inmate Harry Wu in 1992 to carry out research, publish, and publicize the plight of the millions of Chinese held in gulags across China—home to the most extensive forced labor camp system in the world today.

Publications: The organization publishes an annual *Laogai Handbook,* a newsletter, and special reports and assists television journalists in making documentaries exposing the abuse of human rights in the laogai.

Website: www.laogai.org
The LRF webpage has links to foundation newsletters.

Lawyers Committee for Human Rights (LCHR)
333 Seventh Avenue, 13th Floor
New York, NY 10001
Phone: (212) 845-5200
Fax: (212) 845-5299
E-mail: lchrbin@lchr.org

Founded in 1978, the Lawyers Committee for Human Rights works to ensure that all governments are compliant with the International Bill of Human Rights. It supports legal institutions dedicated to upholding human rights for all.

Publications: Extensive publications include books, topical reports, and papers on such varied issues as asylum, freedom of association, international justice, international financial institutions, and international refugee programs. Pertinent issues are also reported with a geographical emphasis, including papers on matters in Africa, Europe, Latin America/Caribbean, and Middle East/North Africa. Publications descriptions are available on the website; most must be ordered from the organization. LCHR's program WITNESS, a partnership with Peter Gabriel and Reebok, releases a biweekly series of human rights videos called "WITNESS Rights Alert."

Website: www.lchr.org/home.htm
The LCHR website is like a newspaper; it has links to articles about the legal aspects of worldwide human rights violations.

Multinational Monitor (Essential Information, Inc.)
P.O. Box 19405
Washington, DC 20036
Phone: (202) 387-8030
Fax: (202) 234-5176

The *Multinational Monitor* is a monthly publication of Essential Information, Inc., an organization that aims to provide provocative information to the public on important topics neglected by the mass media and policy makers. The *Multinational Monitor* examines corporate activity, especially in the Third World, focusing on the export of hazardous substances, worker health and safety, labor union issues, and the environment.

Website: www.essential.org/monitor
The *Multinational Monitor's* website has links to its online issues.

Save the Children Federation
Attn.: Donor Services
54 Wilton Road
Westport, CT 06880
Phone: (800) 243-5075

Save the Children helps impoverished and abused children worldwide, addressing health and educational needs alongside social and economic wrongs.

Publications: The organization has extensive publications available online. This includes Champions Newsbriefs, *IMPACT* newsletter, and annual and special reports. The major report *The State of the World's Mothers* is also available on the website.

Website: www.savethechildren.org

Save the Children's somewhat disorganized website has links to children's rights publications.

Sweatshop Watch
720 Market Street, Fifth Floor
San Francisco, CA 94102
Phone: (510) 834-8990
Fax: (510) 834-8974
E-mail: sweatwatch@igc.org

Sweatshop Watch is a coalition of international human rights organizations. Its goal is ending sweatshop conditions for textile workers.

Publications: Sweatshop Watch publishes a quarterly newsletter, current and back issues of which are available online. The newsletter reports and discusses consumer and labor issues related to human rights violations.

Website: www.sweatshopwatch.org

Sweatshop Watch's website has links to related articles and newsletters.

Transnational Institute (TNI)
The Norwich Center
Box 710
Norwich, VT 05055
Phone/Fax: (802) 649-1000
E-mail: ccgtrans@valley.net
Or:
Paulus Potterstraat 20
1071 DA Amsterdam

The Netherlands
Phone: [31] (20) 662-6608
Fax: [31] (20) 675-7176

Since 1974, the Transnational Institute has worked to find solutions to global problems dealing with militarism, poverty, social wrongs, and the environment. The U.S. branch of the institute has sponsored exchange programs and other projects between the United States and Russia. Over 850 Russian citizens participated in these exchanges, and more than 1,200 U.S. citizens have made the trip to Russia. Now, after the collapse of the Soviet Union, the Transnational Institute continues its exchange program with the Commonwealth of Independent States.

Publications: TNI's global research generates a comprehensive publication program that includes full-length books, topical reports, and a book series published in association with Pluto Press. Also available are publications by TNI fellows. Descriptions of publications and instructions for ordering are available on the website.

Website: www.tni.org

The Transnational Institute's website contains information and links to current news and projects, as well as an extensive online archive of articles and past publications.

UNESCO
3 United Nations Plaza TA-24A
New York, NY 10017
Phone: (212) 824-6380
Fax: (212) 824-6466

The United Nations Educational, Scientific, and Cultural Organization (UNESCO) came into being in 1946, when twenty states ratified its constitution. As of October 19, 1999, the organization has 188 member states. UNESCO's stated goal is "to contribute to peace and security in the world by promoting collaboration among nations through education, science, culture and communication in order to further universal respect for justice, for the rule of law and for the human rights and fundamental freedoms that are affirmed for the peoples of the world, without distinction of race, sex, language or religion, by the Charter of the United Nations."

Publications: UNESCO uses its publications to foster international public awareness of its major programs in literacy, bioethics, education, human rights, women, the environment, sustainable development, and peace. UNESCO's publications catalog includes more than a thousand titles in English, French, Spanish, Russian, Chinese, and Arabic, published under its own imprint or copublished. UNESCO produces books, CD-ROMs, periodicals, and scientific maps derived from UNESCO programs and generally aimed at specialized users. For the general public UNESCO has recently developed news series on key world issues, such as Cultures of Peace. Full listings of UNESCO's publications are available on the website.

Website: www.unesco.org

UNESCO has an extensive website listing the organization's goals, history, and constitution; current events, activities, and programs; and links to related organizations. It is available in English, Spanish, French, Russian, Arabic, and Chinese.

UNICEF: United Nations Children's Fund
UNICEF House
3 United Nations Plaza
New York, NY 10017
Phone: (212) 326-7000
Fax: (212) 887-7465
E-mail: addresses@unicef.org (to find e-mail address of specific person/branch)

Founded in 1946, UNICEF is an advocate of children's rights; it works to protect those rights and helps the young "meet their basic needs and to expand their opportunities to reach their full potential." The organization uses the Convention on the Rights of the Child as its guide in establishing international standards of behavior toward children. UNICEF provides primary health care, basic education, and sanitation in many developing countries.

Publications: UNICEF compiles and makes readily available information on the situation of children, the performance of countries in fulfilling the promise to children, the protection of children's rights, and its own contributions in programs for children. In addition to various news articles, UNICEF's publication program includes annual reports such as *World Summit for Children, Promise and Progress: Achieving Goals for Children, The State of the World's Children, The Progress of Nations 1999,* and the *UNICEF Annual Report.*

Website: www.unicef.org

The UNICEF website is full of reference materials including news articles, publications, statistics, and general and research information.

UNIFEM: Women's Human Rights Program
304 East 45th Street, Sixth Floor
New York, NY 10017
Phone: (212) 906-6400
Fax: (212) 906-6705
E-mail: unifem@undp.org

UNIFEM has worked since 1976 to empower women and to support gender equality. The organization's main goals are strengthening women's economic powers, increasing women's roles in governance and leadership, and promoting women's human rights. *Publications:* UNIFEM publications include books and reports on economic capacity issues, governance and leadership issues, gender mainstreaming challenges, and human rights concerns. UNIFEM and the Center for Women's Global Leadership recently copublished a training manual on women's human rights entitled *Local Action/Global Change, Learning about the Human Rights of Women and Girls.* The manual combines development of rights awareness with issue-oriented actions and includes substantive information about the human rights of women in such areas as violence, health, reproduction and sexuality, education, the global economy, the workplace, and family life. Other publications include videos, annual reports, and speeches and statements on UNIFEM issues.
Website: www.unifem.undp.org
The UNIFEM website has a list of resources and links to the organization's mission statement, press releases, current news regarding women's rights, and other women's rights organizations.

World Vision
34834 Weyerhaeuser Way South
P.O. Box 9716
Federal Way, WA 98063-9716
Phone: (888) 511-6598

World Vision is a Christian organization dedicated to ending poverty, hunger, and human rights abuses worldwide. In India it has developed innovative programs for the liberation and rehabilitation of child bonded laborers.
Publications: Publications include an annual report, a quarterly periodical entitled *World Vision Today,* a monthly commentary and factsheet entitled *Insider,* and policy papers on such issues as landmines and child sponsorship. Most of these publications are available in full text online.

Website: www.worldvision.org/worldvision/master.nsf
The website has current and past press releases, links to current projects, articles about past activities, and links to World Vision sites worldwide.

South America

National Forum on the Prevention and Eradication of Child Labor
SBN Quadra 01
Bloco (F)-Sala 204
Ed. Palacio da Agricultura
SENAR/CA
Brazilia/ DF CEP 70040-000
Brazil
Phone: [55] (61) 226-6815
Fax: [55] (61) 321-5775
E-mail: INFANTIL@senar-rural.com.br

This organization is coordinated by the Brazilian Ministry of Labor and is composed of forty institutions with representatives of workers, employers, the federal government, and NGOs. A methodology of work called "integrated actions" is at the heart of this organization. It means that every institution member of the forum should make an effort to concentrate his/her actions in a specific area at the same time and with the same target group.
Website: None

Organization Indigena Regional de Atalaya (OIRA)
Correo Central, Atalaya
Peru
Phone: [51] (64) 573-469

Formed in 1986 as a federation of local indigenous community groups, OIRA works to organize local people into taking action against the use of slavery affecting the more than ten thousand indigenous peoples in the Atalaya region of Peru. Some of OIRA's achievements include documenting information on sixty communities where slavery was taking place, running literacy courses for indigenous bonded laborers on ranches and estates, persuading authorities to help local indigenous people to be officially registered, and winning an agreement with the authorities over indigenous land rights. OIRA has freed more than six thousand people.
Website: None

Pastoral Land Commission (CPT)
Head Office
Rue 19, No. 34, First Andar
Centro-CEP, 74030-090
Goiania
Goias, Brazil
Phone: [55] (62) 212-6466
Fax: [55] (62) 212-0421
E-mail: cptnac@cultura.com.br

One of the most powerful defenders of land reform in Brazil, the CPT reported five thousand cases of slave labor in Brazil in 1991. CPT is run by a Catholic priest, Father Ricardo Rezende (see Chapter 3), who has consistently denounced the abuse of poor landless Brazilians forced to work as slave labor on estates in the Amazon region and has tried to persuade the national and state governments to take action.
Website: None

South and Southeast Asia

Asian-American Free Labor Institute (AAFLI)
G.P.O. Box 596
Dhaka-1000
Bangladesh
Phone: [880] (2) 88-403
E-mail: aaflibd@pradeshta.net

The AAFLI is one of the AFL-CIO's four international institutes. For the past twenty-five years, the institute has been fighting for and promoting human rights in Asia. It works to eliminate child labor and rehabilitate former child workers. The AAFLI works with trade unions, human rights organizations, and government and NGO groups to promote public policies to enforce labor rights and standards.
Website: None

Bonded Labor Liberation Front, India (BLLF)
7 Jantar Mantar Road
New Delhi 110001
India
Phone: [91] (11) 336-6765/7943
Fax: [91] (11) 336-8355
E-mail: bmm@del2.vsnl.net.in

Founded after police opened fire on a workers demonstration in 1981, the BLLF-India initially aimed to free bonded laborers working in stone quarries near Delhi. It is now a nationwide organization fighting debt bondage in all parts of the economy, including agriculture, where the largest number of bonded laborers exist. It coordinates activities of local centers in identifying, releasing, and rehabilitating bonded laborers; trains activists; educates bonded laborers about their rights; runs education centers; and provides legal advice. The organization established a National Day of Children in Servitude on which rallies and demonstrations are held to highlight the injustices of the debt bondage system.
Website: None

Butterflies
C-7 First Floor
Green Park Extension
New Delhi 110 016
India
Phone: [91] (11) 619-6117
E-mail: bflies@sdalt.erner.in

The Butterflies NGO works specifically with street children around interstate bus terminals in India. It helps to educate the children, provide them with health care, train them in vocations, and file court petitions on their behalf.
Publications: Issues a quarterly magazine that keeps an account of child-related accidents and abuse.
Website: None

Child Workers in Asia (CWA)
P.O. Box 29
Chantrakasem Post Office
Bangkok 10900
Thailand
Phone: [66] (2) 930-0855/6
E-mail: cwanet@loxinfo.co.th

CWA is a network of NGOs and individuals involved with the child labor movement in Asia. Through grassroots efforts and local advocacy, this organization works to foster development of child-focused NGOs. It also analyzes the situation of working children in order to raise awareness of the matter, advise interested organizations, and publish pertinent information.

Publications: Publications include a quarterly newsletter on child labor issues (available on the website).
Website: www.cwa.tnet.co.th
The CWA website offers various declarations on children's rights, an extensive list of references regarding working children (organized by country and by topic, such as "bonded child labor"), statistical information, current research information, and links to related sites.

ECPAT International
328 Phyathai Road
Bangkok 10400
Thailand
Phone: [66] (2) 215-3388
Fax: [66] (2) 612-8272
E-mail: ecpatbkk@ksc15.th.com

The End Child Prostitution in Asian Tourism (ECPAT) campaign began in 1990 in response to concern over increasing child prostitution in Thailand, the Philippines, and Sri Lanka. It aims to persuade governments to introduce effective policing to end child slavery and prostitution, make the promotion of tourism for child prostitution illegal, and encourage legal punishment of abusers, not victims. As a result of its work, these and other governments have introduced stricter laws, and Sweden, Germany, and Australia have passed laws allowing them to prosecute their citizens for sexual abuse of children in other countries. Other offices are established in forty countries, including Australia, Canada, France, Germany, Japan, Switzerland, the United States, and United Kingdom.

Global Alliance Against Traffic in Women (GAATW)
P.O. Box 1281
Bangkok 10500
Thailand
Phone: [66] (2) 215-3388
Fax: [66] (2) 612-8272
E-mail: GAATW@mozart.inet.co.th

Formed at the International Workshop on Migration and Traffic in Women in 1994, the GAATW ensures that human rights of trafficked women are protected by state authorities and agencies. The organization involves grassroots women in practical support and advocacy of international organizations with similar goals.

The GAATW campaigns for a new, broader definition for "trafficked persons" and promotes and facilitates action research in the field of trafficking women.

Publications: The publication program includes practical guidebooks such as *Human Rights in Practice: A Guide to Assist Trafficked Women and Children,* and *The Migrating Women's Handbook.* The organization has also published a regional report entitled *Trafficking in Women in the Asia-Pacific Region,* presenting the background and methods of trafficking in the region, thus giving a clear picture of the conditions and circumstances that characterize the situations faced by trafficked women.

Website: www.inet.co.th/org/gaatw

The GAATW website lists current activities, bulletins and newsletters, documentation and standards regarding women's rights, publications available for purchase, links to other websites, and a questionnaire regarding women's rights.

Human Rights Commission, Pakistan
107 Tipu Block
New Garden Town
Lahore, Pakistan
Phone: [92] (42) 588-3579/583-8341
Fax: [92] (42) 588-3582
E-mail: hrcplhe@brain.net.pk

The Human Rights Commission, Pakistan is an organization working on bonded labor, child labor, and forced marriage. A Special Task Force on the Sindh province has brought the issue of bonded labor and kidnapping of freed laborers to international attention. Over the past five years, the Human Rights Commission has succeeded in freeing over seven thousand bonded laborers.

Website: None

Informal Sector Service Center (INSEC)
P.O. Box 2726
Kathmandu, Nepal
Phone: [977] 270770
Fax: [977] 270551
Email: insec@mos.com.np

INSEC works to promote and protect the human rights of people in unorganized sectors of Nepal. Research into human rights abuses includes the bonded labor system. It also runs human rights and literacy training programs and works with the government to pass effective legislation banning all forms of bonded labor.

Publications: INSEC's documentation center produces and circulates an annual report on human rights issues as well as regular newsletters. It has also published a comprehensive report on bonded labor in western Nepal.

Website: www.hri.ca/partners/insec

The INSEC website provides a history of the organization, a list of accomplishments, current INSEC programs and publications, and general human rights information.

People's Recovery, Empowerment and Development Assistance (PREDA) Foundation, Inc.
Human Development Center
Upper Kalakalan
Olongapo City, Philippines
Phone: [63] (47) 222-5573

PREDA is a not-for-profit human rights organization focusing on women and children's rights. It promotes just laws to empower the poor and protect their rights. PREDA also aims to protect the weak and defenseless, mainly children and women exploited in demeaning labor such as prostitution. The organization assists the sexually abused and leads investigations into allegations of abuse.

Publications: PREDA publishes a regular newsletter, available online. It also posts all articles published externally about or mentioning PREDA on its website.

Website: www.preda.org

The PREDA website has a history of the organization, archives of its newsletter, links to projects, campaign links, and an on-site search engine.

Shoishab
1/20 Humayun Road
Mohammadpu, Dhaka
Bangladesh
Phone: [880] (2) 819-873
Fax: [880] (2) 811-344

Shoishab campaigns nationally on the rights of child domestic workers and has demonstrated the abuses suffered by such children through surveys. It also runs classes for children working as domestic servants and other deprived children.

Website: None

Society for the Protection of the Rights of the Child (SPARC)
P.O. Box 301
Islamabad, Pakistan
Phone: [92] (51) 279-256
E-mail: Sparc@associates.sdnpk.undp.org

SPARC campaigns and researches the problem of bonded labor in Pakistan.
Website: None

South Asian Coalition on Child Servitude (SACCS)
74 Aravali Apartment
DDA Kalkaji
New Dehli 19
India
Phone: [91] (11) 621-0807
Fax: [91] (11) 642-0029
E-mail: mukti@saccs.unv.ernet.in

SACCS is a conglomeration of more than four hundred organizations that work on child labor related issues in Southern Asia. The numerous NGOs, human rights organizations, and trade unions that make up SACCS combat bonded labor and child servitude. Since its creation in 1989, SACCS has liberated forty thousand bonded children from various industries. One SACCS project is the *Mukti Ashram*, a rehabilitation center for freed child bonded laborers.
Website: None

6

Selected Print Resources

In many ways the study of contemporary slavery is in its infancy. The widely held belief that slavery ended many years ago means that it is little studied today. Few organizations, publishers, researchers, and writers work in the area. This in turn means two things: first, that this cannot be a long chapter—there is simply not a wide-ranging literature on the subject; and second, there are still a lot of unanswered questions about slavery today. Some of the most important and basic questions have yet to be answered about new slavery. What, for example, is the best way to rehabilitate ex-slaves? What is the best way to get governments to take action against slavery? And what are the best actions those governments could take? How many people are actually being caught up in international trafficking? And where are they being sent? None of these questions currently have answers. It may be that as you use this book you will also think of questions that are not yet answered. If you do, try to be adventurous in seeking answers. In the fight to end slavery around the world, the questioning and work of every person is important.

Books

Altink, Sietske. *Stolen Lives: Trading Women into Sex and Slavery.* New York: Harrington Park Press, 1995. ISBN 1857270975.

Driven by the desire to start a career or escape poverty, women migrate in search of work and a better life for themselves and their families. For some this search is the beginning of a nightmare experience. From "hotel receptionist" to nightclub "dancer" to "domestic worker," this book exposes how women are hired in their country of origin and then transported, left without money, passports, or permits, to become trapped into prostitution or domestic slavery. Branded as illegal aliens and marooned in a culture they don't understand, they have nowhere to go and no one to help them. With personal testimony from women caught in the trafficking web, *Stolen Lives* reveals the violent inner workings of international crime networks, the routes and methods involved, and how the trafficking gangs are able to circumvent the law.

Anderson, Bridget. *Britain's Secret Slaves—An Investigation into the Plight of Overseas Domestic Workers.* London: Anti-Slavery International and Kalayaan, 1993. ISBN 0900918292.

This book documents the plight of overseas migrant workers in the United Kingdom during a period when returning expatriates and wealthy foreign nationals were allowed to bring domestic staff into the country on a tourist visa. These individuals' lack of independent immigration status tied them to their employer because escape would cause them to lose their right to work at all and be deported. Anderson's investigation uses personal testimony and detailed analysis of the UK concession and wider context of labor migration in a world where economic disparities are increasing. It also looks at the situation of Asian maids plus the situation in Hong Kong and Canada and their attempts to solve the problem.

Anti-Slavery International. *Child Domestic Workers: A Handbook for Research and Action* (Also in French and Spanish) London: Anti-Slavery International, 1997. ISBN 0900918411.

In many countries children working as maids, child-minders, garden boys, and general helpers-about-the-house are a familiar sight. Domestic work is, in fact, one of the most common forms of child employment. But it is not known how many children are involved, nor the age range of the workers, what led to their employment, the terms and conditions of their work, and their feelings about it. This book explores ways of finding out about the situation of these children. This practical guide draws on the experiences and views of NGOs and others working with child domestics in Asia, Africa, and Latin America. Examining the reasons why children working as domestic servants deserve attention, the handbook's step-by-step approach focuses on solutions to research and methodological problems.

Anti-Slavery International. *Enslaved Peoples in the 1990s.* London: Anti-Slavery International, 1997. ISBN 0900918403.

The history of the struggle of indigenous peoples for the recognition of their rights has been intimately connected to the phenomenon of slavery. Throughout the world, indigenous peoples are still subjected to a variety of forms of slavery, and this report charts a cross-section of these terrible experiences in the 1990s varying from the sexual exploitation of women and children in East Asia to debt bondage and serfdom in the Amazon.

Anti-Slavery International. *This Menace of Bonded Labour: Debt Bondage in Pakistan.* London: Anti-Slavery International, 1996. ISBN 0900918357.

This book looks at recent evidence of debt bondage in Pakistan and the failure of the Pakistan People's Party government to enforce the law of 1992, which officially outlawed it—despite the commitment by President Benazir Bhutto, before winning office, to eradicate "this menace of bonded labour." For the use of bonded workers and campaigners on their behalf, the book reproduces in full the text of the 1992 Bonded Labour System (Abolition) Act and the largely disregarded Rules of 1995, which should form the basis for eradicating the bonded system and rehabilitating its victims.

Bales, Kevin. *Disposable People: New Slavery in the Global Economy.* Berkeley: University of California Press, 1999. ISBN 0520217977 (HC), 0520224639 (PB).

This is an investigation of conditions in Mauritania, Brazil, Thailand, Pakistan, and India, revealing the tragic emergence of a "new slavery," one intricately linked to the global economy. Case studies present actual slaves, slaveholders, and public officials in historical, geographical, and cultural contexts. The author offers suggestions for combating the new slavery and provides examples of positive results from organizations such as Anti-Slavery International, the Pastoral Land Commission in Brazil, and the Human Rights Commission in Pakistan. Archbishop Desmond Tutu called this "a well-researched, scholarly, and deeply disturbing exposé of modern-day slavey with well-thought-out strategies for what to do to combat this scourge." (Also available in Spanish, Portuguese, German, Norwegian, and Italian.)

Black, Maggie. *Child Domestic Workers: A Handbook for Research and Action.* London: Anti-Slavery International, 1997. ISBN 00900918411.

A practical "how-to" guide, this book explores ways of finding out about the situation of children working as domestics and examines why children working as domestics deserve attention. It draws on the experiences and views of organizations and others working with child domestics in Asia, Africa, and Latin America. Published with assistance from the ILO's International Program for the Elimination of Child Labor. (Also available in French and Spanish.)

Cadet, Jean-Robert. *Restavec: From Haitian Slave Child to Middle-Class American, An Autobiography.* Austin: University of Texas Press, 1998. ISBN 0292712022.

In his book, Jean-Robert Cadet relates his life in moving, emotional narrative. As a slave-child to a wealthy mistress in Haiti, Cadet endured both physical and mental torture. From the age of four, his childhood ended, and his life became dictated by the whims of his master. As his story unfolds, the reader learns of Cadet's insatiable desire for knowledge and his determination to attend school. Despite Cadet's slave status, he is allowed to attend the Catholic mission schools, where he takes pride in his natural intelligence. Education carries Cadet throughout life—it is his salvation.

Eventually, Cadet is abandoned by his master, only to be reunited with her in America. At school, his abuse is soon found out by a kind schoolteacher, and Cadet is sent to live with foster parents. The young Cadet must now learn to cope with the demons of the past, and the descrimination of white America. As Cadet climbs through the ranks of the U.S. Army, becomes a successful businessman, marries, and begins to teach school, Cadet must still face racism and intolerance. The reader sees that though Cadet's lot has improved dramatically since his childhood, his struggle is not yet over. *Restavec* is a gripping tale of slavery, hardship, and determination.

Colchester, Marcus. *Slave and Enclave: The Political Ecology of Equatorial Africa.* London: World Rainforest Network, 1994. ISBN 9679998762.

The Equatorial Africa of this study—Gabon, the Congo, and the Central African Republic—has a long, sad history of slavery and the deprivations of foreign forest product extraction. For the forest communities of the region the slave wars, conquest, forced resettlement, and labor in extractive industries and the lumber camps has meant the undermining of their ways of life. Deprived of rights and marginal to national economies built upon oil, timber, coffee, and diamonds, these people still find themselves deprived of a political voice or control of their destinies. Leaked studies carried out for the World Bank and published here for the first time show how the foreign-dominated timber companies act with complete contempt for tentative resurgence of community authority and the reawakening of long-submerged indigenous traditions of equality and justice.

Cotton, Samuel. *Silent Terror: A Journey into Contemporary African Slavery.* New York: Writers and Readers, 1998. ISBN 0863162592.

This is the disturbing true account of a black American's journey into the horrors of modern-day slavery in Africa. Cotton's odyssey takes him from New York to Mauritania, where he comes face-to-face with the Arab Berbers' centuries-old practice of enslaving black Africans. The book recounts Cotton's month-long trip to Africa, where he conducted ethnographic research and created a film and audio record of contemporary African slavery under the Arabs of Mauritania. The book is also the story of an African-American's struggle to come to grips with the legacy of slavery and the brutal revelation that slavery continues to thrive in Africa today.

Genovese, Eugene D. *Roll Jordan, Roll: The World the Slaves Made.* New York: Vintage Books, 1976. ISBN 0394716523.

This classic book goes into great detail on the history of slavery in America. The hypocricy and cruelty of the slaveholder class is documented in painful detail. Genovese quotes extensively from court decisions, slaveholder correspondence, and accounts by former slaves and those who fought for their freedom. This is a good introduction to historical American slavery, and you are unlikely to find a more thoroughly documented account of America's most "peculiar" institution.

Gibson Wilson, Ellen. **Thomas Clarkson: A Biography.** York: William Sessions Limited, 1996. ISBN 185072184X.

A biography of a man often slighted in the historical record. His was the first large-scale human rights campaign in human history.

Gifford, Zerbanoo. *Thomas Clarkson and the Campaign against Slavery.* London: Anti-Slavery International, 1996. ISBN 0900918365.

Thomas Clarkson was the "moral steam engine" behind the campaign that led to the abolition of slavery in the British Empire. The story of his commitment and struggle and of the growing abolitionist movement with its setbacks and triumphs provides important lessons for today.

Grieder, William. *One World Ready or Not: The Manic Logic of Global Capitalism.* New York: Simon and Schuster, 1997. ISBN 0140266984.

Although not specifically about contemporary slavery, this is one of the best books to explain the transformations in the world economy that are making new slavery possible. It explores the dynamics of the third industrial revolution by describing a story of human struggle: of diverse peoples and nations faced with the same dangers imposed by unregulated global finance, labor, and competition. The resulting picture is bleak, but Grieder points the way toward solutions.

Hobbs, Sandy, Jim McKechnie, and Michael Lavalette. *Child Labor: A World History Companion.* Santa Barbara: ABC-CLIO, 1999. ISBN 0874369568.

A survey of working children from the Industrial Revolution to the present day, this new reference guide goes beyond the usual Third World confines. The authors analyze the problems and psychological and social development of child workers, then present an overview of child labor in specific countries and world regions. They also examine individuals and organizations devoted to improving the welfare of working children and discuss how various governments, private organizations, and courts have dealt with child labor. This reference contains accurate, up-to-date information on a host of subjects, and the alphabetical entries are cross-referenced by category.

Human Rights Watch. *A Modern Form of Slavery: Trafficking of Burmese Women and Girls into Brothels in Thailand.* New York: Human Rights Watch, 1993. ISBN 156432107X.

Based on in-depth interviews with Burmese trafficking victims, this book documents the violations of internationally recognized human rights committed against them. It also presents detailed

recommendations to the Thai and Burmese (Myanmar) governments and the international community for improving the protection of the thousands of women and girls who are trafficked
into Thai brothels each year and for ensuring the prosecution of
their abusers.

Human Rights Watch. *Pakistan: Contemporary Forms of Slavery.* New York: Human Rights Watch, 1995. ISBN 1564321541.

This book illustrates how throughout Pakistan, employers
forcibly extract labor from adults and children, restrict their freedom of movement, and deny them the right to negotiate the
terms of their employment. It blames the government of Pakistan
for these abuses, both by the direct involvement of the police and
through the state's failure to protect the rights of bonded laborers.

Human Rights Watch. *Rape for Profit: Trafficking of Nepali Girls
and Women to India's Brothels.* New York: Human Rights
Watch, 1995. ISBN 156432155X.

This book focuses on the trafficking of girls and women from
Nepal to brothels in Bombay, where they compose up to half of
the city's estimated 100,000 brothel workers.

Human Rights Watch. *The Small Hands of Slavery: Bonded
Child Labor in India.* New York: Human Rights Watch, 1996.
ISBN 156432172X.

Based on interviews with over one hundred children during a
two-month investigation in India, this report details their plight
in the silk, beedi (hand-rolled cigarettes), synthetic gems, silver,
leather, agricultural, and carpet industries.

Kielburger, Craig, with Kevin Major. *Free the Children: A Young
Man Fights against Child Labor and Proves that Children Can
Change the World.* New York: Harper Collins, 1998. ISBN
0060930659.

This is the dramatic story of one child's transformation from a
normal middle-class kid from the suburbs into an activist fighting against child labor on the world stage of international human
rights. Kielburger founded the organization Free the Children
with his schoolmates at the age of twelve. This book charts the
growing awareness and commitment of these young people and
the experiences that propelled them into the public eye as key
campaigners against child labor.

Kuklin, Susan. *Iqbal Masih and the Crusaders against Child Slavery.* New York: Henry Holt, 1998. ISBN 0805054596.

Here is the powerful story of Iqbal Masih's life and death (see his biography in Chapter 3) and of the movement that continues the struggle against child labor today. This book shows how we are all implicated in the global practice of child labor and how we can all work together to end it.

Lean-Lim, L. (ed). *The Sex Sector: The Economic and Social Bases of Prostitution in Southeast Asia.* Geneva: International Labor Organization, 1997. ISBN 9221095223.

This book focuses on the commercial sex sector and its institutional structures and connections with the national and international economies. It includes case studies of Indonesia, Malaysia, the Philippines, and Thailand, illustrating how vested economic interests and unequal relations betwen the sexes and between parents and children interact with considerations based on human rights, workers rights, morality, criminality, and health threats to influence the legal stance adopted by governments and social programs targetting the sex industry. A chapter specifically addresses child prostitution and why it should be treated as a serious problem.

Lee-Wright, Peter. *Child Slaves.* London: Earthscan Publications Ltd., 1990. ISBN 1853830445.

Based on research done with Anti-Slavery International for a BBC-TV documentary, this book reveals the extent of exploitation of child labor and services throughout the world. It shows how what is eaten, worn, and used every day in Western homes is all too often produced at the expense of poor children's welfare and freedom. It also covers the expansion of the child sex tourism industry as travel to developing countries increases. Includes case studies from India, Bangladesh, Malaysia, Brazil, Thailand, Portugal, Turkey, Philippines, Mexico, and the United States.

McCuen, Gary E. *Modern Slavery and the Global Economy.* Hudson, Wis.: Gary E. McCuen Publications, 1998. ISBN 086596145X.

Part of the *Ideas in Conflict* series, this book is a collection of short articles by experts that explore and sometimes debate the issues of: marginal workers and global slavery, slave labor and child labor, and economic growth and human rights. Blended with the articles are exercises helping the reader to develop reasoning skills, identify editorial bias, and interpret editorial imagery.

Meltzer, Milton. *Slavery: A World History.* New York: Da Capo Press, 1993. ISBN 0306805367.

This is a good introduction to the breadth of slavery's history from ancient times to the present day. It begins with the dawn of civilization and carries the story of slavery forward to the present day. This volume has many illustrations from many cultures and historical periods.

Plant, Roger. *Sugar and Modern Slavery: A Tale of Two Countries.* London: Zed Books, 1987. ISBN 0862325722.

Explores the link between the enslavement of Haitian workers and the Dominican sugar harvest. The sugar produced then flows into U.S. and European markets. Haitian workers are often enslaved in the Dominican Republic during the annual sugar harvest. Brutally used and paid nothing, they do backbreaking work in terrible conditions. Government and police complicity add to their burden.

Robertson, Adam, and Mishra Shishram. *Forced to Plough: Bonded Labor in Nepal's Agricultural Economy.* London: Anti-Slavery International and INSEC, 1997. ISBN 0900918373.

Investigates the situation of some of the most exploited groups of rural workers in Nepal and the conditions that have allowed systems of forced and bonded labor to develop and persist despite the official abolition of slavery in 1926. The book concludes with recommendations for government, trade unions, and development agencies and calls for the introduction of legislation banning bonded labor in Nepal.

Rodriguez, Junius P. *Chronology of World Slavery.* Santa Barbara: ABC-CLIO, 1999. ISBN 0874368847.

This volume traces the course of events, both great and small, that have defined the meaning of slavery throughout human history. Organized by geographic region and time period, it enables readers to gain a quick understanding of how long slavery has been part of human life and where it has occurred. It combines multiple chronologies, sidebars on specialized topics, primary source documents, and illustrations into a compelling portrayal of slavery from the dawn of civilization to the present.

Rodriguez, Junius P., ed. *The Historical Encyclopedia of World Slavery, Volumes I and II.* Santa Barbara: ABC-CLIO, 1997. ISBN 0874368855.

Documenting slavery on a global scale, this work is an invaluable resource for anyone wishing to gain an understanding of the history of slavery throughout the world. With illustrations and maps accompanying essays involving specific geographic locations, the encyclopedia delves into the practice of forced labor in successive centuries. Seven hundred topics of world slavery are presented in short but comprehensive entries that are extensively cross-referenced with bibliographical citations for further research.

Ruf, Urs Peter. **Ending Slavery: Hierarchy, Dependency and Gender in Central Mauritania.** Bielefeld, Germany: Transcript Verlag, 1999. ISBN 3933127491.

Offers insights into the "how" of practices of slavery that persist in parts of Mauritania up to the present day. It brings to light the gendered structures of Moorish slavery and examines their impact on strategies and tactics designed to bring this institution to an end. Underlying this study is empirical data gathered during two periods of field research in rural central Mauritania.

Saunders, Kate. *Eighteen Layers of Hell: Stories from the Chinese Gulag* (Foreword by Harry Wu). New York: Cassell Global Issues, 1996. ISBN 0304332976.

The author shows that millions of people still suffer in *laogai*— forced labor camps—in the People's Republic of China today, and that Western nations participate in slave labor through trading goods produced in the laogai. Among those telling their stories is Harry Wu, a veteran of the laogai who attracted worldwide attention in 1995 when he was arrested by the Chinese authorities while attempting to gather more evidence for his campaign against the laogai.

Sawyer, Roger. *Slavery in the Twentieth Century.* London and New York: Routledge and Kegan Paul, 1986. ISBN 0710204752.

Though now somewhat dated, this is a good review of the state of slavery in the world in the years before the end of the Cold War. Reviews the situation of slavery around the world, looking also at apartheid in South Africa and the case of prison labor in the Soviet Union.

Smith, Paul J., ed. *Human Smuggling: Chinese Migrant Trafficking and the Challenge to America's Immigration Tradition* (**Significant Issues Series**). Washington, D.C.: Center for Strategic and International Studies, 1997. ISBN 0892062916.

Recent cases of the smuggling of Chinese into the United States have brought this issue very much to the fore. Shipping containers holding trafficked Chinese landed in Seattle, Washington, and Vancouver, Canada, in 1999. The dramatic increase in human smuggling has in large part been driven by the significant increase in Chinese citizens being smuggled around the world.

Stearman, Kaye. *Slavery Today* (**Talking Points Series**). Austin, Tex.: Steck-Vaughn, 2000. ISBN 0817253203.

Aimed at young adults, the Talking Points Series looks at some of the most important and controversial current issues. The cause and effects of these subjects are investigated within a global context, with extensive use of illustrations and other evidence. This book highlights the fact that slavery is not a thing of the past and investigates the different circumstances that allow the practice to survive. This is one of the best and easiest-to-use books about contemporary slavery for young people.

Stowe, Harriett Beecher. *Uncle Tom's Cabin.* New York: Harper-Collins (paper), 1987. ISBN 0060806184.

An international bestseller that sold more than 300,000 copies when it first appeared in 1852, *Uncle Tom's Cabin* was dismissed by some as abolitionist propaganda, yet Leo Tolstoy deemed it a great work of literature. Although "Uncle Tom" has become a pejorative term for a subservient black, the Uncle Tom in the book is a man who, under the most inhumane of circumstances, never loses his human dignity. It is an inspiring book that still has the power to give insights into the mindsets of slavery.

Sutton, Alison. *Slavery in Brazil: A Link in the Chain of Modernization.* London: Anti-Slavery International, 1994. ISBN 0900918322.

This is a gripping firsthand account of the spread of slavery across Brazilian society based on six months of field research in Amazonia. It includes accounts of debt bondage in forest clearance, charcoal burning, rubber tapping, and mining in the Amazon region, where more than 70 percent of cases denounced in the previous twenty years had occurred and where all thirteen of the indigenous tribes who have been enslaved at one time or another originate. Concludes with recommendations for action.

Taylor, Yuval, ed. *I Was Born a Slave: An Anthology of Classic Slave Narratives* (2 vols., 1770–1849 and 1849–1866). London: Payback Press, 1999. ISBN 0862419034.

This collection includes narratives from James Albert Gronniosaw, Olaudah Equiano (Gustavus Vassa), William Grimes, Nat Turner, Charles Ball, Moses Roper, Frederick Douglass, Lewis and Milton Clark, William Wells Brown, and Josiah Henson.

Thomas, Hugh. *The Slave Trade: The History of the Atlantic Slave Trade 1440–1870.* London: Macmillan, 1998. ISBN 0333731476.

This book views New World slavery in its international context. The Portuguese and Spanish who first came to Africa arrived in search of gold. They found it, but they also found social systems in which the ransom, buying, and selling of human beings had long been established. These systems had existed in European antiquity, and now they were revived when, shortly after making contact with Africa, the European nations began to establish colonies on the other side of the Atlantic; the horrible traffic continued well into the nineteenth century. Thomas mines vast archives and previously published histories to make his case. This is one of the best and clearest books about the Atlantic slave trade.

United Nations. *Human Rights: A Compilation of International Instruments.* New York and Geneva: United Nations, 1994. ISBN 9211540984.

This is a handy reference book for anyone interested in the international conventions and law on human rights. It includes all the major United Nations conventions that concern human rights.

Verney, Peter. *Slavery in Sudan.* London: *Sudan Update* and Anti-Slavery International, 1997. ISBN 090091839X.

This report gives an outline of the history of slavery in Sudan and its reemergence in the late twentieth century. Peter Verney, editor of *Sudan Update*, puts the slavery issue into context and examines the pitfalls of attributing responsibility solely to the present Sudanese government. He underlines the importance of racial prejudice in Sudan's conflict.

Williams, Phil, ed. *Illegal Immigration and Commercial Sex: The New Slave Trade.* Portland, Ore.: Frank Cass, 1999. ISBN 071464384X.

This volume examines the dynamics of the sex slave trade in both Europe and Asia, identifies the role of organized crime, and considers the countermeasures that governments and law enforcement agencies must take to combat this global problem.

Wu, Harry, and Wakeman, Carolyn. *Bitter Winds: A Memoir of My Years in China's Gulag.* New York: John Wiley and Sons, 1993. ISBN 0471556459.

This is the autobiographical account of Harry Wu—arrested as a student and never formally charged or tried—who spent nineteen years in Chinese prison labor camps and returned twice in disguise to document continuing human rights abuses by the Chinese authorities. He succeeded in capturing on film for the first time footage of life in the camps. Forced to work, starved, and tortured, he watched other prisoners buried in unmarked graves as he was reduced from being a member of the elite intelligensia to an anonymous skeleton.

Briefings and Reports

Anti-Slavery International. *Children in Bondage—Slaves of the Subcontinent.* London: Anti-Slavery International, 1994. ISBN 0900918276.

A useful overview of the variety of slavery to which indigenous peoples are still subjected in the 1990s, from the sexual exploitation of women and children in Southeast Asia to debt bondage and serfdom in South America. The report shows how the history of the struggle of the 350 million surviving indigenous peoples for the recognition of their rights is intimately connected to the phenomenon of slavery and how repercussions of slavery are particularly severe for indigenous people.

Anti-Slavery International. *Debt Bondage.* London: Anti-Slavery International, 1998. ISBN 0900918462.

A provocative and accessible report that provides an overview of debt bondage around the world. Excellent for use with young people; gives case histories, explanations, and recommendations.

Bequele, A., and W. E. Myers. *First Things First in Child Labor: Eliminating Work Detrimental to Children.* Geneva: ILO, 1995. ISBN 922109197X.

Uses numerous case studies to discuss the difficulties in defining work that is hazardous to children and the various preventative approaches that have been used.

Black, Maggie. *In the Twilight Zone: Child Workers in the Hotel, Tourism and Catering Industry.* Geneva: ILO, 1995. ISBN 9221091945.

Children around the world are used and abused in the tourism industry, but this little-studied group of child laborers and their situations are not well known.

Bureau of International Labor Affairs, U.S. Department of Labor. *By the Sweat and Toil of Children: The Use of Child Labor in American Imports—A Report to the Committees on Appropriations, United States Congress* (Vols. 1 and 2). Washington, D.C.: Government Printing Office, 1994.

The U.S. government conducted this review to identify any foreign industry and their host country using child labor in the export of manufactured products from industry or mining to the United States. It includes regional overviews and an overview of the "abolish or regulate" debate. Common kinds of child labor including bonded labor are included. Also provides country profiles.

Bureau of International Labor Affairs, U.S. Department of Labor. *The Apparel Industry and Codes of Conduct: A Solution to the International Child Labor Problem* (Vols. 3 and 4). Washington, D.C.: Government Printing Office, 1996.

Examines nine consumer label programs addressing child labor in the hand-knotted carpet, leather footwear, soccer ball, and tea industries together with other efforts by businesses to develop and implement policies prohibiting child labor. An appendix includes the Adidas, Nike, and Reebok codes of conduct.

Bureau of International Labor Affairs, U.S. Department of Labor. *By the Sweat and Toil of Children: Efforts to Eliminate Child Labor* (Vol. 5). Washington, D.C.: Government Printing Office, 1998.

Reviews the child labor situation in sixteen countries where child labor has been identified as a problem and the levels and types of action being undertaken to reduce child exploitation in those countries.

Cross, Peter. *Kashmiri Carpet Children: Exploited Village Weavers.* London: Anti-Slavery International, 1996. ISBN 0900918357.

Discusses the enslavement of children in the lucrative "Persian" carpet industry.

Effah, Josephine. *Modernized Slavery—Child Trade in Nigeria.* Nigeria: Constitutional Rights Project, 1996. ISBN 97829440804.

Documents the growing incidence of trafficking in young children sold into domestic, sexual, and economic slavery in Nigeria. Includes analysis of the political economy of Nigeria, the smuggling, kidnapping, and recruitment process, role of parents and middlemen, domestic slavery, and forced prostitution. Published with support from the Ford Foundation.

Forcese, Craig. *Commerce with Conscience? Human Rights and Corporate Codes of Conduct, No. 1.,* and *Putting Conscience into Commerce—Strategies for Making Human Rights Business as Usual, No. 2.* Montreal: International Center for Human Rights and Democratic Development, 1997. ISBN 2922084078.

This two-part series presents the results of a survey of Canada's largest corporations and their international operations. The survey showed that only one in seven had codes of conduct with minimal human rights standards, and it examines the effectiveness of those that do exist. The second part provides an overview of the kinds of campaigns that work to make corporations more sensitive to human rights abuses in their international operations—strategies for consumers, shareholders, human rights activists, and businesses campaigning for more accountable human rights policies from governments and companies.

International Labor Organization. *Child Labor—Targeting the Intolerable, Report 6 (1).* International Labor Conference 86th session, 1996. Geneva: ILO, 1998. ISBN 9221103285.

Report submitted to 174 ILO member countries as part of the ILO's campaign against child labor. It surveys international and national law and practice highlighting effective action through new international standards and includes sections on debt bondage, prostitution, and hazardous occupations. For ILO publications in the

United States, Canada, and Puerto Rico contact Ms. Karen A. Lee, International Labor Office, 1828 L Street NW, Washington, D.C., 20036; phone (202) 653–7652; fax (202) 653–7687; e-mail burrylee@ilo.org. (Also published in Arabic, Chinese, French, German, Russian, and Spanish.)

O'Grady, Ron. *The Rape of the Innocent.* London: ECPAT, 1994. ISBN 0959797122.

From the coordinator of ECPAT, an international campaign to end child prostitution, this booklet focuses on children in Asia who are trapped in the slavery of prostitution. Covers trafficking across borders, sex tourism, pornographers, AIDS, and the need for political change and law enforcement. Includes case studies, statistics, and maps outlining the scale and nature of the problem.

Skrobanek, Siriporn. *Human Capital—International Migration and Traffic in Women.* London: CIIR, 1996. ISBN 18252871628.

This report shows how the rights of migrant women in Asia are violated. It discusses the definition of trafficking in international conventions and describes the legal and illegal ways in which women are brought from Thailand to work in other countries. Concludes with recommendations for international action to prevent trafficking. The author is coordinator of the Global Alliance Against Traffic in Women.

Newsletters and Periodicals

Anti-Slavery Reporter
Anti-Slavery International
1755 Massachusetts Avenue NW, Suite 312
Washington, DC 20036-2102
Annual membership/subscription price: $50

A quarterly newsletter free to members of Anti-Slavery International. Covers ongoing campaigns, urgent actions, news from around the world of slavery, child labor, and government action and inaction. Keeps you up-to-date on the latest issues facing abolitionists and organizations.

The New Slavery (**Special Issue of** *Index on Censorship*)
Index on Censorship is a magazine devoted to supporting free journalism and opposing the suppression of the press around the world. For almost thirty years it has campaigned for imprisoned

writers, artists, dramatists, and journalists and published works that have been censored in other parts of the world. Its January 2000 issue was a special issue on new slavery, with contributions from Brian Edwards, Harry Wu, Ali Hassan, and Kevin Bales. Copies of the special issue can be ordered from the magazine's website, www.indexoncensorship.org.

World of Work
International Labor Organization
Attn.: Ms. Karen A. Lee
1828 L Street N.W.
Washington, DC 20036
Phone: (202) 653-7652
Fax: (202) 653-7687
E-mail: burrylee@ilo.org
Website: www.ilo.org

The Bureau of Public Information of the International Labor Organization provides full text (Adobe Acrobat—.pdf—format only) of this magazine at the ILO website. Recent issues contain articles about slavery and forced labor; the global unemployment crisis; child labor; the textile, footwear, and clothing industries; and work stress, among other topics. *World of Work* is a quarterly magazine that does not necessarily reflect the views of the ILO. Note that this is a graphically rich magazine, and the files are correspondingly large. It can be ordered from the ILO or downloaded from the ILO website. Back issues are also stored on the website and can be read or downloaded there.

7

Selected Nonprint Resources

Very often the pioneers that open up a new area of human rights are journalists and filmmakers. That has certainly been the case with new slavery. With so much of the public ignorant of the extent of slavery, television plays an important role in raising awareness. Most of the films and videos listed below were not made by the big Hollywood studios or the main TV networks, but they are strong and sometimes shocking to see. One of the best introductions to new slavery is the documentary *Slavery*, made by British filmmakers Brian Woods and Kate Blewitt and available from the offices of Anti-Slavery International. You will also find magazines and information here that can be downloaded directly from the Internet. If you are interested in learning more about current slavery issues, it is a good idea to keep an eye on current TV listings; news programs are carrying more and more reports on slavery or human trafficking.

Audiotapes

Cause to Communicate
Length: 90 minutes
Cost: $21
Date: 1998
Distributor: Anti-Slavery International
1755 Massachusetts Avenue NW, Suite 312
Washington, D.C., 20036-2102 USA
Phone: (202) 232-3317
E-mail: info@stopslavery.org

Cause to Communicate is an audiocassette and teaching pack on slavery and human rights for English-language teachers and adult learners. It provides resources and skills practice for general English classes and for people learning English as a second or foreign language at the upper-intermediate level. Issues covered include the concept of human rights, the meaning of slavery, cases of forced labor, a look at campaigners past and present, problems for indigenous peoples, children working in the United Kingdom and elsewhere, bonded labor, and views on early and servile marriage.

CD-ROMS

ILOLEX 1999. Windows, ISBN 9220106043. New customers (first-time buyers): US $200; multi-user license: 50 percent surcharge. Order from www.ilo.org.

Since its creation, the International Labor Organization has developed an extensive body of texts in the field of international labor law. However, these texts are contained in numerous publications that are not easily accessible. This has constituted a serious barrier to their dissemination to ILO constituents and other interested institutions, for which the provisions adopted by the ILO on a particular subject and their application around the world would otherwise provide valuable guidance. ILOLEX is a full-text trilingual database (English/French/Spanish) on international labor standards with sophisticated search-and-retrieval software. A single CD-ROM contains all three language versions. Each language version includes:

- the ILO Constitution;
- all the ILO conventions and recommendations;
- the Reports of the Committee on Freedom of Association, from 1985;
- the Comments of the Committee of Experts on the Application of Conventions and Recommendations, from 1987;
- the Annual Report of the Conference Committee on the Application of Standards, from 1987;
- the Reports of Committees and Commissions established under Articles 24 and 26 of the ILO Constitution to examine representations and complaints, from 1985; and
- ratification lists by convention and by country.

In sum, ILOLEX contains about 70,000 full-text documents divided into several chapters. It is possible to search the whole database by subject classification, country, particular convention, or free text query using words or expressions.

Key Indicators of the Labor Market 1999 (KILM). CD-ROM only (single user), US $99.50; ISBN 9221108341; print and CD-ROM set, US $180; ISBN 9221117057. Order from www.ilo.org.

A valuable, wide-ranging reference tool, *Key Indicators of the Labor Market (KILM)* provides the general reader, as well as the expert, with concise explanations and analysis of the data on the world's labor markets, including world and regional estimates. Harvesting vast information from international data repositories as well as regional and national statistical sources, this comprehensive reference offers data on a broad range of countries and issues such as labor force, employment, unemployment, underemployment, educational attainment of the workforce, and more for the years 1980 and 1990 and all available subsequent years. *KILM* is available in two formats—standard print version and CD-ROM. The CD-ROM's interactive design allows users to customize their searches by any combination of indicator, country, year, data inputs, and more and makes searching for relevant information quick and simple.

The World Guide 1999/2000. CD-ROM or book can be ordered at the Third World Institute website at www.guiadelmundo.org.uy or through www.amazon.com. Orders by post can be made to:

Books on Wings
973 Valencia Street
San Francisco, CA 94110
Phone: (415) 285-1145
Fax: (415) 285-3298

The World Guide is an up-to-date reference opus on the past and present of human societies, offering text, maps, graphics, images, music, and statistics on all the nations of the planet. It provides analysis of main international issues from the human rights, social, and environmental angles. Since 1997 it has been published on the Internet along with *The Guide Weekly,* a weekly update service.

The World Guide is divided into two large sections: The first provides analysis of major international problems and tendencies, and the second offers current information on 217 nations of the world, including some still fighting for their independence, and all the current members of the United Nations.

The first section pursues the problems of population, children, food, health, education, women, work, communications, refugees, indigenous people, debt, aid, trade, arms, transnationals, climate change, international organizations, and so on. Within each subject area, a "themes" subsection is renewed periodically according to how issues have evolved over the two-year period. The 1999/2000 issue carries an overview of the twentieth century on the basis of five thematic areas: the Earth and its peoples, society, science and technology, the economy, and international relations.

In the second section, the main text brings together the history of the country since the times of the first peoples, an element corrected and extended in each edition, and the most relevant events of the last two years. The profile and statistics, giving the latest available figures, complete the update.

The book contains more than 750,000 words, including text and statistical data; more than 250 maps of the countries, with their corresponding regional location; some 650 charts; and 10,000 references. *The World Guide* is researched and published in Montevideo, Uruguay, by the Third World Institute (ITeM) in conjunction with an extensive worldwide network of persons and civil organizations.

The new CD-ROM, which appears with the 1999/2000 edition, incorporates multimedia elements. The text, statistics, and maps of the printed version are accompanied by the flags, national anthems, and a selection of photographs of all the countries on the planet. This version also includes the Amnesty International and Social Watch annual reports. All the data, charts, photographs, maps, and texts can be printed or downloaded to your computer.

Exhibits

The Changing Face of Slavery
Anti-Slavery International
1755 Massachusetts Avenue NW, Suite 312
Washington, DC 20036-2102
USA
Phone: (202) 232-3317
E-mail: antislavery@antislavery.org

Designed to appeal to young people, this colorful and innovative twenty-panel exhibition is available in both poster and notebook sizes. This exhibition compliments the teaching pack of the same title, exploring and developing the issues of the transatlantic slave trade and child labor at the time of the Industrial Revolution and today. This is free to rent, but shipping will be charged at cost.

Pamphlets, Photographs and Digital Images, Posters, and Press Kits

The International Labor Organization is the part of the United Nations that is directly concerned with slavery, forced labor, child labor, and trafficking. It produces several kinds of materials in many different languages.

Pamphlets

The ILO provides leaflets that explain its work and deal with subjects like child labor and slavery. These can be ordered from the ILO or printed directly from its website at www.ilo.org. Leaflets include "The ILO: Its Origins and How It Works" and "What We Do: Social Justice and Child Labor."

Photographs and Digital Images

The ILO has photographers around the world documenting the problems of child labor, forced labor, and other work-related issues. Stored on its website are thousands of photographs that can be searched and reproduced. The ILO allows anyone to copy and use these photographs as long as the source is credited. A search on the words "forced labor," for example, will generate ten very good pictures.

Historical and contemporary images are now available from Anti-Slavery International in digital form. Where possible, Anti-Slavery will provide the images at a resolution and format to suit individual needs. These are normally sent as e-mail attachments. Fees to reproduction rights are decided on a sliding scale, starting from $65.00; a minimum search fee may be levied on complex image requests. Orders can be made to:

Anti-Slavery International
1755 Massachusetts Avenue NW, Suite 312
Washington, DC 20036-2102 USA
Phone: (202) 232-3317
E-mail: info@stopslavery.org

Posters

New posters focusing on major areas of ILO activities are now available. Employers' and workers' organizations, trade unions, and other organizations active in the promotion of fundamental human rights in the workplace may receive limited quantities (posters are printed in English, French, Spanish, German, Russian, and Arabic). One poster in the series is concerned with slavery. For information, call the Washington, D.C., ILO office, (202) 653-7652.

Press Kits

When the International Labor Organization does a large-scale investigation or publishes an international report on a subject, it also provides press kits that break down the information into clear and easily used sections. A good example is the 1996 press kit *Stop! Child Labor,* which deals extensively with child slavery as well as child labor more generally and consists of three sections: "Child Labor Today: Facts and Figures," "Child Labor: Action Needed at the National Level," and "International Action: Standards Need Reinforcing." The press kits are available in printed form or can be downloaded or printed directly from the ILO's website, www.ilo.org.

Other Materials

The director general of the ILO makes regular reports to the United Nations. These reports are also available from the ILO office or from its website. Researchers and officers of the ILO also regularly make speeches to conferences around the world. These speeches are usually available in English, French, and Spanish from the website (www.ilo.org) and are cataloged by subject matter.

In the United States, Canada, and Puerto Rico please contact:

Ms. Karen A. Lee
International Labor Office
1828 L Street NW
Washington, DC 20036
Phone: (202) 653-7652
Fax: (202) 653-7687
E-mail: burrylee@ilo.org

Videotapes

Agenda 21

Length:	13 episodes of 26 minutes each
Cost:	Call or e-mail for details
Date:	1994
Distributor:	TVE
	Prince Albert Road
	London NW1 4RZ UK
	Phone: [44] (207) 586-5526
	Fax: [44] (207) 586-4866
	E-mail: tve-uk@tve.org.uk

As the successor to WTN's best-selling Earthfile series, *Agenda 21* offers viewers a popular treatment of topical environment and development issues. The series takes its name from Agenda 21, the agreement signed by over 180 world leaders at the historic Rio Earth Summit in 1992, setting out a blueprint for sustainable development in the twenty-first century. Using this as a framework to explore what sustainable development means in practice, *Agenda 21*'s television magazine format accommodates a mix of topics within each episode and includes episodes such as slave labor in Burma (Myanmar).

The Amahs of Hong Kong

Length:	11 minutes
Cost:	Purchase $95, rental $25 (reduced rates for some groups)
Date:	1995
Distributor:	Bullfrog Films
	P.O. Box 149
	Oley, PA 19547
	USA
	Phone: (610) 779-8226
	Fax: (610) 370-1978

This film explores the lives of Philippina maids, called *amahs*, in Hong Kong. Forced by mass poverty and continuing economic crisis to leave their families and homeland behind, the amahs send 70–85 percent of their earnings back to the Philippines. The women often suffer horrific abuse from their employers, and the sacrifices they make are enormous, but so are the potential rewards: money to educate their children and to improve their own living when retired.

Bonded Labor Campaign
Length: 8 minutes
Cost: $10.00
Date: 1999
Distributor: Anti-Slavery International
1755 Massachusetts Avenue NW, Suite 312
Washington, DC 20036-2102 USA
Phone: (202) 232-3317
E-mail: info@stopslavery.org

This video highlights the work of Anti-Slavery Award winners and human rights activists Vivek and Vidyullata Pandit and the plight of those held in debt bondage.

The Changing Face of Slavery
Length: 30 minutes (plus 60-page booklet)
Cost: $30.00
Date: 1997
Distributor: Anti-Slavery International
1755 Massachusetts Avenue NW, Suite 312
Washington, DC 20036-2102 USA
Phone: (202) 232-3317
E-mail: info@stopslavery.org

This is a well-researched video and teaching pack that focuses on slavery past and present for the 11- to 14-year-old age group. Part one concentrates on the transatlantic slave trade and encourages young people to look at why the trade began and its importance for the growth of wealth in Britain. Part two links the growth of that wealth to the Industrial Revolution and the employment of young children. Part three brings the historical roots and contemporary issues concerning child labor together.

Children's News 1
Length: 26 minutes
Cost: Call or e-mail for details
Date: 1994
Distributor: TVE
Prince Albert Road
London NW1 4RZ UK
Phone: [44] (207) 586-5526
Fax: [44] (207) 586-4866
E-mail: tve-uk@tve.org.uk

This program looks at how the world's governments are responding to UNICEF's call to ratify and implement the Convention on the Rights of the Child. Presented as a "video newspaper," it charts the progress of global ratification since 1990 and focuses on three countries that are taking solid steps to implement the convention: The first is Bolivia, where the government, supported by UNICEF, is undertaking a national drive against infant mortality (one of the highest rates in the world). This is followed by Norway, where the world's first "child ombudsman" speaks in parliament on behalf of children and campaigns for their rights. The focus next shifts to Thailand, where the government and UNICEF are funding projects to provide young girls with skills and self-confidence through the Daughters Education Program to prevent the exploitation of children, particularly through sex tourism. The program ends with a call for global ratification and implementation of the Convention on the Rights of the Child.

Daughters of Africa: Senegal
Length:	15 minutes
Cost:	Call or e-mail for details
Date:	1999
Distributor:	TVE
	Prince Albert Road
	London NW1 4RZ
	UK
	Phone: [44] (207) 586-5526
	Fax: [44] (207) 586-4866
	E-mail: tve-uk@tve.org.uk

Three quarters of Senegal's children don't attend school. Of these, over 60 percent are girls. Child labor is common, and girls as young as nine work as illiterate, domestic servants in the capital city, Dakar. But with support from UNICEF, Tostan—a U.S. NGO—has developed an informal basic education program to provide literacy classes to rural women. Tostan also tries to persuade mothers to attend school with their daughters so they may acquire the basic knowledge that will help them improve their living conditions—and abandon traditional harmful practices like female genital mutilation.

The Face of Decent Work
Length:	18 minutes
Cost:	$12.95
Date:	1996

Distributor: International Labor Organization
In the United States, Canada, and Puerto Rico
contact:
Ms. Karen A. Lee
International Labor Office
1828 L Street NW
Washington, DC 20036
USA
Phone: (202) 653-7652
Fax: (202) 653-7687
E-mail: burrylee@ilo.org
Website: www.ilo.org

This is a riveting expose of the world's most deadly professions
and workplace hazards. By spotlighting mining, agricultural, factory work, and other professions, the video shows how primitive
forms of labor have remained unchanged in their methods for
nearly a thousand years. It shows the victims of the pressure to
produce in an increasingly competitive and global economy—
from the world's deepest mine in India, where men still extract
coal by hand; to the charcoal fields of Brazil, where families are
enslaved in a hellish landscape of smoldering ovens; to the chemical factories of Africa, where innocent children are scarred for
life by the fallout of industrial disaster. In their own words and
voices, the men, women, and children who endure the most intolerable working conditions on earth tell their stories. Available
in English, French, and Spanish.

Going Home Guinea
Length: 31 minutes
Cost: Purchase $150, rental $45 (reduced rates for some
groups)
Date: 1999
Distributor: Bullfrog Films
P.O. Box 149
Oley, PA 19547
USA
Phone: (610) 779-8226
Fax: (610) 370-1978

Mohammed is just ten years old. For most of 1997 he was forced
to act as a young fighter with rebel forces in the jungles of Sierra
Leone. His duties included carrying heavy equipment, acting as
a personal servant to other soldiers, and torturing and disciplin-

ing any of the other child soldiers who stepped out of line. Eventually he escaped to Guinea, where he was one of thousands lining up to register at the Gueckedou refugee camp. In 1997 Guinea was host to an estimated 430,000 refugees: 190,000 Sierra Leoneans and 240,000 Liberians who had escaped the eight-year civil war there. This film evaluates the success of the Guinean government and the UN High Commission for Refugees (UNHCR) in protecting the rights pledged this huge African refugee population under the OAU Convention.

Haiti's Cinderellas: "They Call Me Dog"
Length:	24 minutes
Cost:	Call or e-mail for details
Date:	1994
Distributor:	TVE
	Prince Albert Road
	London NW1 4RZ
	UK
	Phone: [44] (207) 586-5526
	Fax: [44] (207) 586-4866
	E-mail: tve-uk@tve.org.uk

This Danish coproduction focuses on Haiti's population of children from age five to fifteen—three quarters of them girls—who work as domestics in middle-class homes. Forced into unpaid servitude, the majority cannot read or write. Exploring UNICEF's work with such forgotten children, the film shows how—in spite of their bondage—the children find ways to change their lives. Available in English, Spanish, and French.

I Am a Child
Length:	52 minutes
Cost:	$40.50
Date:	1996
Distributor:	International Labor Organization
	In the United States, Canada, and Puerto Rico contact:
	Ms. Karen A. Lee
	International Labor Office
	1828 L Street NW
	Washington, DC 20036
	Phone: (202) 653-7652
	Fax: (202) 653-7687

E-mail: burrylee@ilo.org
Website: www.ilo.org

Neither a catalogue of horrors nor a fairy tale, *I Am a Child* is a fable of despair and hope. Through compelling images and moving personal stories, the viewer learns about children working in the fields and plantations of Kenya and the streets and workshops of Brazil. They are the innocent victims of poverty and exploitation. To rescue them, to return their childhood to them, is the moral imperative for every humane society. This video is intended as a contribution to that cause. Available in English, French, German, Portugese, and Spanish.

Inside Burma, Land of Fear

Length: 51 minutes (2 parts for classrooms: 33 min. and 17 min.)

Cost: Purchase $250, rental $85 (reduced rates for some groups)

Date: 1997

Distributor: Bullfrog Films
P.O. Box 149
Oley, PA 19547
USA
Phone: (610) 779-8226
Fax: (610) 370-1978

Inside Burma exposes the history and brutality of one of the world's most repressive regimes. Award-winning filmmakers John Pilger and David Munro go undercover to expose how the former British colony is ruled by a harsh, bloody, and uncompromising military regime. More than a million people have been forced from their homes and untold thousands killed, tortured, and subjected to slavery.

Nobel Peace Prize winner Aung San Suu Kyi, daughter of the assassinated independence leader Aung San, spent six years under house arrest. In 1990 her party, the National League for Democracy, won 82 percent of the parliamentary seats. The generals, shocked by an election result they never expected, threw two hundred of the newly elected MPs into prison. Suu Kyi's party has never been allowed to take elected office. She warns in the video that far from liberalizing life in Burma, foreign investment and tourism can further entrench the military regime.

**It Takes a Child: Craig Kielburger's Story—
A Journey into Child Labor**

Length: 56 minutes (2 parts for classrooms, 28 min. each)
Cost: Purchase $250, rental $85 (reduced rates for some groups)
Date: 1998
Distributor: Bullfrog Films
P.O. Box 149
Oley, PA 19547
USA
Phone: (610) 779-8226
Fax: (610) 370-1978

This is the video story of Craig Kielburger (see Chapter 3), who was twelve years old when child labor activist Iqbal Massih was killed in Pakistan. A seven-week trip to South Asia made shortly after turned him into a passionate, articulate, and effective advocate on behalf of child laborers everywhere. He started a child-run organization called Free the Children, which now has ten thousand members worldwide. It directs lobbying and petition efforts at governments and big business and has raised over $150,000 to buy children out of bondage and create a school for them, while raising world awareness.

Jessica: A Saudi Slave

Length: 41 minutes
Cost: Call or e-mail for details
Date: 1996
Distributor: TVE
Prince Albert Road
London NW1 4RZ
UK
Phone: [44] (207) 586-5526
Fax: [44] (207) 586-4866
E-mail: tve-uk@tve.org.uk

"Saudi nationals believe that if they have hired a Filipino worker, they have bought the whole life of that worker," comments Mustafa, responsible for protecting the rights of Filipino "guest" workers in Saudi Arabia. Jessica Sumanga was just one of two thousand Filipinos who leave their country every day to work abroad. Her youngest daughter was in need of a heart operation, and so in desperation for money, Jessica left her family two years ago to work in Saudi Arabia. Bruno Sorrentino's horrifying film exposes Jessica's traumatic plight as she runs away from her first employer, who has not only failed to pay her and abused her but has also taken her passport. For the next two years Jessica is passed from household to household, working as an unpaid maid—she is fundamentally a modern slave. Eventually, she has to turn to illegal means to escape her desperate situation. Winner, Best Television Feature Documentary, Asian TV Film Media Academy Awards (1996); Justice Award, One World Broadcasting Trust Awards (1996, UK); and Bronze Plaque, Columbus International Film Festival.

Life on the Line
Length: 38 minutes
Cost: Call or e-mail for details
Date: 1995
Distributor: TVE
Prince Albert Road
London NW1 4RZ
UK
Phone: [44] (207) 586-5526
Fax: [44] (207) 586-4866
E-mail: tve-uk@tve.org.uk

In 1988 troops from SLORC—the Burmese military regime's notorious State Law and Order Restoration Council—brutally suppressed student demonstrations for democracy in Rangoon (Yangon). In protest, Western governments cut off all aid. Since then Burma's military ruler, General Ne Win, has been courting the West again, seeking finance for new infrastructure and tourist development in the country. Director Damien Lewis and anthropologist Tom Sheahan spent eight months in Burma (Myanmar) investigating how this is affecting ordinary Burmese citizens. Traveling through the countryside, they filmed evidence that Ne Win's government has been forcibly clearing whole villages, raking the houses with machine guns and rounding up the inhabitants to work—in chain-gangs—on clearing jungle and building roads for a new pipeline carrying gas from the coast to Rangoon.

No Holidays for Us
Length: 26 minutes
Cost: Call or e-mail for details
Date: 1997
Distributor: TVE
Prince Albert Road

London NW1 4RZ UK
Phone: [44] (207) 586-5526
Fax: [44] (207) 586-4866
E-mail: tve-uk@tve.org.uk

Statistics don't account for the millions of children who live invisible lives as unregistered laborers—their special needs unseen and unmet. But in Bangladesh, Haiti, and India new organizations are investigating their problems, as shown in this video.

Our News, Our Views

Length: 30 minutes
Cost: $30.00
Date: 1999
Distributor: Anti-Slavery International
               1755 Massachusetts Avenue NW, Suite 312
               Washington, DC 20036-2102
               USA
               Phone: (202) 232-3317
               E-mail: info@stopslavery.org

This video pack examines children's rights, child labor, and the media and is made up of eight news reports written, produced, and presented by groups of young people. Designed for 14- to 18-year-olds, the activities encourage individuals to develop and express their own ideas.

Out of Sight, Out of Mind

Length: 15 minutes
Cost: $15.00
Date: 1999
Distributor: Anti-Slavery International
               1755 Massachusetts Avenue NW, Suite 312
               Washington, DC 20036-2102
               USA
               Phone: (202) 232-3317
               E-mail: info@stopslavery.org

An estimated one million girls under age eighteen work as maids in the Philippines for little or no pay and unlimited hours. Produced with local NGO Visayan Forum, this campaign video was given extensive airing on Philippine television and was also shown in the U.S. Congress. This exposure added to Visayan Forum's work on this issue and has resulted in a new law being proposed to protect child domestic workers.

The Price of Progress

Length: 54 minutes
Cost: Purchase $250, rental $75 (reduced rates for some groups)
Date: 1989
Distributor: Bullfrog Films
P.O. Box 149
Oley, PA 19547
USA
Phone: (610) 779-8226
Fax: (610) 370-1978

This classic film investigates three huge resettlement schemes in India, Indonesia, and Brazil—all sponsored by the World Bank, the world's largest lending institution. Some $30 billion in grants and loans are provided each year by development banks and other institutions to developing countries, frequently for mega projects that involve uprooting indigenous peoples. Using the World Bank's own documents, the film analyzes the social, environmental, and economic costs of some of the bank's lending policies. As one person says, "Next to killing them, the worst thing you can do to a people is to force them to move."

Rights and Wrongs

Length: 3 episodes of 26 minutes each
Cost: Call or e-mail for details
Date: 1995
Distributor: TVE
Prince Albert Road
London NW1 4RZ
UK
Phone: [44] (207) 586-5526
Fax: [44] (207) 586-4866
E-mail: tve-uk@tve.org.uk

These episodes from the British series *Rights and Wrongs* concern issues of new slavery: "Child Labor" reports from Pakistan and elsewhere on the millions of child workers systematically abused, despite international treaties drawn up to protect their rights; "Human Rights in Asia" marks the sixth anniversary of Tiananmen Square and the twentieth anniversary of the end of the Vietnam War by reviving the debate about human rights in Asia; and "Human Rights Progress in South Africa" examines that country's difficult journey toward its objectives in the year following democratic elections.

Rights, Camera, Action

Length:	30 minutes with booklet
Cost:	$30.00
Date:	1999
Distributor:	Anti-Slavery International
	1755 Massachusetts Avenue NW, Suite 312
	Washington, DC 20036-2102
	USA
	Phone: (202) 232-3317
	E-mail: info@stopslavery.org

A video and booklet education pack plus evaluation form examining the sensitive subject of the commercial exploitation of children for use with 14- to 18-year-olds. Covers childhood, the UN Convention of the Rights on the Child, selling children, child prostitution and pornography, trafficking. Aims to develop awareness of and take action against this growing global problem, and also explores techniques and issues concerning video production.

Slavery

Length:	78 minutes
Cost:	Call or email for details
Date:	2000
Distributor:	Anti-Slavery International
	1755 Massachsetts Avenue, NW, Suite 312
	Washington, DC 20036-2102
	(202) 232-3317
	Email: info@stopslavery.org

This is the first major film made about new slavery. It was produced by Home Box Office and the British Network Channel 4, and made by the award-winning filmmakers Brian Woods and Kate Blewitt. Filmed in India, Brazil, West Africa, London, and Washington, D.C., it shows real slavery and explains how it fits into the global economy. The filmmakers actually buy slaves in Africa and help to free child slaves in India. This is the most important film made about contemporary slavery.

A Sporting Chance

Length:	9 minutes
Cost:	$20.00
Date:	1997
Distributor:	Christian Aid (UK)
	35 Lower Marsh Waterloo
	London SE1 7RT UK

Phone: [44] (207) 620-4444
Fax: [44] (207) 620-0719

About 55 million children work in all kinds of trades in India from sewing sports shoes to serving as domestic servants. Some of these children work long hours making sporting goods that they will never be able to use. The video looks at the work these children do and how local organizations are seeking to improve their lives.

Sudan—The Secret Story
Length: 26 minutes
Cost: Call or e-mail for details
Date: 1998
Distributor: TVE
               Prince Albert Road
               London NW1 4RZ
               UK
               Phone: [44] (207) 586-5526
               Fax: [44] (207) 586-4866
               E-mail: tve-uk@tve.org.uk

Filmmaker Damien Lewis traveled secretly to an area placed off-limits to UN aid workers to uncover evidence of a deliberate campaign of genocide by the regime. His film shows that the roots of the problem are manmade and lie in a deliberate policy by the government in the north to clear out the black non-Islamic peoples and impose an Islamic Arabic-speaking state and gain control of the south's oil fields.

Tomorrow We Will Finish
Length: 26 minutes
Cost: Call or e-mail for details
Date: 1995
Distributor: TVE
               Prince Albert Road
               London NW1 4RZ
               UK
               Phone: [44] (207) 586-5526
               Fax: [44] (207) 586-4866
               E-mail: tve-uk@tve.org.uk

Over 150,000 girls between the ages of five and sixteen work in Nepal's two thousand carpet factories. The stories portrayed in this program are based on cases complied by Child Workers in

Nepal, a children's labor organization. They include the history of three girls, Suri, Tama, and Maya, forced by poverty to work in the city's carpet factories for sixteen hours a day and denied their rights as children.

Ujeli: A Child Bride in Nepal
Length: 60 minutes
Cost: Call or e-mail for details
Date: 1992
Distributor: TVE
Prince Albert Road
London NW1 4RZ
UK
Phone: [44] (207) 586-5526
Fax: [44] (207) 586-4866
E-mail: tve-uk@tve.org.uk

Filmed on location in the Rasuwa district of Nepal, this is the story of ten-year-old Ujeli. Against the advice of her teacher and doctor, who warn of the dangers of early child bearing, Ujeli's parents arrange for her to be married. Excluded from school and forced to work from dusk to dawn, Ujeli rapidly assumes the responsibilities of an adult woman, including motherhood. This tragic tale unfolds in a land where an estimated 40 percent of women get married before they reach age fourteen. As a result, Nepal's maternal mortality rate of 850 per 100,000 live births is among the highest in the world. In Nepali with English subtitles.

Under the Carpet—Bihar's Lost Boys
Length: 15 minutes
Cost: $20.00
Date: 1994
Distributor: Christian Aid (UK)
35 Lower Marsh Waterloo
London SE1 7RT
UK
Phone: [44] (207) 620-4444
Fax: [44] (207) 620-0719

This documentary takes a look at child labor in the Indian carpet industry and at international campaigning efforts against child labor. For students aged sixteen or older.

Websites

There are a few websites that exist independently of any other publications or organizations, some of which are the work of students. The ones listed here are excellent introductions to child labor and slave labor.

Global March against Child Labor
www.globalmarch.org

The Global March movement began when thousands of people marched together to jointly put forth the message against child labor. The march, which started on January 17, 1998, touched every corner of the globe, built immense awareness, and led to a high level of participation from the masses. This march finally culminated at the ILO Conference in Geneva. The voices of the marchers were heard and reflected in the draft of the ILO Convention against the worst forms of child labor. The following year the Convention was unanimously adopted at the ILO Conference in Geneva. The movement is soon going to publish a "worst forms of child labor" report that shall state the situation a year from the time the Convention was adopted unanimously. The site keeps you up-to-date with anti–child labor action around the world.

ILO U.—The Child Labor Website for High School and College Students
http://www.us.ilo.org/ilokidsnew/ILOU/ilou.html

Sponsored by the Washington, D.C., branch of the International Labour Organization of the United Nations. At this site you can take a crash course in child labor, find out how students can make an impact in the fight against child labor, and join the ILO Student Leader Network to get alerts and updates via e-mail.

Immaculata High School (Somerville, New Jersey) Child Slave Labor News
www.geocities.com/Athens/Styx/7487

The students and faculty of Immaculata High School are very concerned about the problem of child slave labor. Each year, the senior U.S. History II Honors class, taught by Miss Joann Fantina, publishes numerous newsletters covering many aspects of child slave labor. A new group of students takes over the project each year as the previous class graduates. It is a common interest among the students and is continued enthusiastically year after year.

Glossary

chattel labor   the traditional form of slavery—when one person totally owns another.

child labor   parents pass their child on to another person whether or not money is exchanged and that person gains control of the child and the child's labor. Children are extremely vulnerable to physical abuse—beatings and sexual—excessively long hours, and/or being made to work in dangerous or cramped conditions. Girl domestic servants are especially vulnerable to sexual abuse. Some children are enslaved in debt bondage (see below), in which a parent or relative pawns the child, sometimes at a very young age, in return for loans that they can never repay.

Some employers argue they need the "nimble fingers" of children, but they really mean a docile and controllable labor force. A good example would be a 10-year-old boy working 14-hour days at a carpet loom. At night he sleeps under the loom while his parents are hundreds of miles away in his home village. He may be chained, especially if he tries to escape.

convention or covenant   agreement in international law between sovereign states, but one that is less formal than a treaty.

debt bondage (also called bonded labor)   when an individual works for another indefinitely to pay off a debt. A person becomes a bonded laborer when his or her labor is demanded as a means of repayment for a loan. The person is then tricked or trapped into working for very little or no pay, often for seven days a week. The value of the laborer's work is greater than the original sum of money borrowed. Can be inherited from one generation to another, maintaining members of a family in permanent bondage in return for an old loan, the details of which have long been forgotten. In some cases employers owed money sell the debt to a new employer. Some bonded laborers receive no payment at all for their work; other may be bonded by relatively small advances on their wages that are endlessly repeated.

forced labor   any work or service that a person does not do voluntarily and which is only done because of a threatened punishment or penalty. Forced labor is often a feature of war. There are exceptional circumstances when it is seen as acceptable under international law. A country may make convicted prisoners perform forced labor or compulsory military service. In countries affected by war or civil conflict, such as Burma, those enslaved are often the weak or defenseless such as refugees, members of ethnic minorities, women, or children.

globalization   that process of social change that is making the world seem "smaller." Features of globalization are the way that time and distance are no longer seen as barriers to communication and the way that people all over the world are now exposed to the same products, media, and ideas. One result of globalization is that national governments are less able to control the flow of money, products, information, and people across their borders.

indigenous (people)   native or original to an area, as in "indigenous culture," often used to refer to the inhabitants of a territory prior to invasion or colonization and to their descendants. Indigenous peoples, such as the native Indian tribes of the Amazon, are particularly vulnerable to slavery.

migrant labor   Some domestic workers are subjected to slavery, particularly children and immigrants who work and live in the same house or premises as their employer and are paid little or nothing for their work, often on grounds that they receive food and lodging. They are cut off from families, local society, and possible protection. Cases continue to be uncovered in countries such as the United States where servants are brought in from abroad, either legally or illegally, and then treated like slaves.

nongovernmental organization (NGO)   independent organizations that are not part of any state or interstate agency—includes charities, nonprofit organizations, voluntary groups, professional associations, trades unions, and human rights bodies.

NGO's do a great deal of the research and work liberating and rehabilitating slaves around the world.

serfdom   when agricultural workers cannot leave the place where they live and work—often very similar to debt bondage in practice—or when a tenant is bound to live and labor on land belonging to another person and provide him or her with a service in return, whether for reward or not, and the tenant is not free to change his or her status. In many countries, individuals, families, or entire social groups have traditionally been obliged to work for others for little or no reward. This status usually has no basis in law, but the practice persists and is often enforced with violence.

servile marriage   where a young girl or women has no right to refuse being entered into a marriage. In servile marriage a young woman is often given in exchange for money or other payment, and she can sometimes be inherited by another person if her husband dies, or she can even be sold to someone else. A typical case is when a 12-year-old girl is told her family has arranged a marriage with a 60-year-old man. She has no opportunity to exercise her right to refuse and is unaware that she can do so. Servile marriage is listed in United Nations conventions as "a practice similar to slavery."

slave   The word *slave* comes from the word *Slav* (as in Slavic peoples), derived in Middle English from Old French *esclave* and medieval Latin *sclavus, sclava,* meaning *Slavonic* (captive). It comes from Roman times when German tribes supplied the slave markets of the Roman Empire with captured Slavs.

slavery   For the purposes of this book slavery is defined as "a social and economic relationship in which a person is controlled through violence or its threat, paid nothing, and economically exploited." (See pp. 78–80 for the official U.N. definitions of slavery.)

social clause   a general term that refers to the introduction of social standards into trade agreements that have usually been driven by economic considerations only. For example, the NAFTA (North American Free Trade Agreement) now has a "social clause" making international trade agreements conditional on respect for a number of internationally recognized labor standards. The question of a "social clause" is one of the areas of controversy in the World Trade Organization (WTO). Many people believe that a "social clause" is an important way to prevent the importation of goods made with slave labor to countries such as the United States. On the other hand, many developing countries resist a "social clause" because they feel it will only work to keep their imports from being purchased abroad.

state(s) party In the United Nations conventions or in international law a state party is a country whose government has signed a treaty or agreement and is legally bound to follow its provisions.

untouchables/outcasts a term used to describe all those in Hindu society, primarily in India, who do not belong to the four major Hindu castes. Untouchables are now designated in India as "scheduled castes." Discrimination against these castes is pervasive in India and Nepal. In Nepal one will even find segregated water fountains in public places for "untouchables." This discrimination is linked to slavery in that most people enslaved in South Asia come from these castes.

Index

A-3 visas, 28–29, 152
AASG. *See* American Anti-Slavery Group
Abd (Mauritanian slaves), 68
Abolition Act 1833 (Britain), 37, 38
Abolitionists' biographical sketches, 49–71
Action pour le Changement, Mauritania, 95–96
Adoption of Children Ordinance Law 1941, Sri Lanka, 41
Adut, Angelina, 98–99
Africa
    African Network for the Prevention and the Protection Against Child Abuse and Neglect (ANPPCAN), 137
    anti-slavery organizations, 137–138
    chattel slavery, 92, 150–151
    contemporary slavery, 173
    Equatorial, 172
    North, 150–151
    Organization of African Unity (OAU), 57
    WAO-Afrique, 137–138
    West, 125, 127
    See also individual countries
Agency for International Development, USA, 133
Agenda 21 (videotape), 193
Agnivesh, Swami, 49–50
Agricultural debt bondage, 8–9, 35, 177
AIDS/HIV, 10, 113, 115–116, 120, 122

Akorli, Enyoham, 104
Albania, 125
Altink, Sietske, 169–170
The Amahs of Hong Kong (videotape), 193
American Anti-Slavery Group (AASG), 27–28, 150–151
    foundation, 44, 56
    Internet, 102
    Mauritania, 45, 69
American Colonies, 36
American South (nineteenth century), 7, 8, 11
Amnesty International USA, 151
Anderson, Bridget, 170
Anthony, Susan B., 70
Anti-Slavery International, 135–136
    antecedents, 42
    Child Domestic Workers, 170–171
    Children in Bondage, 181
    Debt Bondage, 181
    digital images, 191
    Enslaved Peoples in the 1990's, 170–171
    objectives, 25–26
    reports, 22, 108–110, 181–182
    This Menace of Bonded Labor, 171
    United Nations, 26
Anti-slavery organizations, 25–31
    Africa, 137–138
    Asia, 138–139, 163–168
    Australia, 138
    Europe, 139–150
    North America, 150–162
    South America, 162–163
Anti-Slavery Reporter, 184

211

Anti-Slavery Society of Australia, 138
Anti-Slavery Society. *See* Anti-Slavery International
Anti-Slavery Squadron, British Navy, 37, 38
Apartheid, 43
The Apparel Industry and Codes of Conduct, 182
Arab slaveholders, Mauritania, 11
Argentina, 37
Armenians, 54
Asia
    Asia Monitor Resource Center, 139
    Child Workers in Asia (CWA), 138–139, 164–165
    migrants, 138–139
    sex tourism, 113, 115, 144, 153–154, 165, 176
    South, anti-slavery organizations, 163–168
    South Asian Coalition on Child Servitude, 58–59, 67, 168
    Southeast, 4, 12, 163–168, 176
Asian Migrant Center (AMC), 138–139
Asian-American Free Labor Institute (AAFLI), 152, 163
Athie, Mohamed, 27, 44
Atlantic slave trade, 36, 180
Audiotapes, 187–188
Australia, Anti-Slavery Society of, 138
Azerbaijan, 54

Baltimore Sun, 99–101
Bangladesh, 128–129
Beedis industry, 15–16, 129–130, 131
Benin, 14, 103
Bequele, A., 182
Bidis. *See Beedis* industry
Bihar, 205
Bill of Sale (1992), 93
Bitter Winds: A Memoir of My Years in China's Gulag, 181
Black, Maggie, 127, 171–172, 182
Boilil, Aichana Mint Abeid, 93–94
Bonded labor, 83–90
    Bonded Labor Act 1992, Pakistan, 44

Bonded Labor Campaign (videotape), 194
Bonded Labor Law, India, 50
contract slavery, 9–10, 13, 90–92
definition, 207–208
India, 43, 50, 62–63, 84–89
Nepal, 166–167, 177
Pakistan, 47, 83, 89–90, 168, 171
Bonded Labor Liberation Front, India (BLLF), 50, 163–164
Books, 169–181
Bosnia, 108–110
Boulkheir, Messoud ould, 95–96
Branding, 81
Brazil
    chattel slavery, 92
    child labor, 133
    contract slavery, 90–92
    domestic slavery, 1, 13
    Executive Group for the Repression of Forced Labor, 91
    forced labor, 59–60
    Lei Aurea (Golden Law), 39
    National Forum on the Prevention and Eradication of Child Labor, 162
    Para state, 65
    Pastoral Land Commission, (CPT) 163
    Queirós Law, 38
    Slavery in Brazil, 179–180
Briefing papers, 181–184
Britain
    Abolition Act (1833), 37, 38
    British Empire, 25, 40, 53
    British Navy Anti-Slavery Squadron, 37, 38
    domestic slaves, 170
    Factory Act, 1833, 7
    Peruvian Amazon Company, 39–40
    prostitution, 14
    slave trade, 52, 53
    See also England
Britain's Secret Slaves—An Investigation into the Plight of Overseas Domestic Workers, 170
Brothel economics (Thailand), 113–117
Bureau of International Labor Affairs, 182, 183

Burma
Burma Peace Foundation, 139
Burma Project, 140
Inside Burma, Land of Fear
(videotape), 198
See also Myanmar
Butterflies (anti-slavery organiza-
tion), 164
Buxton, Thomas F., 38, 40
By the Sweat and Toil of Children,
182, 183

Cadet, Jean-Robert, 50–52, 172
Cady Stanton, Elizabeth, 38, 70
CAFOD (Catholic Fund for
Overseas Development),
140–141
Cambodia
Cambodian Human Rights and
Development Association,
122
Cambodian Women's Crisis
Center, 123
government action, 121–124
Sex Workers' Union of Cambo-
dia, 117
sexual slavery, 117–121
Campaign for Education, 59
Campaign for Migrant Domestic
Workers Rights, 28–29, 152
Canada, 154–155
Caribbean, 38, 125
Caste systems, 11, 26, 68, 86, 211
Catholic Church, 59, 65
Catholic Fund for Overseas De-
velopment (CAFOD),
140–141
Cause to Communicate (audiotape),
187–188
CCEM. *See* Committee Against
Modern Slavery
CD-ROMS, 188–190
Ceylon. *See* Sri Lanka
Chan, Dina, 117–121
Chand, David, 27, 44
The Changing Face of Slavery (exhi-
bition), 190–191
The Changing Face of Slavery
(videotape), 194
Chattel labor, definition, 207
Chattel slavery
Africa, 92, 150–151

Brazil, 92
definition, 12
Mauritania, 56, 93–97
North Africa, 150–151
Sudan, 28
*Child Domestic Workers: A Hand-
book for Research and Action*,
170–171
Child labor
Asia, 138–139, 164–165
Bangladesh, 128–129
bans, 46
Bill Clinton's speech, 130–134
Brazil, 133, 162
By the Sweat and Toil of Children,
182, 183
Caribbean, 154–155
Child Domestic Labor (report),
127
*Child Domestic Workers: A Hand-
book*, 170, 171
*Child Labor: A World History
Companion*, 174
Child Labor Coalition (CLC),
152–153
Child Labor Deterrence Bill
(USA), 128–129
*The Child Labor Website for High
School and College Students*,
206
and child slavery, 128–134
Child Workers in Asia (CWA),
138–139, 164–165
debt bondage, 22–23
definitions, 23, 207
domestic, 167, 170, 171, 181
Dominican Republic, 63–64
Free the Children (FTC), 57–58,
154–155
Free the Children, 175
Global March Against Child
Labor, 23, 46, 61, 206
Guatemala, 133
International Organization of
Employers resolution, 83
International Program on the
Elimination of Child Labor
(IPEC), 22, 23
Kashmir, 183
National Forum on the Preven-
tion and Eradication of Child
Labor, 162

Child Labor, *continued*
  Pakistan, 133
  South Asian Coalition on Child
    Servitude (SAACS), 58–59,
    67, 168
  Supplementary Convention on
    the Abolition of Slavery, the
    Slave Trade, and Institutions
    and Practices Similar to Slav-
    ery, 80
  Website, 206
  See also Convention Concerning
    the Prohibition and Immedi-
    ate Action for the Elimination
    of the Worst Forms of Child
    Labour
*Child Labor—Targeting the Intolera-
  ble,* 183–184
Child rights
  Child Rights Information Net-
    work (CRIN), 142
  Children's Rights Project,
    155
  Convention on the Rights of the
    Child, 44, 82
  Defence for Children Interna-
    tional (DCI), 144
  Group for the Convention on
    the Rights of the Child, 147
  Philippines, 167
Child slavery, 15–16, 44, 50–51, 83,
    137–138, 210
  African Network (ANPPCAN)
    and sexual slavery, 137
  Asian tourism and sexual slav-
    ery, 153–154, 165
  and child labor, 128–130
  Child Slave Labor News (web-
    site), 206–207
  Child Slaves, 176
  End Child Prostitution in Asian
    Tourism (ECPAT), 153–154,
    165
  Ghana, 14
  Hong Kong, 40
  India, 26–27, 67–68, 129–130
  *Iqbal Masih and the Crusaders
    against Child Slavery,* 176
  Japan, 42
  Mauritania, 68–69
  prostitution, 16, 83, 153–154
  restavecs, 14, 125, 127–128

restavecs testimonies, 50–52,
    63–64
  Rugmark campaign, 26–27
  sexual, 42, 45, 123
  West Africa, 125
  World Congress Against Com-
    mercial Sexual Exploitation
    of Children, 45
*Children in Bondage—Slaves of the
  Subcontinent* 181
Children's News 1 (videotape),
    194–195
Chile, 37
China, 44–45
  Bitter Winds, 181
  laogai (forced labor system), 42,
    110–111, 178, 181
  Laogai Research Foundation,
    156–157
  migrant trafficking, 179
  war slavery, 42
Christian Aid, 141
Christian Solidarity International
    (CSI), 45, 54, 56, 100, 102–103
Christian Solidarity Worldwide
    (CSW), 54, 142
Chronology of World Slavery,
    177
Chronology, slavery, 35–47
Clarkson, Thomas, 25, 37, 52–53,
    173, 174
Clean Clothes Campaign, 143
Clinton, Bill, 130–134
Coalition Against Slavery in
    Sudan and Mauritania (CAS-
    MAS), 153
Colchester, Marcus, 172–173
Comite Contre L'Esclavage Mod-
    ern (CCEM), 17, 29–30, 143
Commission on Human Rights,
    22
Committee Against Modern Slav-
    ery (CCEM), 17, 29–30, 143
Comparison, old and new slavery,
    7–10
Congo Reform Association
    (CRA), 39
Congress of Vienna, 37
Consumption, slave-made goods,
    21, 27
Contemporary slavery, 15–18,
    24–25, 173

Contract slavery, 9–10, 90–92
Convention Concerning the Prohibition and Immediate Action for the Elimination of the Worst Forms of Child Labour, 22, 23, 26, 130–134
effects of legislation, 128
extract, 83
passed by ILO, 46–47
Convention for the Suppression of the Traffic in Persons and Exploitation of the Prostitution of Others, 42
Convention on the Rights of the Child, 44, 82
Conventions
definition, 207
evolution of (table), 77
extracts, 78–83
Coolie labor, 38, 40
Corruption, 6–7, 76, 123
Cotton, Samuel, 173
Covenant, definition, 207
Cox, Caroline, Baroness of Queensbury, 53–54
Credit, 66–67, 133
Crime networks, 24–25
Cross, Peter, 183
CSI. *See* Christian Solidarity International
CSW. *See* Christian Solidarity Worldwide
Cuba, 37
Czech Republic, 146–147

Daobadri, Julie, 104–105
Daughters of Africa: Senegal (videotape), 195
Debt bondage, 12–13
Agricultural, 8–9, 35, 177
beedis, 15–16, 129–130, 131
child labor, 22–23, 83
contract, 9–10
Debt Bondage, 181
definition, 207–208, 210
India, 8–9, 50, 61–62, 66–67
Nepal, 30
Pakistan, 60–61, 64–65, 171
peshgi, 44, 89
prostitution, 9–10, 116
Supplementary Convention, 80

Debt, international, 59, 76–77
Declaration of the Rights of Man, 36
Defense for Children International (DCI), 144
Definitions
bonded labor, 207–208
chattel labor, 12, 207
child labor, 207
conventions, 78, 207
covenants, 207
debt bondage, 207–208, 210
forced labor, 208
globalization, 208
indigenous people, 149, 208
migrant labor, 208
NGOs, 208–209
outcasts, 211
serfdom, 209, 210
servile marriage, 209
servile status, 82
slave, 209
slave trade, 82, 209–210
slavery, 2–3, 78–79, 82, 209–210
social clause, 210–211
State(s) party, 211
untouchables, 211
worst forms of child labor, 83
Denmark, 36
Devadasi women, 14
Digital images, 191
Disposability, 7, 171
Disposable People: New Slavery in the Global Economy, 113–117, 171
Domestic slavery
Brazil, 1, 13
Britain, 170
Campaign for Migrant Domestic Workers Rights, 152
children, 125
France, 16–18, 29–30
Haiti, 51–52, 127–128
Indonesia, 127
Philippines, 126–127
United States, 1, 28–29, 125–126
Venezuela, 127
West Africa, 125, 127
Dominican Republic, 21, 63–64, 125
Douglass, Frederick, 54–55, 70

Drug trafficking, 83
Dutch colonies, 39

Economic and Social Council, 22
Economic change, 5–6
Economic, Social, and Cultural Covenant, 77
Economic vulnerability, 76
Economy, global, 176–177
ECPAT. *See* End Child Prostitution in Asian Tourism
Education, Campaign For, 59
Effah, Josephine, 183
Egypt (Ancient), 35
Eighteen Layers of Hell: Stories from the Chinese Gulag, 178
El Hor movement, Mauritania, 43
Emancipation Proclamation, United States, 1863, 39
Emergence, modern slavery, 5–7
Employers, International Organization of, 45
End Child Prostitution in Asian Tourism (ECPAT), 153–154, 165
Ending Slavery: Hierarchy, Dependency and Gender in Central Mauritania, 178
England. *See* Britain
England (tenth century), 35
Enslaved Peoples in the 1990's, 170–171
Equatorial Africa, 172
Essential Information Inc., 157
Europe
    anti-slavery organizations, 139–150
    European Community, 4
    European Union, 25
    human trafficking, 147
    slave trade, 36
Executive Group for the Repression of Forced Labor (Brazil), 91
Exhibitions, 190–191
The Face of Decent Work (videotape), 195–196
Factory Act 1833 (Britain), 37
Farrakan, Louis, 99–100
Forced labor
    Bosnia, 108–110

Brazil, 59–60, 91
China, 42, 110–111, 178, 181
    conventions, 41, 106, 110
    definition, 208
    Myanmar (Burma), 105–108
    Tibet, 110–111
Forced Labor Convention, 41, 106, 110
Forced to Plough: Bonded Labor in Nepal's Agricultural Economy, 177
Forcese, Craig, 183
Forms of slavery, 4, 7–10, 12–14
Foundation Against Trafficking in Women, 144
France, 16–18, 29–30, 38
Free the Children: A Young Man Fights against Child Labor and Proves that Children Can Change the World, 175
Free the Children (FTC), 32, 57–59, 154–155
Free will, loss of, 3, 13

G-5 visas, 28–29, 152
Garment industry, 146, 182
Gatos ('cats') (contract slave recruiters), 91–92
Gender, 178
Geneva Conventions, 109
Genovese, Eugene D., 173
Germany, 41, 45
Ghana, 103–105, 137
Ghandi, Mahatma, 50
Gibson Wilson, Ellen, 173
Gifford, Zerbanoo, 174
Global Alliance Against Traffic in Women (GAATW), 165–166
Global economy, 176–177
Global March Against Child Labor, 23, 46, 61, 206
Global slavery, responsibility, 20–21
Globalization, 4, 18–21, 208
    International Forum on, 155–156
Going Home Guinea (videotape), 196–197
Government corruption, 6–7, 65, 76
Greece (Ancient), 35
Greider, William, 6, 20, 174

Gross domestic product (GDP), 76
Guatemala, 133
Guinea, 196–197
Gyatso, Palden, 110–111

Haiti
   Haiti's Cinderellas: "They Call Me Dog" (videotape), 197
   independence, 36
   refugees, 64
   Restavec: From Haitian Slave Child to Middle-Class American, 172
   restavecs, 14, 51, 125, 127–128
   testimonies, 50–52, 63–64
Haratin (Mauritanian ex-slaves), 93, 95–96
Harkin Bill, United States, early 1990s, 128–129
High Commission for Refugees, United Nations (UNHCR), 197
The Historical Encyclopedia of World Slavery, Volumes I and II, 178
History of slavery, 35–47
HIV/AIDS, 10, 113, 115–116, 120, 122
Ho, Catherine, 111
Hobbs, Sandy, 174
Hong Kong, 40, 193
Household slavery. *See* Domestic slavery
HRW. *See* Human rights, Human Rights Watch
Human rights
   Commission on, 22
   Human Rights: A Compilation of International Instruments, 180
   Human Rights Commission of Pakistan (HRCP), 64, 89–90, 166
   Human Rights Information and Documentation Systems International (HURIDOCS), 144–145
   Human Rights Lawyers Committee, 157
   Human Rights Watch (HRW), 155, 174–175
   A Modern Kind of Slavery, 174–175

   Pakistan: Contemporary Forms of Slavery, 175
   Rape for Profit, 175
   The Small Hands of Slavery, 175
   Universal Declaration of Human Rights, 21, 42, 77, 79
   women's, 155, 161, 167
Human Smuggling: Chinese Migrant Trafficking and the Challenge to America's Immigration Tradition, 179
Human trafficking
   Cambodia, 121–122
   Chinese migrants, 179
   Convention for the Suppression of the Traffic in Persons, 42
   description, 23–25
   estimate of size, 19
   Europe, 147
   Foundation Against Trafficking in Women, 144
   Global Alliance Against Traffic in Women, 165–166
   Human Smuggling: Chinese Migrant Trafficking and the Challenge to America's Immigration Tradition, 179
   India, 175
   international debt relation (figure), 77
   Kosovo, 124–125
   Nepal, 175
   Rome Final Act, 1998, 77
   Ukraine, 23
   United States, 24, 47, 179

I Am a Child (videotape), 197–198
I Was Born a Slave: An Anthology of Classic Slave Narratives, 180
Illegal Immigration and Commercial Sex: The New Slave Trade, 181
ILO. *See* International Labour Organization
IMF. *See* International Monetary Fund
Immaculata High School, Child Slave Labor News (website), 206–207
Indentured servitude, Pakistan, 44
Index on Censorship, 184–185

India
  beedis (cigarette) industry,
    15–16, 129–130, 131
  bonded labor, 43, 62–63, 83–89
  Bonded Labor Liberation Front
    (BLLF), 50, 163–164
  Butterflies, 164
  caste system, 11, 68, 86
  child slavery, 26–27, 67–68,
    129–130
  coolie labor, 38, 40
  debt bondage, 8–9, 50, 61–62,
    66–67
  devadasi women, 14
  Nepali female trafficking, 175
  Shramjeevi Sanghatana (trade
    union), 85
  street children, 164
Indigenous peoples, 149, 162, 208
Indonesia, 6, 26, 127
Infant mortality, 76
Informal Sector Service Center
  (INSEC), 30–31, 166–167
IN-Ghana, 137
Inside Burma, Land of Fear (video-
  tape), 198
Institut Psycho-Social de la
  Famille (IPSOFA), 128
International Child Labor Elimi-
  nation bill, 46
International Confederation of
  Free Trade Unions (ICFTU),
  145
International Convention for the
  Suppression of the White
  Slave Trade, 39
International Convention on the
  Suppression and Punishment
  of the Crime of Apartheid, 43
International debt, 59, 76, 77
International Forum on Global-
  ization (IFG), 155–156
International Labor Organization
  (ILO), 43, 46–47, 146
  *The Child Labor Website for High
  School and College Students,*
  206
  *Child Labor—Targeting the Intol-
  erable,* 183–184
  Convention Against Forced
  Labor, 106, 110
  Convention Concerning the

Prohibition and Immediate
  Action for the Elimination of
  the Worst Forms of Child
  Labour, 22, 23, 26, 40, 46–47,
  83, 128, 130–134
  ILOLEX 1999 (CD-ROM),
  188–189
  International Labor Conference,
  146
  International Organization of
  Employers, 45
  on Myanmar, 13–14
  objectives, 22
  pamphlets, 191
  posters, 192
  press kits, 192
  reports to United Nations,
  192
  Tripartite Declaration of Princi-
  ples Concerning Multina-
  tional Enterprises and Social
  Policy, 43, 44
International Labor Rights Fund,
  156
International law, 21–23, 78–83
International Monetary Fund
  (IMF), 133
International Needs (IN), Nigeria,
  104, 137
International Organization for
  Migration (IOM), 23
International Organization of Em-
  ployers, 45
International Program on the
  Elimination of Child Labor
  (IPEC), 22, 23
International Textile, Garment
  and Leather Workers Federa-
  tion, 146
Internet, 102
IPEC. *See* International Program
  on the Elimination of Child
  Labor
*Iqbal Masih and the Crusaders
  against Child Slavery,* 176
Islam, 11, 42–43
*It Takes a Child: Craig Kielburger's
  Story—A Journey into Child
  Labor* (videotape), 199

Jacobs, Charles, 27, 44, 55–56
Japan, 4, 11, 41, 42

Jessica: A Saudi Slave (videotape), 199–200

Kamara, Cheikh Saad Bouh, 56–57
Kashmir, 183
Key Indicators of the Labor Market 1999 (CD-ROM), 189
Kielburger, Craig, 57–59, 154, 175, 199
King, Martin Luther, 55, 87
Kosovo, 59, 124–125
Kuklin, Susan, 176
Kuwait, 11

La Strada Ceska Republika, 146–147
Labor concerns, 139
Labor rights, 156, 163–164
Laogai (forced labor camps)
China, 42, 178, 181
Laogai Research Foundation, 156–157
Tibet, 110
Lavalette, Michael, 174
Law, international, 21–23, 78–83
Lawyers Committee for Human Rights (LCHR), 157
League of Nations Slavery Convention (1926), 21, 40–41, 78–79
Lean-Lim, L., 176
Leather workers, 146
Lee-Wright, Peter, 176
Legal ownership, 2, 7, 9, 19
Lei Aurea (Golden Law), Brazil, 39
Levels of slavery (figure), 75
Liberation, problems of, 30, 31–32
Libya, 69
Life on the Line (videotape), 200
Lincoln, Abraham, 39, 522
Loans, microcredit, 133
Lopez Loyola, Dona Pureza, 59–60

Major, Kevin, 175
Malaya, 40
Mandela, Nelson, 89
Marriage, 80, 209
Masih, Iqbal, 57–58, 60–61, 176
Mauritania

abd (slave), 68
Action pour le Changement, 95–96
Arab slaveholders, 11
chattel slavery, 56, 93–97
child slavery, 68–69
Coalition Against Slavery in Sudan and Mauritania (CASMAS), 153
dependency and gender, 178
El Hor movement, 43
Haratin, 93, 95–96
Mauritanian Human Rights Association (MHRA), 57
racism, 11
SOS Enclave, 96
SOS Slaves, 94
U.S. relations, 27, 45, 95
World Bank, 96
McCuen, Gary E., 176–177
McKechnie, Jim, 174
Meltzer, Milton, 177
Mexico, 112
Microcredit loans, 133
Migrants
Asia, 138–139
definition, migrant labor, 208
domestic labor, 28–29, 152, 179
Model Business Principles, United States, 44–45
A Modern Form of Slavery: Trafficking of Burmese Women and Girls into Brothels in Thailand, 174–175
Modern Slavery and the Global Economy, 176–177
Modernization, economic, 6
Money, morality of, 11
Morel, E. D., 39
Morocco, 69
Mortality, infant, 76
Mott, Lucretia, 38
Mukti Ashram, 67–68
Multinational Monitor (Essential Information Inc.), 157
Multinationals, Tripartite Declaration of Principles Concerning, 43, 44
Murahliin, Sudan, 97–99
Muslim World Congress, 42–43
Mutilation, 81

Myanmar (Burma)
  abolition of slavery, 41
  Burma Peace Foundation, 139
  Burma Project, 140
  forced labor, 105–108
  ILO report, 13–14
  Thai brothel trade, 174–175
  U.N. Commission of Inquiry,
    46, 106–108
  videotape, 198
  war slavery, 13–14
Myers, W. E., 182

NAFTA. *See* North American Free
  Trade Agreement
Nankar, Keshav, 61–62, 84–86
National Forum on the Preven-
  tion and Eradication of Child
  Labor, 162
Native Americans, 70
Nazi Germany, 41
Nepal, 4
  bonded labor, 30, 166–167, 177
  caste discrimination, 26
  child brides, 205
  child slavery, 26
  female trafficking, 175
  Informal Sector Service Center
    (INSEC), 30–31, 166–167
Netherlands, 37, 39
The New Slavery, 184–185
Newsletters, 184–185
NGOs. *See* nongovernmental
  organizations
Nigeria, 14, 103, 104, 137
No Holidays for Us (videotape),
  200–201
Nongovernmental Organizations
  (NGOs), 147, 208–209
North Africa, 150–151
North American Free Trade
  Agreement (NAFTA),
  210–211
Norwegian Institute of Interna-
  tional Affairs (NUPI), 147–148
Number of slaves, estimate, 3–4

OAU. *See* Organization of African
  Unity
O'Grady, Ron, 184
*One World Ready or Not: The Manic
  Logic of Global Capitalism*, 174

Organization Indigena Regional
  de Atalaya (OIRA), 162
Organization of African Unity
  (OAU), 57
"Otherness," 10
Our News, Our Views (videotape),
  201
Out of Sight, Out of Mind (video-
  tape), 201
Outcasts, definition, 211
Ownership, legal, 2, 7, 9, 19

Pakistan
  bonded labor, 44, 47, 83, 168
  child labor, 133
  debt bondage, 60–61, 64–65,
    171
  Human Rights Commission of
    Pakistan, 64, 89–90, 166
  Human Rights Watch (HRW),
    175
  *Pakistan: Contemporary Forms of
    Slavery*, 175
  peshgi system, 44, 89–90
Pamphlets, 191
Pandit, Vidyullata, 61, 62–63
Pandit, Vivek, 61, 62–63, 86–89
Paraison, Father Edwin, 63–64
Pastoral Land Commission, Brazil
  (CPT), 163
Patan, Shakil, 64–65
People trafficking. *See* Human
  trafficking
People's Recovery, Empowerment
  and Development Assistance
  Foundation (PREDA), 167
Periodicals, 184–185
Peru, 37, 39–40, 162
Peshgi (debt bondage system), 44,
  89–90
Philippines, 11, 126–127, 167
Photographs, anti-slavery, 191
Plant, Roger, 177
Police corruption, 6–7, 76, 123
Political prisoners, 110
Population, world trends, 5, 76
Posters, 192
Practices defined as forms of slav-
  ery, 78, 79–82
PREDA. *See* People's Recovery,
  Empowerment and Develop-
  ment Assistance Foundation

Predictors of slavery, 76
Press kits, 192
The Price of Progress (videotape),
    202
Prostitution
    Britain, 14
    child, 16, 42, 83, 153–154, 165
    debt bondage, 9–10, 11
    End Child Prostitution in Asian
        Tourism (ECPAT), 153–154,
        165
    Japan, 11
    Nepali women, 175
    Philippine women, 11
    Southeast Asia, 176
    Thailand, 9–10, 11, 113–117
    tourism, 144, 153–154, 165, 176
    See also sexual slavery

Quakers, 52–53, 70–71
Queensbury, Baroness of (Caro-
    line Cox), 53–54
Queirós Law, Brazil, 38

Race, 10–12
Racism, 8, 11, 52
Rädda Barnen (Sweden), 148
*Rape for Profit: Trafficking of Nepali
    Girls and Women to India's
    Brothels*, 175
Refugees, 59, 64, 124–125, 197
Rehabilitation issues, 17–18,
    31–32, 62–63
Religion
    Catholic Church, 59, 65
    Islam, 11, 42–43
    links with slavery, 14, 50,
        103–105, 137
Reports, anti-slavery, 181–184, 192
Responsibility, global slavery,
    20–21
Restavecs (child domestic slaves),
    14, 51, 125, 127–128
    testimonies, 50–52, 63–64
*Restavecs: From Haitian Slave Child
    to Middle-Class American*
    (Cadet 1998), 172
Retailers, slave-free goods, 27
Rights
    child, 144
    Child Rights Information Net-
        work, 142

Children's Rights Project, 155
Convention on the Rights of the
    Child, 44, 82
    See also Human rights
Rights, Camera, Action (videotape),
    203
Rights and Wrongs (videotape),
    202
Rights of Man, Declaration of, 36
Ritual slavery, 14, 137
Rizende, Father Ricardo, 65, 163
Robertson, Adam, 177
Rodriguez, Junius P., 177, 178
*Roll, Jordan, Roll: The World the
    Slaves Made*, 173
Rome (Ancient), 35
Rome Final Act, 1998, 77
Ruf, Urs Peter, 178
Rugmark, 26–27, 45, 148–149
Russia, 38. *See also* Soviet Union

Sanders Amendment, 1997
    (United States), 129
Saran, Amar, 65–67
Saudi Arabia, 11, 41, 199–200
Saunders, Kate, 178
Save the Children Federation,
    158
Save the Children Fund, Swedish
    Division, 148
Sawyer, Roger, 178
Scheduled castes. *See* Caste sys-
    tems
Seattle protest, 1999, 19
Senahe, Mercy, 105
Senegal, 56, 195
Serfdom
    children, 83
    definition, 209, 210
    Holy Roman Empire, 36
    Russia, 38
    Supplementary Convention,
        80
Servile marriage, definition, 209
Servile status, definition, 82, 209
*The Sex Sector: The Economic and
    Social Bases of Prostitution in
    Southeast Asia*, 176
Sex tourism, 113, 115, 144, 176
    ECPAT, 153–154, 165
Sex Workers Union of Cambodia,
    117

Sexual slavery
  Cambodia, 117–124
  Child, 42, 45, 123, 153–154, 165
  Commercial, 111–124
  Thailand, 113–117
  United States, 112
  See also prostitution
Shishram, Mishra, 177
Shoishab (anti-slavery organization), 167
Shramjeevi Sanghatana (Indian trade union), 85
Sierra Leone, 37, 41
Silent Terror: A Journey into Contemporary African Slavery, 173
Slave and Enclave: The Political Ecology of Equatorial Africa, 172
Slave definition, 209
Slave labor, Nazi Germany, 41
Slave raids, Sudan, 97–99
Slave trade
  Atlantic, 36, 180
  Britain, 52, 53
  Conventions, 7, 39, 42, 79–82
  Cuba, 37
  Danish ban, 36
  Definition, 82, 209–210
  estimated size, 23–24
  European, 36
  The Slave Trade: The History of the Atlantic Slave Trade 1440–1870, 180
  trans-Saharan, 35–36
  white, 39
  See also Human trafficking
The Slave Trade: The History of the Atlantic Slave Trade 1440–1870, 180
Slave-free goods, 27
Slaveholders, 9, 11
Slavery
  Definitions, 2–3, 78–79, 82, 209–210
  estimated number of slaves, 3–4
  facts and figures, 74–78
  global responsibility, 20–21
  institutions and practices similar to, 210
  international debt, 76
  levels of, 75
  nature of, 4
  predictors of, 76
  profitability of, 76
  Slavery Convention of the League of Nations, 77, 78–79
Slavery (videotape), 203
Slavery: A World History, 177
Slavery in Brazil: A Link in the Chain of Modernization, 179–180
Slavery in Sudan, 180
Slavery in the Twentieth Century, 178
Slavery Today, 179
The Small Hands of Slavery: Bonded Child Labor in India, 175
Smith, Paul J., 179
Social change, 5–6
Social clause, definition, 210–211
Social Policy, Tripartite Declaration of Principles Concerning, 43, 44
Social vulnerability, 76
Society for the Protection of the Rights of the Child (SPARC), 168
SOS Enclave, 96
SOS Slaves, 94
South America, 4, 39, 162–163. *See also individual countries*
South Asian Coalition on Child Servitude (SACCS), 58–59, 67, 168
Southeast Asia, 4, 12, 163–168, 176. *See also individual countries*
Soviet Union, 23, 54. *See also* Russia
Spain, 37
A Sporting Chance (videotape), 203–204
Spread of slavery, 75–77
Sri Lanka, 41
State, role of, 21–23
State(s) party, definition, 211
Stearman, Kaye, 179
Still, William, 69
Stolen Lives: Trading Women into Sex and Slavery, 169–170
Stop Slavery that Oppresses People (STOP), 28, 45, 56

Stowe, Harriet Beecher, 179
Street children, 164
Strobanek, Siriporn, 184
Student activism, United States,
   101–103
Subcommission on Prevention of
   Discrimination and Protec-
   tion of Minorities, 22
Sudan
   Activists, 56
   Anti-American Slavery Group,
      27–28
   chattel slavery, 28
   Christian Solidarity Interna-
      tional, 45
   civil war, 44, 46, 54
   Coalition Against Slavery in
      Sudan and Mauritania
      (CASMAS), 153
   evidence of slavery, 99–101
   Murahliin, 97–99
   slave raids, 97–99
   Slavery in Sudan, 180
   Sudan—The Secret Story (video-
      tape), 204
   war slavery, 14, 97–103
*Sugar and Modern Slavery: A Tale of
   Two Countries,* 177
Sugar industry, 21, 31, 63–64
Suman (abolitionist), 67–68
Supplementary Conventions on
   the Abolition of Slavery, the
   Slave Trade, and Institutions
   and Practices Similar to Slav-
   ery, 42, 78, 79–82
Survival International, 149–150
Sutton, Alison, 179–180
Sweatshop Watch, 158
Sweden, 37, 148

Taylor, Yuval, 180
Textile workers, 146, 158, 182
Teyeb, Moctar, 68–69, 93
Thailand
   brothel economics, 113–117
   Burmese women trafficking,
      174–175
   debt bondage, 116
   HIV/AIDS, 113, 115
   Prostitution, 9–10, 11
   sexual slavery, 113–117
This Menace of Bonded Labor: Debt

Bondage in Pakistan, 171
Thomas Clarkson: A Biography,
   173
*Thomas Clarkson and the Campaign
   against Slavery,* 174
Thomas, Hugh, 180
Tibet, 110–111
Togo, 14, 103
Tomorrow We Will Finish (video-
   tape), 204–205
Torres, Dominique, 29–30
Tostan (NGO), 195
Trade unions, 85, 145
Transnational Institute (TNI),
   158–159
Trans-Saharan slave trade,
   35–36
Tripartite Declaration of Princi-
   ples Concerning Multina-
   tional Enterprises and Social
   Policy, 43, 44
Trokosi system, Ghana, 103–105
Trust Fund on Contemporary
   Forms of Slavery, 50, 57
Tubman, Harriet, 69–70

Ujeli: A Child Bride in Nepal
   (videotape), 205
UK. *See* Britain
Ukraine, 23
UN. *See* United Nations
Uncle Tom's Cabin, 179
Under the Carpet—Bihar's Lost Boys
   (videotape), 205
Underground Railway, Pennsyl-
   vania, 69–70
UNESCO. *See* United Nations,
   Educational, Scientific, and
   Cultural Organization
UNHCR. *See* United Nations,
   High Commission for
   Refugees
UNICEF. *See* United Nations,
   Children's Fund
UNIFEM. *See* United Nations,
   Women's Human Rights
   Program
United Kingdom. *See* Britain
United Nations (UN)
   Anti-Slavery International, 26
   Children's Fund (UNICEF),
      127, 160

United Nations (UN), *continued*
Commission on Human Rights, 22
Convention on the Rights of the Child, 44, 82
Economic and Social Council, 22
Educational, Scientific, and Cultural Organization (UN-ESCO), 159–160
employees' domestic slaves, 125
forced labor Myanmar (Burma) Commission of Inquiry, 106–108
High Commission for Refugees (UNHCR), 197
Human Rights: A Compilation of International Instruments, 180
human trafficking estimate, 19
reports to, 192
role of, 21–23
Security Council, 21–22
Subcommission on Prevention of Discrimination and Protection of Minorities, 22
Trust Fund on Contemporary Forms of Slavery, 50, 57
Women's Human Rights Program, 161
Working Group on Contemporary Forms of Slavery, 22, 43
United States of America (USA)
Agency for International Development, 133
American Anti-Slavery Group (AASG), 27–28, 44, 45, 56, 102, 150–151
American Colonies, 36
American South (nineteenth century), 7, 8, 11
Amnesty International, 151
anti-slavery organizations, 150–163
Baltimore Sun, 99–101
Child Labor Deterrence Bill, 128–129
China, 110
contemporary slavery, 24–25
domestic slavery, 1, 28–29, 125–126

Emancipation Proclamation, 1863, 39
Harkin Bill, early 1900s, 128–129
human trafficking, 24, 179
importation of slaves ban, 37
India's *beedis* industry, 15–16, 129–130, 131
International Child Labor Elimination bill, 46
Mauritania, 27, 45, 54, 69, 95
Model Business Principles, 44–45
Native Americans, 70
North American Free Trade Agreement (NAFTA), 210–211
racism, 52
Sanders Amendment, 1997, 129
sexual slavery, 112
slave-produced imports, 4
student activism, 101–103
Underground Railway, 69–70
Voice of America, 99–101
Universal Declaration of Human Rights (1948), 21, 42, 77, 79
Untouchables, definition, 211
USA. *See* United States of America (USA)

Venezuela, 127
Verney, Peter, 180
Videotapes, 193–205
Vienna, Congress of, 37
Vietnam, 123
Violence, 2–3, 6–7
Virgin premium, 115
Visas, 28–29, 152
Vogel, Barbara, 28, 45, 101–103
Voice of America, 99–101
Vulnerability, 11, 76

Wakeman, Carolyn, 181
WAO-Afrique, 137–138
War slavery
China, 42
definition, 13–14
Myanmar (Burma), 13–14
origins, 35
Sudan, 14, 97–103
Websites, 206
West Africa, 125, 127

White slave trade, 39
Wiebalck, Gunnar, 102
Wilberforce, William, 37, 52, 53
Williams, Phil, 181
Women, inheritance of, 80
Women's rights
  Philippines, 167
  UN Women's Human Rights
    Program (UNIFEM), 161
  Women's Rights Project, 155
Woolman, John, 70–71
Working Group on Contemporary
  Forms of Slavery, 22, 43
World Anti-Slavery Convention,
  38
World Bank
  employees' domestic slaves,
    125
  international debt to, 76–77

Mauritania, 96
  U.S. relations, 133
World Congress Against Com-
  mercial Sexual Exploitation
  of Children, 45
The World Guide 1999–2000 (CD-
  ROM), 189–190
World Muslim Congress, 42–43
World of Work (magazine), 185
World Trade Organization (WTO),
  19, 133, 150, 211
World Vision, 161–162
WTO. *See* World Trade Organiza-
  tion
Wu, Hongda Harry, 111, 156, 181

Yemen, 42

Zarempka, Joy, 29